Dear Mike,

Enjoy!

The Lean Extended Enterprise

Moving Beyond the Four Walls
to Value Stream Excellence

TERENCE T. BURTON
STEVEN M. BOEDER

J.ROSS
PUBLISHING

APICS.
THE EDUCATIONAL SOCIETY
FOR RESOURCE MANAGEMENT

Copyright ©2003 by J. Ross Publishing, Inc.

ISBN 1-932159-12-6

Printed and bound in the U.S.A. Printed on acid-free paper.
10 9 8 7 6 5 4 3 2 1

Library of Congress Cataloging-in-Publication Data

Burton, Terence T., 1950–
    The lean extended enterprise : moving beyond the four walls to value stream excellence /
by Terence T. Burton and Steven M. Boeder.
        p. cm.
    ISBN 1-932159-12-6
    1. Total quality management. 2. Reengineering (Management). 3. Industrial management.
I. Boeder, Steven M.   II. Title.
    HD62.15 .B867 2003
    658.4′013—dc21   2002156194

Phone: (561) 869-3900
Fax: (561) 892-0700
Web: www.jrosspub.com

TABLE OF CONTENTS

PREFACE

This book has evolved into a challenging and rewarding work with several purposes. Many of our professional colleagues have encouraged Steve and me to write an implementation book about lean. For the past decade, both of us have been involved in many non-traditional applications of kaizen, lean, Six Sigma, and enterprise resource planning (ERP) that you will not find in any previous textbooks. In addition, we have integrated these methodologies, tools, and enabling technologies into a more holistic version of lean across the total value stream. We understand the critical success factors of strategic improvement programs such as lean and Six Sigma, and we have dozens of successful implementations behind us. This book project, however, has been indicative of many improvement programs in industry. We *wanted* to write a book, but we muddled around for two years because we were too busy. We also invented many other convenient excuses to justify postponing the writing of this book. Then we decided to get serious, get down to business, focus our objectives, leverage our knowledge and experiences — and the first draft was completed within a few months.

In retrospect, the muddling and the evolution of this text have been very positive in that they have allowed us to cultivate our ideas and concept-engineer the final product. We started this project with the goal of writing a more hands-on implementation book about lean, but we aborted this option because we felt that the outcome would be *just another book* about lean. The next evolution involved the integration of lean and Six Sigma, but it was just too limiting because it involved writing about something that is so obvious. We understand the controversy and confusion that exist with the integration of all improvement methodologies, tools, and enabling technologies — kaizen, lean, Six Sigma, and ERP — and we have blended these methodologies for years with great success. So integration needs to incorporate all of these methodologies, not just lean and Six Sigma or lean and ERP. This led to the need to present why some organizations achieve great success with these methodologies while others fail miserably. Then we decided we needed to discuss the major *soft-side* elements of success: leadership, strategy, deployment, and execution. We know from our experiences that the tools themselves play a minor role in success because they are the *means,* not the *ends.* Then we decided that we needed to discuss how to move off the shop floor and go after the high-impact opportunities of lean — on the soft core-business processes of the enterprise. More recent experiences with enabling technology beyond ERP — for example, supply chain management (SCM), advanced planning and scheduling (APS), customer relationship management (CRM), supplier relationship management (SRM), product life cycle management (PLM), networks and portals, and Internet-based applications — showed us how to reduce variability and manage demand across the total value stream. Furthermore, these applications enabled many lean practices via collaboration on new product development, planning and order fulfillment, supplier management, sales force automation, and many other value-enhancing activities. During this stage we became familiar with the business models of leading organizations such as Dell, Taylor Made, Best Buy, Herman Miller, Southwest Airlines, Colgate-Palmolive, and many others pursuing excellence across their total value streams. The details of these business models revealed that industry was approaching the next generation of lean very quickly and that many of these organizations had already arrived at these new levels of performance. Business models are moving away from building products, filling up warehouses, and hoping consumers will buy their products and services. The driver of change is a new "demand-slide" economy characterized by dynamic mass-customized demand streams for instant availability of products, in whatever quantity and flavor that appeal to the particular customer. The basics remain the same as they did 100 years ago when people were buying and selling goods off of wagons. However, the value proposition of innovative product development, delivery, customerization, and service is radically different.

Let's clarify something before we go further into this book. Organizations always begin their strategic improvement initiatives with the greatest of intentions — but many fall down in the execution and sustaining phases. For decades, the most common approach for organizations has been to jump sequentially from one improvement program to the next, with a primary focus on disconnected islands of improvement. In retrospect, it seems a bit presumptuous to expect that five lean principles, seven basic QC tools, ERP, a few kanbans, a 5S checklist, a DMAIC framework, a SCOR model, one-minute management, or a reengineering toolbox by themselves would solve the vast array of challenges facing most organizations. A few years ago, some organizations began shifting their improvement focus and began pursuing broader silos of improvement, like product development excellence, customer service and order fulfillment improvements, and supply chain excellence.

Most recently, the emergence of enabling information technology beyond ERP is driving these silos of improvement to a point of convergence. For example, it requires a broad spectrum of integrated methodologies and tools (kaizen, lean, Six Sigma, ERP, etc.) to address total value stream opportunities. It just doesn't work with a *pick one* strategy. Another reality is mass customization and short life cycles. It no longer makes sense to improve a link in the supply chain or the new product development process or customer requirements for existing and new products in isolation of each other. Think about toys, digital electronics, printers, durable goods, automotive components, or fashion merchandise for a minute. Then think about all of the critical customer and supplier information that is floating around among hundreds of people in your organization. It is very possible to have a great product development process but miss significant market opportunities due to supply chain issues, not product development issues. Getting product to the right selling channels and retailers, in the right stockkeeping unit (sku)/store/quantity combinations to satisfy seasonal or cyclical demands is becoming a more precise science. SCM, APS, PLM, CRM, and SRM are enabling organizations to view these activities as seamless, single-process streams.

Let's return to our muddling conversation. This muddling bought us time to combine our experiences, knowledge, leadership and implementation expertise, and emerging enabling technology to create a totally new perspective of lean. The Lean Extended Enterprise is our name for this next generation of lean. The final evolution of our efforts is our book, *The Lean Extended Enterprise: Moving Beyond the Four Walls to Value Stream Excellence.*

WHY THIS BOOK IS A MUST-READ

Before we move on, let's revisit reality for a moment. Pick up any book on lean and what do you see? Most of what is written is about the shop floor. For decades, many of our lean improvement efforts have focused on the production areas because people can *see, touch, feel, hear, and smell* tangible things such as equipment speeds, scrap parts, downtime, bottlenecks, and excess inventory. People talk a good Lean Enterprise game, but the applications of kaizen, lean, and Six Sigma have been focused primarily on "hard processes," isolated islands of improvement, and *Lean Manufacturing*. Many of these books provide the solid philosophy and presentation of kaizen, lean, or Six Sigma tools, but they leave you doing the mambo when it comes to implementation and results. *The Lean Extended Enterprise* fills in these gaps between philosophy and rubber-on-the-road success.

Manufacturing is no longer a competitive weapon; it's just a link in the chain. Optimizing the total value stream is the most critical factor in improving competitiveness. In this total value stream context, most organizations have been focusing their lean efforts in the middle of the process and on the wrong opportunities. For those who really understand root cause analysis and wish to be honest, ask yourself: Where do most of the root causes of shop floor problems occur? The answer to this question is why we now need to focus more attention on the Lean Extended Enterprise.

It's no surprise that many organizations have "hit the wall" with their lean efforts, and several factors contribute to this dilemma:

■ Our leadership and industrial culture demand instant gratification: *Let's hurry up and finish those continuous improvement programs! Let's get ERP up in three months! Let's get Six Sigma going — our customer is visiting us next month! Let's get the lean posters and cell signs hung up! Let's fix everything with a blitz!* Seriously, organizations have a sincere interest and great intentions in improvement, but they are unwilling to make the human investment required to achieve tangible and sustaining success.

■ Many organizations have deployed a shotgun approach to improvement with an overzealous focus on the methodologies and tools themselves. This has produced many splintered, "flavor-of-the month" programs and isolated islands of improvement, but total business performance has not improved as expected. For some of these organizations, their employees "cringe and balk" at the thought of another improvement program. Unfortunately, we cannot blame the methodologies and tools because they work well when deployed correctly to the right opportunities.

■ Organizations refuse to recognize that strategic improvement is a core competency — a core competency that many executives are missing when they begin their improvement journeys and a core competency that they often fail to develop within their organizations. You don't wake up one day, flip a switch, and have these competencies in place throughout your organization. Intention is a right first step, but intention is nothing more than emotion. It takes a big commitment to define and organize a strategic improvement initiative and then integrate strategy, leadership, execution, the right methodologies, and achieve permanent culture change. Those organizations that have achieved impressive results from their strategic improvement programs do so because they understand this fact. They have developed this core competency and they invest years of consistent effort to become best-in-class organizations.

The Lean Extended Enterprise provides a more holistic total value stream approach to lean and builds a greater appreciation of the leadership, strategy, execution, and soft cultural practices that contribute to success. If you're stuck at the perpetual lean wall, this book will help you to knock it down and move on to much higher levels of improvement opportunity across the total value stream.

NEXT-GENERATION LEAN: THE LEAN EXTENDED ENTERPRISE

The next frontier of improvement is the *Lean Extended Enterprise*. This is where organizations migrate from the production floor to the support areas and pursue the "soft process" areas such as new product development, sales and marketing, purchasing and material planning, distribution and logistics, customer/field service, and finance. Organizations find themselves dealing more with information flows than product flows, and these soft processes are the real opportunities for value stream improvement. The further upstream we apply lean, the more significant the benefits, and the benefits increase exponentially. However, we need to expand our methodologies and tools beyond the *five key principles of lean* because we are dealing with a broad range of operational issues that require a broader range of solution sets. In addition, there are the complexities of cross-functional and cross-enterprise business processes and unexplainable process variation. Integration of kaizen, lean, Six Sigma, ERP, and other enabling technologies becomes very important in this transition. There is also a need for stronger and fully engaged leadership to facilitate improvements across the traditional boundaries.

The *Lean Extended Enterprise* views all the entities in the total value stream (e.g., suppliers, subcontractors, the company, and customers) as if they were a single enterprise. The Lean Extended Enterprise is an expansion of our traditional notion of lean to improve velocity, flexibility, responsiveness, quality, cost, and process optimization across the total value stream. The speed and effectiveness of each partner in the total value stream determine how successful the overall value stream will be among competing value streams. This is a gold mine of opportunity because 70 to 95% of many organizations' product cost, lead time, design, supply chain planning, and manufacturing are outside of their four walls. However, it requires deployment and integration of various improvement methodologies to the broader nature of process improvement opportunities. It also requires migrating beyond ERP to other enabling technologies such as SCM, APS, CRM, PLM, SRM, and other Internet-based applications that enable real-time upstream/downstream collaboration. Many Fortune 1000 corporations have already discovered the potential power of the Lean Extended Enterprise, even though they might not call it that exact name, and are well into execution. Many organizations are years into implementation, but for industry as a whole it is the new frontier of improvement — a frontier with order-of-magnitude opportunities and larger benefits than any single improvement initiative that preceded it. The combined benefits of market dominance, benchmark profitability, and total value stream optimization are worth millions to billions of dollars in benefits.

THE LEAN EXTENDED ENTERPRISE: OBJECTIVES AND CONTENTS

We are extremely pleased with the final version of this book because it's not just another book on lean. *The Lean Extended Enterprise* incorporates many new concepts, practices, and principles of the total value stream. The objectives of this book are to:

- Provide a working reference model for the Lean Extended Enterprise that addresses strategy, implementation planning, deployment, execution, and integration of improvement methodologies, tools, and enabling technologies
- Build awareness and importance of soft-side improvement issues, help organizations and individuals avoid the most common pitfalls of strategic improvement, and steer clear of "flavor-of-the-month" fad programs
- Increase acceptance that the Lean Extended Enterprise is a strategic improvement initiative and that it takes continued effort and years to build cultures and organizations such as Dell, Nokia, Caterpillar, Harley Davidson, and other leading value-stream-focused enterprises — but it also results in enormous rewards and market dominance
- Recognize the importance and logic of integrating core business processes, the total value stream, and improvement methodologies such as kaizen, lean, Six Sigma, ERP, and other enabling technologies
- Provide a framework for gauging current strengths and weaknesses vis-à-vis the Lean Extended Enterprise, and assist organizations in refocusing their improvement efforts on the highest value stream opportunities

We are confident that you will find many new and interesting concepts in *The Lean Extended Enterprise.* Our comprehensive Lean Extended Enterprise

Reference Model (LEERM) is included in Chapter 2. The LEERM is comprised of various Panels of Value Stream Integration that provide a step-by-step guide for strategy, implementation planning, deployment, and execution. A crucial dilemma in organizations is the resolution of gaps between the various business improvement methodologies that executives and their people are exposed to and the conflicting actions of what organizations must do, are capable of doing, and would like to do. This book will help you to lead and close these gaps and improve performance across the total value stream. The LEERM provides the foundation, bricks and mortar, and tools to resolve these complicated dilemmas. The Strategy of Improvement process and our Plan-Deploy-Execute framework will help you to remove the emotions and focus on fact-based strategic improvement.

The Lean Extended Enterprise Assessment Process (LEEAP) is presented in Chapter 8. LEEAP is our structured performance measurement instrument for the LEERM. LEEAP includes a detailed assessment and scoring process for the Lean Extended Enterprise across 7 best practice categories and 42 best practice criteria. Chapters 4, 5, and 6 provide discussions about kaizen, lean, and Six Sigma, respectively, and how these methodologies enable the Lean Extended Enterprise. The power of lean and IT (Chapter 7) is phenomenal for upstream/downstream collaboration and real-time demand management. We suggest that you read "Leadership and Infrastructure Development for the Lean Extended Enterprise" (Chapter 3), "Value Stream Integration: A Key Element of Success" (Chapter 9), and "The Lean Extended Enterprise: Bring It On!" (Chapter 10) several times because these are the elements of strategic improvement that make or break your improvement programs. Each chapter includes a summary of key points and a list of selected readings that provide more detailed information about specific topics. You will discover very quickly that this book is definitely a *no-spin zone* version of the Lean Extended Enterprise and strategic improvement. To make the book an interesting read, we have also included anonymous examples and experiences to drive home some of our points. These stories have served as the fodder for increasing our own knowledge and wisdom, and we hope they do the same for you.

Each chapter provides a summary of take-away points and selected further reading and other more detailed resources and Internet references. In addition, free downloads of templates and tools are available from J. Ross Publishing (www.jrosspub.com).

The *Lean Extended Enterprise* is unfolding rapidly before our very eyes. Demand-driven value streams require quick response — beyond the current capabilities of present ERP applications. They require instant collaboration and response across the total value stream. This in turn requires a high degree of integration and comprehensive, more accurate, faster, and more actionable information. The methodologies and enabling technology are available and work well when deployed correctly to the right process improvement opportunities. The super booster enabling technology beyond ERP, such as SCM, APS, CRM, SRM, PLM, networks, portals, and exchanges, is available and is enabling the Lean Extended Enterprise for hundreds of companies and their trading partners.

There is no need to wait for the next silver bullet. We have everything we need to achieve total value stream excellence. It does not matter what color the ribbon is on your improvement box; it's the content of the box that matters. It does not matter what label you assign to your corporate improvement umbrella; it's the substance that counts. If your organization has achieved less than desirable results with previous improvement programs, the Lean Extended Enterprise is a huge opportunity to cultivate these dormant improvements and save millions or billions of dollars. The rest is up to you. Good luck on your challenging and rewarding journey.

Terence T. Burton, President
The Center for Excellence in Operations, Inc.

Steven M. Boeder, Plant Manager
Traex Company, A Unit of Libbey, Inc.

ACKNOWLEDGMENTS

One of the problems with acknowledgments is that we end up in a situation where we can't possibly mention the name of everyone who has influenced our work. Even if we tried, we would inadvertently forget someone. At the top of our list are our own companies, families, friends, and professional colleagues that provided constant encouragement and helped us through this project. In the process of writing this book, we had to transform ourselves into Lean Extended Enterprise monks and disappear on many weekends, forfeiting more precious time than we expected with family and friends.

The next group of people we wish to acknowledge are the hundreds of companies and clients, thousands of executives, and hundreds of thousands of people with whom we have collectively worked over the years. This book would not be possible without the resulting experiences, education, and knowledge gained by our affiliation with you. You represent all of the trails and stepping-stones of wisdom that suddenly fell into place and enabled us to create our book.

Another group we wish to acknowledge is the American Production and Inventory Control Society (APICS) family. We have crossed paths with thousands of fellow professionals over the years. APICS has enabled us to grow from entry-level planners and schedulers into executives, SIG Chairs, instructors, international conference presenters, and thought leaders on the Lean Extended Enterprise. APICS has taught us a great lesson about life: The most rewarding part of learning is giving back and helping to develop others in your profession.

Our careers have also benefitted from the constant stream of new information about leading management topics. We thank the universities, educators, and authors for the thousands of textbooks, trade publications and articles, websites, webinars, workshops and seminars, and other learning opportunities that are available to all of us. Writing this book has created a new level of appreciation for the commitment and efforts of fellow authors. It also makes one appreciate the great education/professional development infrastructure we all have available to us throughout our entire lives.

Many executives and professional colleagues provided their time, invaluable insights, feedback, and thought leadership ideas for our Lean Extended Enterprise mission: Frank Colantuono, Mark Hendricks, Ed Cholmeley-Jones, Marty Mrugal, John Reichard, Ray Rossi, and Norman Scobie of SAP America; Hiten Varia of I2 Technologies; Gary Cone and Aimee Cowher of Global Productivity Solutions; Alec Lengyel and Tom Shaw of the Government Electronics and Information Technology Association of the Electronic Industries Alliance (GEIA); Steve Schaus of Sequa Corporation; Sherry Gordon of ValuEdge; Kelly Marchese of Deloitte Consulting; Paul Matthews of Cap Gemini Ernst & Young; Art Dirik of Demantra Systems; Don Blake, Bill Garrison, Chuck Concannon, and Kurt Robertson of Boeing; Dave Byrne of General Cable; Oddie Leopando and Terry Bell of Maxima Technologies; Gary McCarthy of UPS; Tim Andreae of MCA Solutions; John Tallis of Thomas & Betts; Bob Watson of the Juran Institute; Paul Robinson, Joanne Kalp, and Dave Gronewald of Tyco Healthcare; Linda Hitchens and Paula Smith of APICS; Jack Murray of KPMG Peat Marwick; Bob McInturff of McInturff & Associates; Chris Christensen of the University of Wisconsin Madison; Douglas McGill of Lockheed Martin; Jeff Sams and Eric Lussier of Atlantic Research Corporation; Nikki Savramis of GoodIdea; Vicki Lynch and Jay Zook of CEO; Dan Marconi of Hubbell; Chris Heidelberger of ChannelWave; Dennis Grahn of Menasha Corporation; Bill Heiselman and Jeff Miller of Harris Corporation; Jennifer Cornelssen of EMC; Tony Rudd of Mercury Marine; and Mike Gastonguay of General Electric.

We wish to acknowledge the Massachusetts Institute of Technology (MIT) for its decades of research in lean and, in particular, its leadership of the Lean Aerospace Initiative (LAI). This important collaborative effort between MIT and its coalition partners (e.g., aerospace and defense companies, unions, and government agencies) established an enterprise-wide lean framework for this complex industry. We particularly appreciate the efforts of Professor Deborah Nightingale, Co-director of the LAI, for her thought leadership in the LAI and for promoting the principles and practices of lean across the total enterprise.

Special thanks to Drew Gierman, Publisher at J. Ross Publishing, and the entire J. Ross Publishing team. Without the entrepreneurial and publishing competencies of these individuals, our book would not have been possible.

Through the professional collaboration of everyone we have mentioned, this book was born. This was a professionally rewarding experience for both of us, especially now that we can share the results of our efforts with you.

THE AUTHORS

Terence T. Burton is Founder and President of The Center for Excellence in Operations, Inc. (CEO). He has over 30 years of experience in manufacturing, quality assurance, engineering, materials management, purchasing, distribution, and management consulting. Terry holds a B.S. and M.S. in Industrial Engineering from the University of New Haven and an M.B.A. from Boston University. He is a certified Six Sigma Black Belt, National LEAN SIG Chairman, and CPIM certified member of APICS. He is a frequent instructor/educator, speaker and author at various industry association events, and writes for numerous trade publications. Terry has written hundreds of articles on lean, Six Sigma, supply chain, and accelerated product development and is the author of four books published by Prentice-Hall and Harcourt Brace.

Steven M. Boeder is currently Plant Manager at Traex Company, A Unit of Libbey, Inc. He has over 23 years of experience in production, materials management, purchasing, distribution, quality, and information technology. Steve has extensive implementation experience in Lean Manufacturing and serves as a frequent instructor on the subject at the University of Wisconsin's Management Institute. He holds a B.S. in Business Administration from the University of Wisconsin and an M.B.A. from Edgewood College. He is a CPIM and CIRM certified member of APICS. He has also served as National LEAN SIG Chairman of APICS.

ABOUT APICS

APICS — The Educational Society for Resource Management is a not-for-profit international educational organization recognized as the global leader and premier provider of resource management education and information. APICS is respected throughout the world for its education and professional certification programs. With more than 60,000 individual and corporate members in 20,000 companies worldwide, APICS is dedicated to providing education to improve an organization's bottom line. No matter what your title or need, by tapping into the APICS community you will find the education necessary for success.

APICS is recognized globally as:

- The source of knowledge and expertise for manufacturing and service industries across the entire supply chain
- The leading provider of high-quality, cutting-edge educational programs that advance organizational success in a changing, competitive marketplace
- A successful developer of two internationally recognized certification programs, Certified in Production and Inventory Management (CPIM) and Certified in Integrated Resource Management (CIRM)
- A source of solutions, support, and networking for manufacturing and service professionals

For more information about APICS programs, services, or membership, visit www.apics.org or contact APICS Customer Support at (800) 444-2742 or (703) 354-8851.

Free value-added materials available from
the Download Resource Center at www.jrosspub.com

At J. Ross Publishing we are committed to providing today's professional with practical, hands-on tools that enhance the learning experience and give readers an opportunity to apply what they have learned. That is why we offer free ancillary materials available for download on this book and all participating Web Added Value™ publications. These online resources may include interactive versions of material that appears in the book or supplemental templates, worksheets, models, plans, case studies, proposals, spreadsheets and assessment tools, among other things. Whenever you see the WAV™ symbol in any of our publications, it means bonus materials accompany the book and are available from the Web Added Value Download Resource Center at www.jrosspub.com.

Downloads available for *The Lean Extended Enterprise: Moving Beyond the Four Walls to Value Stream Excellence* consist of lean, kaizen, and Six Sigma implementation tools, assessment guides, templates, and worksheets.

INTRODUCTION
TO THE LEAN
EXTENDED ENTERPRISE

Thirty years ago I (TB) started my industrial engineering career as a time study and methods analyst for one of the world's leading brass manufacturers. It was one of those old-line industries in the Naugatuck Valley area of Connecticut where grandpa, dad, his sons, relatives, and in-laws all worked. At that time, employees had on average around 25+ years of service. The company hired me and Dan, a classmate of mine, as their first two degreed industrial engineers. It was a tremendous transition from academia to the real world of manufacturing. Dan and I were quickly counseled that our long hair, bell-bottoms, platform shoes, and loud ties were inappropriate dress code for the copper and brass industry. Academia could never prepare us for what we were about to experience during those first few years of employment. We were the "hippy-dippy" time study kids in a Theory X (brush cut, white shirt, black tie, polyester sport coat) company.

Dan and I talked off-line a lot, and we agreed that while we might be going through major personal and cultural adjustment, it was an industrial engineer's gold mine, a place where we could directly apply basic industrial engineering skills and make quick improvements. I remember implementing all kinds of state-of-the-art improvements on the shop floor, like rearranging equipment and creating shadow boards for tools to improve workplace organization and flow. We performed setup and changeover studies to reduce downtime and improve delivery flexibility. We conducted man/machine interference and work-sampling studies to reduce idle time. We charted out the flow of many production and overhead operations. People called these our "meat paper" charts because we drew them on a roll of brown butcher paper and covered the walls with them. We set up very clever FIFO cycle die and saw-sharpening practices so they would be ready in the bins the next time they were needed. We held work orders back so we could regulate work in process around the real bottlenecks and drain the swamp of partially completed work on the shop floor. We established standards for engineering and maintenance activities based on reasonable expectancies. We did preventive maintenance/repair kitting and process improvements in the bottleneck areas. I remember clutching my triple watch clipboard as I followed people performing all kinds of jobs around, from the overhead crane operators to the billet extruders. I would time study their every move and later summarize the results into Pareto charts, then categorize their tasks into necessary versus created activity, then redesign the process. I remember standardizing machine adjustments, measuring critical parameters, and performing manual statistical specification studies. I worked with several suppliers on scheduling, cost, and technical tooling issues.

We were clearly dropped into an "us versus them" environment. Initially, we were confronted daily by a plant full of intimidating cigar-chomping union guys. They would tap their machines with one of their metal tools to give everyone a heads-up that the time study guys were walking through. Occasionally, a few of them would wave their wrenches in the air and scream about their machines or if the shop steward knew we were in their area. A few operators would tell us stories of a time study engineer's bones found in the pickling tanks 20 years earlier. Being fresh out of engineering school, we did not confront or tease these guys, as some of our co-workers did. We listened to their concerns. Why? Not because we believed in employee involvement but because we were plain scared! I remember listening carefully to the operators on the floor, asking their opinions and getting them involved in our projects, treating them with dignity and respect, allowing them to help us implement improvements and modify the incentive system so they could still make a few extra bucks for good performance.

One of my first assignments was with "Benny," a second-generation employee and shop steward (Benny's son also worked there). Benny was an intimidating monster of a guy, about 6'5", who wore denim overalls and had fingers like Italian sausages. Benny was a bull worker, and he knew how to work hard and smart. He was a real gentleman — until something set him off. Then he was like a freight train off the track. I heard the old stories about his infamous fistfights in the parking lot and decided very quickly that I never wanted to see that side of him.

Benny and I got off to a good start. We collaborated on how to improve his operation, and, being green, I listened a lot and gained Benny's trust. One day, he said with a grin, "Hey kid, let me show you something. Then you can do whatever you want. You're the time study guy." Benny showed me how to adjust his machine and boost output by 20%, and he also showed me how to adjust the incentive system fairly, honestly, and equitably. When I asked him why he was not running his operation this way, he said, "The other time study men don't even talk to us when they come down here. They told us we *had* to do it this way. They're giving us incentive pay to do things wrong, and they'll write us up if they catch us doing anything different. Pretty dumb, huh." Benny was testing me. We made *his* changes, everybody won, and Benny became a good friend and shop floor ally. I always confided in Benny and tapped his wisdom and his advice on other assignments.

Back then, I could not spell empowerment, but I was practicing it. We were learning firsthand that these operators were only as good as their processes, and we did everything we could do to make their jobs better. They would tip us off and show us how to make improvements, and we would adjust the incentive schedule so they were not penalized for making improvements. The operators on the floor soon became our buddies and showed us the ropes because we gave them a big say in what we were doing. We were successful at winning over many gruff old-timers by making their jobs a lot safer, easier, and higher paying to boot. The shop stewards began requesting that Dan and I be assigned to their studies. Even though shipping performance, profitability, and employee relationships were clearly improving, a few folks in management began accusing us of getting too friendly with the union workers instead of playing the expected management role.

Then there were those incentive systems that made people work like maniacs so they could bring home a few extra bucks for their families. No matter what the other time study guys changed, those workers were clever enough to make it even faster as soon as they walked away. Why? Because nobody listened to them and it was their way of getting even. Faster meant "more money." They even had an acronym for it — IGYYSOB (pronounced "iggysob," which stood for "I'll get you, you SOB"). I remember developing incentive schedules for those big, burly, third-shift casting shop guys dressed in their green asbestos suits, hard hats, and shields, covered from head to toe in lampblack, stirring orange molten metal casting pots. That lampblack penetrated everything and took months to work its way out of your pores. I remember thinking that hell must be like this place. A lot of these guys couldn't speak English, that is until you cheated them out of a nickel on their premium earnings. I remember the heated fist-pounding grievance meetings and flat tires, the "KBATN" (kick butt and take names) culture, the adversarial up-from-the-ranks managers who used the two new industrial engineering college whiz kids as their cost reduction pawns. We were out there like quail foraging for berries (*mils* of savings).

The general manager was like the "Pig Vomit" character in *Private Parts,* the Howard Stern movie, when it came to our dress, but he was usually supportive of our work. For years I wondered why he hired us. We were clearly two square pegs in a bunch of round holes. I never had the opportunity to ask him, but years later Dan and I figured out that he knew exactly what he was doing. The industrial engineering department had a poor reputation, but the work itself was critical to the success of the business. Almost every industrial engineer was previously an operator on the floor, either reluctant to make waves or converted to a time study tyrant. These industrial engineers had the "one to two years of experience 20 times over" disease. The industrial engineering department ran the same way as it did 20 to 30 years earlier, and there was a procedure for everything. These people cut their teeth in the shop on these procedures and viewed them as dictates of behavior. We walked into a "for God's sake don't think, just follow the recipe" job. Some of the process documentation dated back to before we were born. The general manager recruited two inexperienced but energetic industrial engineers with no industry experience and no previous bad habits to bust their old industrial engineering mold. He let us go and we did what we did because we didn't know any better. Some of our co-workers were jealous of our degrees and the fact that we got away with not following departmental procedures. But they could not see that our initial success on the floor was due to listening to operators and new ideas, not a sheepskin or a procedure that did not work anyway. Dan and I joked about our jobs and compared them to cheating on a test because the operators gave us most of the answers!

I will never forget the sounds of the industrial engineering and premium departments' mechanical Frieden calculators that clickety-clicked, clanged, and ka-chinged along all day. Each premium clerk had a huge green binder full of incentive schedules; it was so thick you could use it as a step stool. The clerks would open their green premium schedule binders and begin simultaneously with the 8:00 a.m. bell. Then they would close the binders and wait for the 5:00 p.m. bell almost as if on cue. They did the same thing at lunch and breaks. You could tell the time of day within two or three minutes by the sound of those big binders closing. Technology blessed us with a GE time-sharing system with a teletype machine and a 150-pound Wang scientific calculator. Soon, the whiz kids automated the entire premium department with Data General Novas and eliminated those grotesque green binders. That was an industrial engineer's utopia back then! The oil embargo of 1973 hit us very hard, and everyone in the company suddenly became interested in all of these improvement activities. These efforts made us *lean and mean,* and after the embargo we emerged as a much stronger organization as many of our competitors went belly up.

We did not call what we were doing back then lean or just-in-time (JIT) or Six Sigma, pull systems or kanban or synchronous scheduling or takt time or work cells, reengineering or enterprise resource planning (ERP) or supplier partnering, value stream mapping or non-value-added work, setup reduction or total preventive maintenance, kaizen or 5S, and certainly not cross-functional teaming. But I know our efforts made a big difference in profitability; those mils of savings added up. The time study tools we used were not new. Our co-workers had been using many of these tools for decades. What *was* new was the approach and the execution.

What is the point of telling you this 30-year-old story? Because we want to help you get more results from business improvement. There are at least three universal lessons that are very relevant to business improvement in 2003.

Lesson #1: Business Conditions Change, But the Fundamentals of Business Improvement Do Not

There really is not much new in business improvement when you peel back the onion. We refer to this as the "same box with a different ribbon wrapped around it" syndrome. If you go back and read some of the early 20th century writings of Henry Ford, Fredrick Taylor, and Frank Gilbreth, these people were right on the mark in terms of what we're still trying to get right 100 years later. There has been a parade of buzzword improvement programs during the past few decades. However, the contents of the box remain pretty much the same. Regardless of the ribbon du jour, business improvement is more common sense than rocket science. But it does require strong leadership and breaking the mold of old habits. Sometimes our buzzwords and enabling technologies overcomplicate the simple notion of understanding what the customer wants, when and how much the customer needs, and then delivering on our commitments. Sure, there are legitimate reasons why this is not a perfect science, but the tools themselves are not one of them.

There's nothing new in terms of the tools of lean, kaizen, and Six Sigma themselves; many of these tools have been around for years. What is very new is the enabling technology. We are in such an infancy stage with enabling technologies such as ERP, digitization, advanced planning and scheduling (APS), collaborative development, e-business, digital auctions, and other Internet applications. These enabling technologies are evolving daily, and our children will one day smile about how we used to do things today. There is no need to wait for the next silver bullet — we have all the methodologies and enabling technologies we need. Put these factors together into a cohesive Lean Extended Enterprise initiative and you have literally millions of times the power and opportunities of that GE time-sharing teletype machine or that 150-pound Wang scientific calculator. Leading organizations such as Dell, Ford, Boeing, Bombardier, and others are now integrating all of these elements into their total value chain improvement programs. If you do business with them or any other Fortune 1000 company, your future success will be directly related to how well you hook your wagon into their Lean Extended Enterprises.

Lesson #2: Humbling Experiences Jolt Our Thinking and Force Us to Look at Things Differently

Never underestimate the opportunities growing under your feet. We do not always appreciate some of our career experiences, but eventually the purpose of those experiences falls into place. Thirty years ago I couldn't wait to get a few years of experience behind me so I could move on to a different company, and I did just that, many times over. Many of Dan's and my improvements humbled the place, but we were also painfully humbled back into our place — especially when we tried to introduce our improvement ideas in the exempt office areas (salaried employees thought that they were exempt from the industrial engineering department). Dan and I were too inexperienced to be products of the habits, norms, and practices of our environment, so we ended up doing a lot of things differently. We were blessed with learning about business improvement and cultural change from the first minute of our careers. It was an introduction to the harsh realities of change and how our industrial engineering logic, reason, and tools by themselves were no match for entrenched cultural norms.

Back then, I could not have possibly realized how those valuable experiences would ultimately influence my career and the direction it took — and, more importantly, the collective education, knowledge, and industry experiences that led me to start up a successful company and be capable of writing this book. It's funny how all of the experiences and situations stick in your mind, and then one day you understand the purpose of all those stopping-off points in your career and how they all fit together. It's called wisdom, and you collect it by opening your mind to a wide variety of situations and by being a participant in many humbling experiences. Sometimes you get to play the *humbler* and sometimes you're the *humblee,* but it's all wisdom. Exposure to these humbling experiences opens the mind's eye to change. Soak up every learning experience available to you like a sponge, and listen to everyone's point of view. Stop complaining about inefficiency and bad practices — challenge them and chase down better alternatives with real data. Don't be afraid to become involved in these situations, and always act professionally and with the facts. If you are painfully humbled, step back and look for the lessons learned because you probably deserved it. Humbling experiences jolt our thinking and force us to look at things differently. Keep your attitude in check, and don't let it get in the way of new ideas. Pay attention to those precious learning opportunities. You never know how those stepping-stones will fall into place someday to your personal and professional advantage. Business improvement is a journey of fun, personal growth, professional accomplishment, and human fulfillment.

Lesson #3: Business Improvement Is a Fact of Life

Organizations can be involved in many of these improvement programs and not gain any tangible benefits or competitive ground. We have all experienced the billions of dollars spent on total quality management (TQM), JIT, total employee involvement (TEI), total preventive maintenance (TPM), lean, kaizen, reengineering, ERP, Six Sigma, and many other strategic improvement programs only to fall short on delivering the results promised. We have watched these various methodologies achieve breakthrough improvement in some organizations and fail miserably in others. There are a number of factors that cause results way below expectations, and we will cover most of them in this book. The good news is that many previous improvement programs provide an excellent springboard for the Lean Extended Enterprise. Better yet, those sunk costs can be leveraged into larger breakthrough improvements. Whether you have achieved raving success or total failure with prior improvement programs, strategic business improvement is a fact of life if you want to be a competitive player in your markets.

Improvement is not success or failure dependent, it's not product or industry dependent, and it's not program or customer dependent. Improvement is always necessary, especially in today's competitive global economy. Too many executives view improvement as a response to something bad, and if things are okay, then there is no need for it. Maybe it's ingrained thinking because "needs improvement" was often affiliated with report cards, warning slips, and performance appraisals. Another common dilemma is the across-the-board freezes when things get tight. This strategy has never made sense because it freeze-frames organizations, people, learning and development, processes, and performance. It is a guaranteed strategy that nothing will improve. The fact is, every enterprise needs to make improvement as important as booking an order, paying vendors, and closing the books every month. And every organization needs to make improvement both real and real-time to customers and its own bottom line.

The Lean Extended Enterprise represents an enormous opportunity to recapture all that money left on the table. Those investments are sunk costs if you choose the "let's wait and see" mind-set and do nothing. Sure, we can sit back and blame 9/11 or the slump in the economy or our customers for these problems. The hard fact of the matter is that, in many cases, there is no correlation between the internal excuses and the external world of events. When executives choose to think that there *is* a correlation and act accordingly, it all becomes a self-fulfilling prophecy. You had these problems before 9/11 and the market crash, and you will have bigger problems when things get better if you choose to do nothing. Pretty soon, this leadership style becomes an all too familiar tune. A comment by one executive to his staff says it all: "There's only two outcomes in business and in life — performance and excuses."

THE LEAN EXTENDED ENTERPRISE: THE NEXT FRONTIER OF IMPROVEMENT

The concepts, definitions, and methodologies of lean have been present in American industry for decades. Probably the most well-known example of lean is Toyota, when it developed its Toyota Production System (TPS) after World War II; it finally caught the Western world's attention after the 1973 oil crisis. For over 20 years before anyone knew it, Toyota pursued the TPS primarily to eliminate waste and reduce costs in its production system — it was the obvious solution to manage the constraints of space, people, and limited resources. But the reality is that many of the basic concepts of lean have been kicking around for nearly a century, going back as far as Fredrick Taylor's Principles of Scientific Management, Dr. Shewhart at Western Electric, and Henry Ford's mass production system. A big breakthrough occurred in 1996 with the book *Lean Thinking* by James P. Womack and Daniel T. Jones. Although most industries "dabbled" in many "flavor-of-the-month" improvement programs, *Lean Thinking* brought a more focused and disciplined approach to lean with the five key principles: specify value, create the value stream, flow, pull, and perfection.

Through the 1980s and up to the present time, most organizations have been involved in a variety of formal improvement programs such as MRP II, JIT, bar coding, TQM, ERP, reengineering, kaizen, lean manufacturing, and team-based problem solving. More recently, there are bold initiatives in the areas of lean, Six Sigma, supply chain management, and many enabling technologies such as collaborative product development, collaborative forecasting and planning, and digitization. Much of these efforts has focused primarily within the four walls of an enterprise and on the production floor. For this reason and many others, it is not surprising that the benefits have not been as great as expected, particularly when one considers all the "money left on the table" in the total value stream.

The next frontier of opportunity for lean exists in the end-to-end value stream. This means getting off the production floor and attacking the "soft process" areas such as new product development, sales and marketing, purchasing, distribution and logistics, customer/field service, and finance. It means connecting the dots on your current fragmented improvement efforts. This also means walking outside of your four walls and building nimble lean supply and customer networks. Finally, it means recognizing that you are just a small piece of the total improvement opportunity. We refer to this as the Lean Extended Enterprise. The Lean Extended Enterprise views every entity in the total value stream (e.g., suppliers, subcontractors, your company, and customers) as if they were a single enterprise. The Lean Extended Enterprise also views every activity in the stream, from design to delivery and post-sales service/support, as opportunities for improvement. This shift is happening fast, and the early leaders are achieving best-in-class performance with revenue growth, faster cash-to-cash cycles, lower operating costs, and a much more challenged workforce. Figure 1.1 provides an overview of the Lean Extended Enterprise.

The Lean Extended Enterprise is gaining momentum rapidly because it provides a model in which companies and trading partners interact across key processes of sales, sourcing, procurement, product development, manufacturing, order fulfillment, and customer service. No longer is the production floor by itself a competitive advantage. The Lean Extended Enterprise is an expansion of our traditional notion of lean to improve velocity, flexibility, responsiveness,

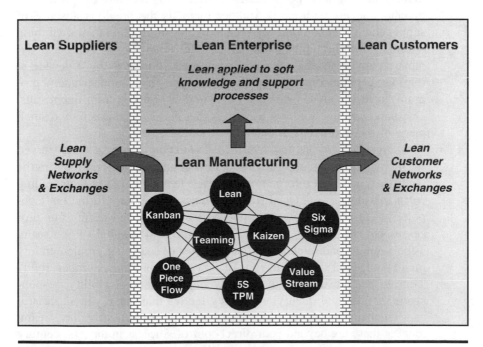

FIGURE 1.1 The Lean Extended Enterprise

quality, and cost across the total value stream. In short, it means deciding on the best collaborative courses of action and then acting on those decisions quickly so everyone in the value stream benefits. The speed and effectiveness of each partner in the total value chain determine how successful the overall value chain will be among competing value chains.

A number of factors are driving this new movement to the Lean Extended Enterprise:

1. The manufacturing landscape has changed dramatically in the past few decades. There is a much larger electronics and software content in most production operations, resulting in less intensive, smaller shop floor activity and much more "knowledge-based" activity. Another factor is globalization and a move to smaller nimble operations more contiguous to the markets they serve. A third factor is the whole offshore movement. A fourth factor is shorter life cycles and a much faster paced, much more competitive industrial world. A good example of a major manufacturing landscape change is high-tech hardware production, which is much smaller than it was 20 years ago.

2. Most improvement programs typically begin in production and materials management because people can see, touch, and measure the product or inventory levels with ease. Another factor is the previous absence of supply chain collaboration, which led organizations to do their own thing internally with little thought about the total value stream. Quite frankly, most organizations have made great progress during the past decade in improving production and quality. However, many improvement programs have run out of steam and failed to deliver real bottom-line results. One important fact we have learned is that the shop floor is only a small piece of the improvement pie.

3. Most organizations are now overloaded with conflicting data and starved for high-quality factual information. Few companies are confident in the quality of their own information and even less confident in their trading partners' information. Our ERP, e-business, and other information technology (IT) initiatives were supposed to simplify and define our processes, but they have complicated many aspects of the total value stream. Take a minute and think about the total cost of acquiring, implementing, maintaining, and supporting your ERP system. It's a huge number, right?

4. Time to market, innovation, velocity improvement, flexibility, responsiveness, cost, and quality are all key factors that make you successful as a company. If you consider every activity in the total value stream, most of these are beyond your direct control. Success in the 21st century depends on how the Lean Extended Enterprise operates, not how you

operate as a single link in the chain. Sure, some links have more power than others, but even corporate giants like GE, Ford, and Boeing are highly dependent on the Lean Extended Enterprise.

5. Think about developing a profit-and-loss and a value stream map for your own Lean Extended Enterprise. Guess what you would learn. Based on our benchmarking and client experiences, you would find that as much as 70 to 95% of product cost is generated outside of your company. You would find that as much as 75 to 95% of lead time is consumed outside of your company. You would learn that 95%+ of the key activities of design, supply chain planning, and manufacturing (and the associated employees) are outside of your company. You would learn that there is a whole stream of conflicting performance measurements in place, creating conflicts between various elements of the total value stream. And finally, you would wonder why your organization is not in hot pursuit of this gold mine of collective opportunity. That's why the Lean Extended Enterprise is so critical to future success and collaborative competitiveness.

BENEFITS OF THE LEAN EXTENDED ENTERPRISE

Why should an organization be interested in another improvement program? What does all of this Lean Extended Enterprise stuff equate to in terms of return on investment (ROI) and benefits? How is it different from Six Sigma or your ERP implementation? First, the Lean Extended Enterprise is not another new program. In some cases, it builds upon previous successes with these individual improvement methodologies to take the organization to a higher level of excellence. In other cases, it means going back and learning how to harvest all the fruit not harvested from your previous efforts. In every strategic improvement initiative from reengineering to Six Sigma there have been successes and failures. We understand the differences and have provided much of this new knowledge in this book. One of the major themes of this book is that all of the improvement methodologies are not new, but they all work well when applied to the right opportunities. They work even better when integrated and deployed across the total value chain. That's a major message of this book. There's no other way to say it: If you failed at any previous improvement programs, it's not the tool's fault. But the money is still on the table.

Second, the cash-to-cash implications of the Lean Extended Enterprise are enormous. The potential benefits of the Lean Extended Enterprise are equal to a conservative 3 to 7% of revenues annually, depending on your starting point. Smaller organizations may be at the lower end of the spectrum, although not necessarily. Larger organizations tend to achieve benefits in the upper end of the spectrum and beyond because their value streams are more complex and contain more waste. We are not insinuating that smaller organizations are more efficient than larger organizations. Larger organizations have more links in their customer and supply chains and therefore more layers of opportunity across the entire value stream. Think about this for a minute. A $100 million company might be looking at $3 to $5 million a year in savings, and a $5 billion company might be looking at $50 to $70 million a year in savings. In terms of incremental profitability, this equates to 20 to 50% revenue growth. That's real money! When the Fords, the Unilevers, the Harley Davidsons, and Daimler Chryslers ask their suppliers for cost reductions that seem off the wall, they're not. They are very achievable with the right improvement strategy and execution plan.

To achieve these dramatic results, executives must embrace two distinct levels of performance: strategic performance and operating performance. At the strategic level, executives must lead, mentor, and live the change process until it becomes embedded in the organizational culture. For example, GE defines Six Sigma as "the way they work — in everything they do and in every product they design." It is not a program; it is within the core values of how GE conducts its business. At the operating level, executives must build the right infrastructure and execute change in a way that produces an ROI for the business. Organizations deserve, and should achieve, a return on their improvement initiatives and tie the results of their efforts directly to operating performance. Organizations that are maniacs about the first level of performance usually achieve significant benefits at the second level, regardless of the particular improvement methodology. Some organizations do not embrace strategic performance. They might achieve some temporary improvements, but they usually drift back into old habits. Others delegate major improvement to a committee or get bogged down in tunnel vision justifications and ROI calculations that they will never see. Major strategic improvement requires a healthy balance between strategic performance and operating performance to be successful.

LEARN BEFORE YOU LEAN

Implementing the Lean Extended Enterprise is more difficult and challenging than any other improvement effort an organization may have pursued in the past. It requires a value stream mind-set, strong leadership, a precision-driven improvement strategy, collaboration, and deployment of the right improvement tools to the right opportunities. The good news is that it's more common sense than rocket science. Unlike our traditional lean viewpoint, it takes a lot more than the *five key principles of lean* applied to the shop floor to succeed.

Two of the most disturbing trends in organizations attempting to implement business improvements such as lean, kaizen, Six Sigma, or ERP are (1) the tendency to get it done and over with and (2) the fascination with improvement tools and techniques. We will cover this topic in more detail in Chapter 3, but it is worth mentioning right up front. Many organizations skip the most important element of improvement — the Strategy of Improvement. We believe that much of the blame rests on that quarterly performance mind-set. Instead, organizations hold their finger to the wind, then launch the popular buzzword program. First it's TQM, then JIT, then reengineering, then ERP, then kaizen, then lean, then Six Sigma in hopes that one of these programs will fix everything. Managers go off to a workshop or visit a customer, then grab hold and implement tools and techniques in an effort to get quick results. They attempt to solve every perceived problem in the company with the same tools. Before you know it, equipment is rearranged in a U-shaped layout, cell signs are hung up, bright kanban squares are painted on the floor, and everything looks better. There must be thousands of organizations with their nice-looking, cherry-picked work cells in the corner of the plant. Everyone is chest thumping because they blitzed it into place in three days. People are out for the next few months giving speeches about their accomplishments, and if they're really lucky, a trade publication writes an article about it. But their customers see no difference in their performance. Then you hear the questions: Should I implement lean before or after Six Sigma? Should I implement kaizen before lean? How do I implement a pull system with an inaccurate sales forecast? Which is better, lean or the TPS? Isn't Six Sigma the same as TQM? Will lean foul up our ISO certification? Can you help me set up a DOE on shop rag usage? Their intentions are good, but the execution is poor. The focus is often on the tools rather than the problem. Their actions are "perception driven" versus "fact driven" and not focused on true pain points and causal factors of the business. The improvements are heavy on the hype, light on results, and transparent to the customer and the bottom line. But everyone receives their coffee mug. The real root cause? Leadership. Executives and managers always ask, "What are the major pitfalls of kaizen, lean, ERP, Six Sigma?" Believe us, it isn't the tools, and it isn't the software because these elements work well. It is strategy, deployment, and execution, all of which fall into the domain of leadership. Regardless of the name you assign to your corporate improvement umbrella — lean, Six Sigma, extended enterprise integration, or hocus pocus — remember that success is 80% leadership and 20% tools. When we refer to leadership, we are not placing the blame on your executives, as you will see in Chapter 3. Leadership incorporates a continuum of factors that touches everyone in the organization.

Enough cynicism. It's too easy to blame leadership. But have you either heard about or been part of, although you may not want to admit it, an improvement program like this? This approach may produce a few short-term benefits, but it never becomes a sustaining improvement process embedded in the company's culture. It's very frustrating to get involved in another one of these programs; people eventually question the results, and it degenerates into another "flavor-of-the-month" improvement program. It creates a very skeptical "oh oh, here we go again" culture that resists change. Leadership has set people up to balk and cringe at the thought of another improvement program. You cannot order people to change by edict; the most successful changes occur when people understand and play an active role in change. When discussing this topic, the words spoken by an executive a few years back come to mind: "We need lean because we finished our continuous improvement programs years ago!" He caught himself and quickly became amused by his off-the-cuff comment.

This "flavor-of-the-month" approach also becomes a convenient way to define and pass along problems or point fingers. At one organization that really got into kaizen blitzes (as opposed to kaizen as a longer term improvement philosophy), the executive team was your familiar "get it done and over with" taskmaster group. They brought in a kaizen blitz consulting firm and pursued this effort for nearly a year. They blitzed everything from the incoming quality control department to the cafeteria food. They used the words blitz and lean interchangeably. Every time there was a problem, someone would say, "Hey, we need Joe to come over and do a kaizen on this problem." They blitzed a welding operation to death, trying to fix complex process variation. Sorry, wrong tool. If the problem wasn't resolved, it always seemed to be Joe's fault. It reminded me (TB) of my early career when a production foreman would call the quality control manager and say, "You better get out here. *You* have a quality problem," or when my phone would ring and the vice-president of finance would tell me that *I* have an inventory problem. Did Joe or the quality control manager or I create these problems? Of course not, but they are the convenient excuse, the point people to pass on the hot potato. In all fairness, did this organization achieve any benefits? Sure, everyone has low-hanging fruit. Today, however, the low-hanging fruit and their kaizen blitz program are both gone. Remember that quality, inventory, delivery performance, profitability, and process variation are outcomes. To eliminate these problems you need to understand and deal with the root causes. You cannot fix outcomes.

Figure 1.2 includes two very important formulas for success on your Lean Extended Enterprise journey. They are two formulas we all intuitively know, but often do not put into daily practice.

Our intent is not to be negative, but we want you, the reader, to reflect on these discussions as a wake-up call because they cause most improvement

Same People *Same Thinking* *+ Same Process* ························ *Same Results!* *Improvement requires a* *change in the input* *factors.*	$Problem = f\,(Root\ Causes)$ *You cannot fix a problem unless you* *eliminate the root causes.* *You must calibrate and measure root causes,* *before and after change.* *If the problem gets smaller or goes away,* *you addressed the correct root cause.*

FIGURE 1.2   Lean Extended Enterprise 101: two important formulas to remember

programs to fail. They will cause the Lean Extended Enterprise to fail. If your organization is guilty of any of the areas we discussed above, then recognize that you will need a leadership and cultural mind-set change before you embark on your Lean Extended Enterprise journey. Otherwise, you will add another "flavor-of-the-month" improvement program to your collection. We will expand on these two areas in much more detail in Chapter 2.

The benefits of the Lean Extended Enterprise (3 to 7% of an organization's total revenues) are very real. However, the benefits are outcomes of a successful implementation. Organizations will succeed by pursuing this journey along three vectors of improvement: They must continue with their operational focus and wring out every possible opportunity on the manufacturing shop floor. They need to expand their operational focus to a business or enterprise focus and go after the opportunity-rich soft process areas such as product development, inventory management, sales and marketing, finance, distribution, and customer service. Finally, they need to expand their enterprise focus to a shareholder focus and pursue value creation across the extended enterprise. Organizations can close the gap between current and best-in-class performance with great leadership coupled with relentlessly tracking down the causal factors. There is no shortcut or magic improvement dust, just a lot of hard work. It will not happen in 60 days or 6 months. It's an industrial mind-set change, a cultural transformation. The best-in-class performers are reaching this improvement plane in three to four years. Many organizations are well into this journey, and many will never get there if they do not begin now. As one executive said, "I'm not going to implement Six Sigma until my customers make me do it."

The Lean Extended Enterprise focuses on creating the right infrastructure to achieve total value stream success: faster cycle times, instantaneous visibility and synchronization, increased flexibility and responsiveness, higher quality, lower supply chain costs from your business networks, and increased profitability and competitiveness. The Lean Extended Enterprise expands the scope of our traditional view of lean beyond the four walls and targets the most significant *pain-point* collaborative processes as opportunities for breakthrough improvement.

The Lean Extended Enterprise is the total value stream equivalent of a Cirque Du Soleil play. Unbelievable acts are happening at varying degrees of speed. The acts and the music tell a visual story. Individual actors are paying meticulous attention to their own roles and the other details around them. There is real-time communication and information exchange. Every movement is an example of perfection, with very tight margins for error. Every motion of every act is in perfect harmony via quick response and instantaneous adjustment. Timing and delivery are precise. Whether it's Boston, Orlando, Montreal, or Las Vegas — whether it's Quidam, La Nouba, Mystere, or Alegria with different actors — the process is perfect. The customers are always astonished and thunderstruck by the experience.

RESPONDING TO THE DEMAND-SLIDE ECONOMY

For most organizations, lean is still more of an operational tactic than an all-encompassing business strategy. Most of the books to date address lean as a manufacturing tool or give a 75,000-foot view of lean as an overall organizational architecture. Other books invent new ribbons for the same old box. The five principles of lean fit best with production operations, and that's where most people start and stop. The Lean Extended Enterprise expands our traditional perspective of lean. This broader vision of lean recognizes that eliminating waste and improving competitiveness are universal strategies that apply to the total value stream. One of the objectives of this book is to show you that no matter what the label on your improvement umbrella reads, it is your actions that ultimately count.

It has taken us only 200 years to destroy the notion of supply-side economics. The world is moving away from building products, filling up warehouses, and hoping consumers will buy those products. We are in a new *demand-slide* economy characterized by dynamic mass-customized demand streams for instant availability of products, in whatever quantity and flavor that appeal to the particular customer. No, it's not a Freudian slip. It's short for *demand landslide* because that is exactly how it is hitting organizations that are ill prepared to respond to these new order-of-magnitude market demands. A good example of this is cell phones. Beyond the initial purchase, just think of all the calling plans, keyboard styles, phone covers, antenna and battery lights, and other customized add-ons available in the marketplace. The only way to define, develop, manage, and deliver on customer requirements and these tight windows of opportunity is through instantaneous upstream/downstream collaboration.

The Lean Extended Enterprise is very real. There are already many terms — the extraprise; the value chain; the extended enterprise; collaborative production, forecasting, and replenishment; collaborative commerce; demand-chain management; and others — to describe this evolution. Many organizations are years into implementation, but for industry as a whole it is a new frontier of improvement — a frontier with larger opportunities and larger benefits than any single improvement initiative that preceded it. The Boeings, Dells, Fords, Lockheed Martins, and Rockwells have already discovered the power of the Lean Extended Enterprise, even though they might not call it that exact name. The knowledge, the upstream/downstream collaboration, the methodologies and tools, and the enabling technologies are available. It's now a matter of putting it all together into an integrated approach and executing.

We will integrate lean thinking vertically — implementing lean beyond the production floor to the high-impact "soft process" areas. We will integrate lean thinking horizontally beyond the four walls to cover the highly leverageable total value stream opportunities in the customer and supplier domains. And we will integrate lean thinking laterally — success through empowered people and teams, through cultural transformation, and through integration of kaizen, lean, Six Sigma, ERP, and other enabling technologies. Organizations such as Dell, Daimler Chrysler, Boeing, and many other smaller ones have applied many of these concepts correctly to their operational, business, and shareholder opportunities and have achieved great results. They live the Lean Extended Enterprise every day.

The goal of this book is to provide a practitioner's text on how to implement the Lean Extended Enterprise based on our experience with hundreds of companies. We will support our text with case studies and examples and also discuss many of our experiences to make the book more fun. Our intent is not to belittle anyone, but rather to help the broader readership avoid common mistakes in its Lean Extended Enterprise implementation efforts. As always, remember that total wisdom equals positive wisdom plus negative wisdom plus neutral wisdom.

CASE STUDY 1: BOEING*

Across the enterprise, Boeing is attacking waste and streamlining processes. The goal? Cost competitiveness. These days, it isn't enough for a company to merely cut costs. It needs to streamline processes while improving quality, becoming nimble while responding quickly to customer demand, and empowering employees while increasing profits. In the early nineties, Boeing faced a deregulated commercial airline industry that had begun to focus on profitability and realized it needed to become leaner in order to offer its customers airplanes at reduced costs and improved quality. Company executives traveled to Japan, where they studied concepts that would become known as lean — just-in-time delivery, error-free production, and continuous flow. Boeing initially focused on Commercial Airplanes, but crossed business units and helped drive lean improvements in the groups now comprising Integrated Defense Systems (IDS). Although lean often is viewed as a factory floor concept, its philosophy stretches across the Boeing enterprise, touching everything from suppliers and procurement to engineering and design to manufacturing and delivery. Stunning results have been achieved even in the areas of aircraft modification and support. In fact, all these systems must be integrated and embrace lean concepts in order for progress to occur across the value stream.

Boeing's mid-nineties shift to lean is already reaping tangible dividends. Consider:

- The F/A-18E/F Super Hornet program aimed to reduce defects by 90% from 1998 to 2003, but reached this goal two years early. The program also continues to operate under budget, realizing a savings of 1.5 million labor hours while having delivered each of its 100 aircraft on or ahead of contract delivery dates.

- By incorporating lean tactics throughout the design and construction phase, the Delta IV facility in Decatur, Alabama shrank from a planned 4 million square feet to 1.5 million square feet. Rather than building multiple rocket assembly lines, a lean process helped create a single continuously moving line. Also, thanks to better space utilization, the facility was able to bring in Delta II fabrication and tank production work.

- Two of Phantom Works' technology thrusts specifically address lean, funneling what they learn across the Boeing enterprise. The "Lean Sup-

---

* Summarized from Boeing's *Frontiers* magazine article entitled "Getting Lean." Reprinted with permission.

port and Service Initiatives" thrust designed processes for streamlining the KC-135 facility in San Antonio, Texas, as well as processes that helped IDS compete for the extension of the Payload Ground Operations Contract.

■ Using a lean-derived "kaizen" process, Shared Services Group tape librarians at a Boeing Data Center in Puget Sound reduced the footprint of the tape library used by the Enterprise Server by more than 90% while significantly shortening the tape-handling cycle time.

■ Since 1998, the AH-64D Apache multi-role combat helicopter final assembly line in Mesa, Arizona has used lean tactics and tools to create a pulse moving line. The Apache program has realized a 54% reduction in build hours and 218% increase in its build rate.

■ Workers in so-called "moonshine shops" team up to create right-sized production equipment that is more precise and requires less space and maintenance — and costs less — than monument-sized machines purchased by outside suppliers. Right-sized equipment is designed for a very specific purpose, usually for one task or set of tasks for one part or part family, whereas "monuments" tend to be multi-purpose and support a wide range of work statements. For example, workers replaced a $2 million three-axis router used in airplane stow bin production at Everett's Interior Responsibility Center with a "homemade" version for just $50,000. And that's what it used to cost annually just to repair the more expensive machine.

■ The 757 program's field processes have transferred to Final Assembly, saving one day of flow time. Also, Systems Installation has moved into Final Assembly, housing all assembly and integration processes under one roof. To date, the 737 program has shaved its flow time by 30 percent, reduced its crane moves by 39%, lowered its inventory levels by 42%, and reduced its needed floor space by 216,000 square feet.

Analyst Howard Rubel of Goldman Sachs noted Commercial Airplanes' lean improvements in a June 20, 2002 report, following his visit to the 737 and 757 production lines in Renton, Washington: "Boeing's plan to change the way it manufacturers jetliners appears to be delivering results," he wrote. "We believe that productivity initiatives adopted through the introduction of lean manufacturing processes have reshaped the company's learning curve and enabled it to enjoy far less disruptions than planned, especially as it reduces production to match the current market environment. We believe that the company is ahead of its long-term operating plan and that the reduced costs can flow into profits."

Suppliers and Procurement Are Key

Boeing suppliers are integral parts of the value stream, from both cost and logistics standpoints. Across the company, lean practitioners are sharing their knowledge with suppliers, helping them streamline their operations and thus become better partners to Boeing. The Supplier Management Process Council, which predates the Boeing merger and acquisitions of the late 1990s, oversees this process. It's about leading by example, says council chairman Bill Stowers.

Woven Electronics supplies wiring harnesses for the JDAM program, and the Simpsonville, South Carolina–based firm embraced the chance to learn lean. Woven has been part of the U.S. Air Force–sponsored Small/Medium Enterprise Initiative, designed to help small- and medium-sized firms improve their manufacturing technology practices. Since starting lean activities on its first harnesses in January 2000, Woven has improved its inventory turns from 7 turns a year to its current 26 turns. It is very close to a one-piece flow, which means it doesn't have all the work-in-progress inventory, and cycle time has been reduced from weeks down to hours. The company has gone from producing 30 cables each week to 90 cables per day to keep up with JDAM's ramped-up production.

Boeing isn't just focusing on manufacturing suppliers. Even Boeing Library Services recently introduced its own lean ordering process, turning the ordering of all books, except those not available through Boeing-approved supplier Barnes & Noble, over to each organization or group. The goal: to remove the library as a middleman. Eliminating this step lowers the end price to the ultimate Boeing customer, as overhead finance costs are no longer added to the price of publications.

Inevitable Culture Shift

Change — even when inevitably for a company's good — is never easy. But engaging employees in the process, from conception to development and delivery, is critical to lean's success at Boeing and beyond. While some shop floor workers used to refer to lean scornfully as "Less Employees Are Needed," many who implement its concepts every day have become believers. To maintain the free flow of ideas, the company may soon host a competition between moonshine shops to reward the most creative approaches to factory floor problems.

CASE STUDY 2: DELL COMPUTER CORPORATION

Dell Computer is the poster child of the Lean Extended Enterprise. Using a web-based direct-to-customer business model, Dell has revolutionized the way that computers are configured, priced, and sold. Over 50% of Dell's sales come over the web. At the same time, more than 85% of Dell's suppliers are electronically integrated, resulting in a seamless and quick value stream. Every 20 seconds Dell aggregates customer orders and instantly analyzes material requirements and checks stock availability in its 7 hours worth of inventory. If the inventory is not on hand, Dell's suppliers have 90 minutes to assemble the order and drive it to Dell's plant. Dell then unloads and positions inventory on the assembly line within the next 30 minutes — in the exact order that it is needed for assembly.

Dell has the end-to-end visibility of demand and supply. Instead of the tedious approach of forecasting, master scheduling, ERP explosion, purchase order processing, and expediting, Dell and its suppliers collaboratively plan and receive the exact material needed to support customer orders every two hours. Dell's competitors, such as Compaq, IBM, and HP, rely more on the sales channel business model, which requires about three to four weeks of inventory in the channel pipeline. This leads to slower response to change, higher inventory investment, more obsolescence, and lower profitability. These factors are very important indicators in the PC marketplace. When cycle times are reduced to the Dell levels, the need for forecasting and planning becomes less important. Velocity is the key to managing variation. The Dell value chain discovers situations and acts on them in real time, so the variation within these 20-second and 90-minute windows is a lot less. Dell is measuring performance in minutes and hours, while the rest of the world thinks in terms of weeks or months.

CASE STUDY 3: ROCKWELL AUTOMATION POWER SYSTEMS*

Rockwell Automation Power Systems chose the name Power Lean for its Lean Enterprise implementation effort because the business philosophy of Lean Enterprise has been "super-charged" with the tools and methodologies of Six Sigma. The objective of Power Lean is to enable growth of the business by using the tools and methodologies of lean and Six Sigma to reduce lead times, reduce cost, improve quality, and improve delivery performance. Power Lean combines the structured training and certification approach of Six Sigma Black Belts with the hard-hitting, bias for action approach of kaizen teams. Power Lean is a holistic approach in which the efforts of strategic sourcing, lean manufacturing, design, e-commerce, and total quality are well coordinated and

---

* Summarized from an SAE article entitled "Seamless Integration of Lean Enterprise and Six Sigma." ©2003 SAE International. Reprinted with permission.

properly linked to Rockwell's stakeholders and financial metrics. Quantitative three-year goals were established for Power Lean, which are focused on quality, cost, and delivery performance. These key elements of business performance are critical factors in satisfying existing customers and winning new business. They are also the metrics most impacted by the tools and methodologies of lean and Six Sigma.

Lean Enterprise is centered on the concept of flow. Once value has been clearly and accurately defined, value stream mapping, pull production systems, and continuous improvement systems are all designed to enable and maintain flow. Two of the major inhibitors to flow in a production environment or business process are variation and defects. Although the philosophy of Lean Enterprise recognizes this critical element, reduction of variation and defect elimination can be greatly enhanced by the adoption of Six Sigma tools and methodologies. It is for this reason that Lean Enterprise and Six Sigma make for an ideal merger. The benefits of Six Sigma cannot be fully realized in an organization that is not lean and a process cannot flow when there is excessive variation and defects.

CASE STUDY 4: FORD MOTOR COMPANY

Ford purchases over $100 billion of products and services from its supply base. Two hundred suppliers provide nearly 90% of the materials and components used in the production of Ford cars and trucks. Approximately 10,000 suppliers provide Ford with all of the other products and services it needs to run its business, ranging from capital equipment to advertising. Ford's interface with suppliers has evolved from one focused through global purchasing to a broad-based network of relationships spanning people in many activities across Ford and supplier organizations. This strategy has allowed Ford to focus the effort of all its people on improving quality, increasing customer satisfaction, and working more efficiently and effectively.

Today, suppliers are closely integrated into Ford's product development process and, in many cases, have direct responsibility for the design and engineering of components and complete systems. To promote the closest possible ties in these programs, Ford and supplier employees engage in a Business Leadership Implementation program aimed at strengthening cross-company relationships on program development teams and focusing their combined energy on delivery of new vehicle and powertrain programs that satisfy customers. Ford works together with its suppliers to find new ways to improve quality, enhance efficiency, spur innovation, and meet social and environmental expectations simultaneously. The goal is to increase the overall value the total value stream provides to Ford customers, shareholders, and society. Ford is working so closely with many of its suppliers that, to an outside eye, they sometimes are indistinguishable from Ford Motor Company.

Ford is also working more closely with its inter-plant product manufacturing and assembly. For example, at Ford's new Northeast Industrial Complex in Bahia, Brazil, 29 suppliers will be working with Ford to launch an innovative process that will take Ford and its suppliers to new levels of cooperation. Suppliers are providing higher levels of value-added, including design expertise and value chain management. Ford and its suppliers will be sharing the site, services, and management of the plant.

Ford's International Supplier Advisory Council provides an opportunity for Ford's senior leaders to meet with the CEOs of their leading suppliers. The council provides an opportunity for these leaders to discuss emerging industry issues and establish strategies for coordinated deployment at Ford and supplier companies. Over the last two years, for example, the council championed a focused effort to improve the high-mileage reliability of Ford's products. Ford is extremely committed to maintaining strong links with its suppliers through ongoing executive-level dialogue. The Executive Champion Program connects a Ford senior executive with the CEO of each major supplier. Together they address major cross-company issues and ensure the overall alignment of Ford and supplier businesses. Ford has developed the capacity to communicate quickly and easily with its entire supplier community. The Ford Supplier Network brings nearly 1,900 suppliers, representing the vast majority of Ford's production supply base, online for communication and training. Ford has also developed a unique network of programs and training facilities to help create shared knowledge with its key suppliers. In a given year, most of Ford's major suppliers participate in one or more of these programs.

During the past several years, Ford product teams, which include Ford employees and key suppliers, have met with customers at the Consumer Insight Center to gain firsthand knowledge of customer needs and desires. Developing a deep, shared visceral understanding of its customers enables Ford and its suppliers to design, develop, and manufacture products that meet and exceed customers' expectations. Ford's Technology Review Center facilitates collaboration on new technologies that promise competitive advantages in vehicle function and efficiency.

Ford operates centers focusing on Consumer Driven 6-Sigma quality methods, total cost management, and lean production methods. Ford's major suppliers provide feedback about how to make those centers more effective. For example, executives from Arvin-Meritor, Donnelly, Lear, Midway Stamping, and Ford (with expert consultants from Kettering University, Ohio State University, the University of Michigan, and Productivity, Inc.) participate in the Lean

Advisory Board, which promotes and assists in the deployment of lean manufacturing methods in the supply base.

The Product and Value Benchmarking Center helps Ford employees and key suppliers learn about best practices and evaluate their actions against other companies. In addition, Ford offers suppliers an extensive curriculum of training programs that are available around the world. It has begun providing online training to suppliers through the Ford-Supplier Learning Institute.

Ford uses a set of Supplier Improvement Metrics to help its purchasing managers and suppliers track real-time performance on issues including quality, cost, and delivery. The web-based system allows Ford employees and suppliers to monitor performance and take steps to resolve problems quickly and collaboratively. Suppliers give Ford high marks for communicating openly and sharing quality data to facilitate resolution of quality and customer satisfaction concerns.

When problems arise, members of Ford's Supplier Technical Assistance and Lean Engineering groups work with suppliers to resolve the situation. The entire team is guided by Ford's values: *We do the right thing for our customers.* Ford is continuing to evolve its version of the Lean Extended Enterprise and is sharing its knowledge with suppliers. Consumer Driven 6-Sigma methodology has been shared with top suppliers. Ford has recently opened a new quality learning center, the Corporate Quality Development Center, with the latest in quality tools and processes.

Ford's relationships with suppliers are far from perfect and the execution of its business objectives is not flawless, but Ford has an excellent game plan in place to strive for perfection and flawlessness in the total value stream. Ford's underlying Lean Extended Enterprise approach is solid, and it is striving to improve and make the execution flawless. By fostering an atmosphere of open communication, knowledge sharing, and collaboration, Ford is continually enhancing the capacity of the Ford–Extended Enterprise team to develop and build great products.

CASE STUDY 5: LOCKHEED MARTIN TACTICAL AIRCRAFT SYSTEMS*

The Lockheed Martin Tactical Aircraft Systems (LMTAS) Lean Enterprise Initiative is a three-phase major reengineering effort begun in 1991. Prior to that

---

* From research conducted by Best Manufacturing Practices, a partnership among the Office of Naval Research's BMP Program, the Department of Commerce's Bureau of Industry and Security, and the University of Maryland's Engineering Research Center.

time, as production declined, the company was experiencing quality and schedule difficulties, which prompted LMTAS to reexamine its business. The Lean Enterprise perspective encompasses the whole company and the customer. It focuses on two concepts: effectiveness (doing the right things) and efficiency (doing things the right way). LMTAS' approach to lean emphasizes effectiveness first, systematically eradicating areas the company should not be pursuing, and then doing the rest efficiently.

Using total weapon system cost as the integrating metric, the company began eliminating the non-value-added costs and activities from all aspects of its operation. Many operations such as machining, sheet metal fabrication, and most other fabrication operations were outsourced. Only those operations that were considered strategically important were retained and streamlined. The number of employees was reduced from over 30,000 to 12,000. A program cancellation also contributed to the downsizing.

Phase I began in 1991 and set the vision and targets for the change. Phase II, begun in 1992, positioned the company for low-rate production, and in 1993 Phase III emphasized redesigning the entire business (and is now complete). The company is now oriented around nine core business systems: Customer Value Determination, Business Area Management, Planning and Controlling, New Business, Business Engagement, Product Definition and Design, Product Delivery, Product Support, and Infrastructure.

LMTAS has moved from a traditional fabrication and assembly operation to an assembly and composite fabrication operation with Integrated Product Team participation by its fabrication suppliers. Weapon system production costs are decreasing dramatically. The per unit cost to the government for the F-16 has been reduced by $3 million, and the company is looking to its proposed commercialization approach as offering the best potential for further reductions.

CHAPTER 1 TAKE-AWAYS

- Many of the basic concepts of lean have been kicking around for nearly a century, going back as far as Fredrick Taylor's Principles of Scientific Management, Dr. Shewhart at Western Electric, and Henry Ford's mass production system.
- The Lean Extended Enterprise is an expansion of our traditional notion of lean to improve velocity, flexibility, responsiveness, quality, and cost across the total value stream.
- The Lean Extended Enterprise is gaining momentum rapidly because it provides a model in which companies and trading partners interact

across key processes of sales, sourcing, procurement, product development, manufacturing, order fulfillment, and customer service.

- The annualized benefits that an organization can expect to achieve from
a fully functional Lean Extended Enterprise are a conservative 3 to 7%
of total revenues.

- The Lean Extended Enterprise is more difficult and challenging than
any other improvement effort an organization may have pursued in the
past. It requires a value stream mind-set, strong leadership, a precision-
driven improvement strategy, collaboration, and deployment of the right
improvement tools to the right opportunities.

- Same People + Same Process + Same Thinking = Same Results. Improvement requires breaking the mold and changing the factors in this
equation. If we hold the factors constant and add automation, we get
faster Same Results.

- Improvement tools and methodologies such as kaizen, lean, Six Sigma,
ERP, and other IT enabling technologies all have their place in the Lean
Extended Enterprise. The Lean Extended Enterprise is not an "either/or"
decision. It can only be achieved by applying all of these methodologies
correctly, to great opportunities, to achieve great results.

SUGGESTED FURTHER READING

Ford, Henry, *Ford — Today and Tomorrow,* Productivity Press, 1988.
Monden, Yashiro, *Toyota Production System,* Engineering and Management Press, 1998.
Mosser, Ralph and Ralph Barnes, *Motion and Time Study,* 7th edition, John Wiley and Sons,
    1980.
Murman, Earll, Thomas Allen, Kirkor Bozdogan, Joel Cutcher-Gershenfeld, Hugh McManus,
    Deborah Nightingale, Eric Rebentisch, Tom Shields, Fred Stahl, Myles Walton, Joyce
    Warmkessel, Stanley Weiss, and Sheila Widnall, *Lean Enterprise Value,* MIT Press,
    2002.
Ohno, Taiichi, *Toyota Production System,* Productivity Press, 1988.
Shewhart, Walter, *Economic Control of Quality of Manufactured Product,* 1931.
Taylor, Fredrick, *The Scientific Method of Assembly,* 1903.
The AT&T (Western Electric) Statistical Quality Handbook, 1956.
Womack, James and Daniel Jones, *Lean Thinking,* Simon and Schuster, 1996.
Womack, James, Daniel Jones, and Daniel Roos, *The Machine That Changed the World,*
    Simon and Schuster, 1990.

THE LEAN
EXTENDED ENTERPRISE
REFERENCE MODEL

In this chapter we will begin to dissect the inner workings of the Lean Extended Enterprise Reference Model and focus on explaining the various panels of value stream integration. We will also present barriers to success and common pitfalls as organizations go through the framework of the model.

OVERVIEW OF THE LEAN EXTENDED ENTERPRISE REFERENCE MODEL

The Lean Extended Enterprise Reference Model (LEERM) in Figure 2.1 is a structured framework for assisting companies, their customers, and suppliers in their transition to a total value stream conversion of lean. The model provides a structured methodology for creating a customer-centric enterprise followed by aligned execution to increase customer value. The LEERM is a never-ending pursuit of perfection and velocity improvement targeted across the total value stream. New product launches, new customer requirements, acquisitions, or other major events create the need for organizations to either continue in their current cycle of improvement or shift back to a previous cycle.

The architecture of the LEERM includes four layers, which we refer to as Panels of Value Stream Integration (Figure 2.2). There are four distinct Panels of Value Stream Integration:

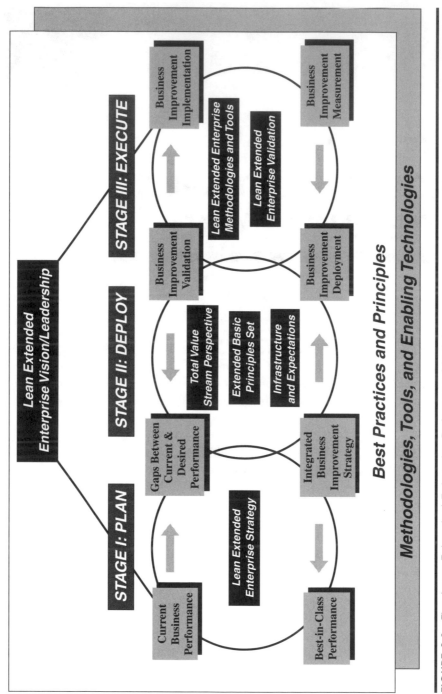

FIGURE 2.1   The Lean Extended Enterprise Reference Model

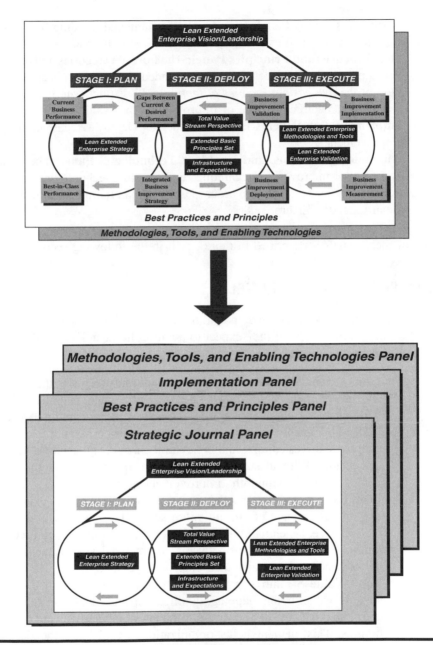

FIGURE 2.2   LEERM Panels of Value Stream Integration

1. **Strategic Journey Panel:** Includes the fundamental building blocks for an inter-, intra-, and extra-enterprise-wide lean initiative.
2. **Best Practices and Principles Panel:** The flow of categories and criteria for implementing a successful Lean Extended Enterprise. It is an expansion of the *five basic principles of lean* into 42 distinct criteria covering the entire breadth and scope of improvement in a value chain.
3. **Implementation Panel:** CEO's familiar Plan-Deploy-Execute model of improvement.
4. **Methodologies, Tools, and Enabling Technologies Panel:** The broad spectrum of improvement techniques and enabling technologies that organizations need to deploy in order to achieve maximum benefit from the Lean Extended Enterprise.

Each of these panels is described in more detail in the following sections.

STRATEGIC JOURNEY PANEL

This panel contains the seven fundamental building blocks that executives must instill in their organizations if they expect to achieve the Lean Extended Enterprise improvement initiative:

1. **Lean Extended Enterprise Vision/Leadership:** This is the engine and power train behind any strategic improvement initiative. This building block aligns strategy, deployment, and execution. Vision/leadership mentors the organization through the correct improvement pathways, drives cultural and behavioral change, and achieves financial results. Without strong vision/leadership, it's just another fizzling "flavor-of-the-month" improvement program.
2. **Lean Extended Enterprise Strategy:** This is the thorough examination and assessment of current value stream business processes and performance, benchmarking of best-in-class performance, and recognition of/consensus on gaps between current and desired value stream performance from an extended enterprise perspective.
3. **Total Value Stream Perspective:** This recognizes multiple value streams, value stream mapping, qualification and root cause analysis, and "chunking out" of high-impact, manageable improvement opportunities. This element helps organizations avoid "boil the ocean" improvement initiatives.
4. **Expanded Basic Principles Set:** This is the notion of integrated methodologies and tools that enable a Lean Extended Enterprise (e.g., kaizen, lean, Six Sigma, enterprise resource planning [ERP],

and other enabling technologies). The basic premise of the LEERM is that organizations must do all of these things great; they do not have the luxury of islands of isolated improvement.

5. **Infrastructure and Expectations:** This establishes the values and basic rules of conduct and behavior by establishing a sense of urgency and recognition of the need to change. This element also promotes the organizational values required for success, such as trust, mutual respect, empowerment, teaming practices, change management, awareness/communication, recognition and rewards alignment, and other behavioral adjustments.

6. **Lean Extended Enterprise Methodology and Tools:** This includes education via certification and deployment of an expanded arsenal of tools that address the broader spectrum of requirements encountered in a collaborative, total value stream setting. The total value stream consists of issues that require a much broader spectrum of improvement methodologies than the *five basic principles of lean.*

7. **Lean Extended Enterprise Validation:** This includes the correct metrics to align improvement initiatives and link daily activities to the Lean Extended Enterprise improvement strategy. This element also includes verification of success by linking value stream performance to financial performance. Validation closes the loop between improvement strategy and improvement outcomes.

The Strategic Journey Panel is shown in Figure 2.3.

BEST PRACTICES AND PRINCIPLES PANEL

This panel includes the underpinning best-in-class practices and principles of lean applied across the total value stream. It expands upon the five basic principles and incorporates improvement thinking from other initiatives traditionally not included under the lean umbrella.

This panel incorporates the flow of categories and criteria for implementing a successful Lean Extended Enterprise and is organized somewhat similarly to the Baldrige structure. Best practices categories include:

- Leadership
- Customer and market focus
- Uniform improvement infrastructure
- Value stream processes
- Extended enterprise integration

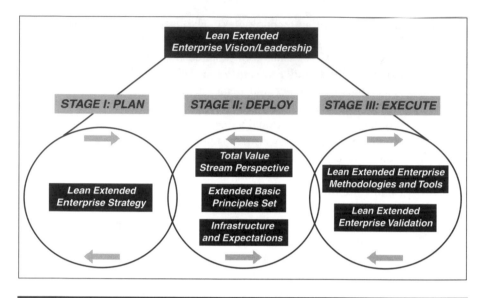

FIGURE 2.3   LEERM Strategic Journey Panel

- Organizational learning
- Performance measurement

Within each of the seven categories are six specific criteria which serve as the underpinning practices and principles of value stream excellence. It is an expansion of the *five basic principles of lean* into 42 distinct criteria that cover the entire breadth and scope of improvement in an organization. Our intention with the LEERM is to address all hard and soft process areas, internal and external activities, simple to complex operations problems, and leadership to rubber-on-the-road issues with this framework.

The Best Practices and Principles Panel is shown in Figure 2.4. The criteria are self-explanatory in most cases, and we have chosen not to provide pages of text to describe every box in this panel. In Chapter 8 we provide a Lean Extended Enterprise Assessment Process which will help clarify some of the questions about each best practices and principles criterion.

IMPLEMENTATION PANEL

This is CEO's familiar Plan-Deploy-Execute model of improvement. These three stages in the model have overlapping paths and directions. In other words,

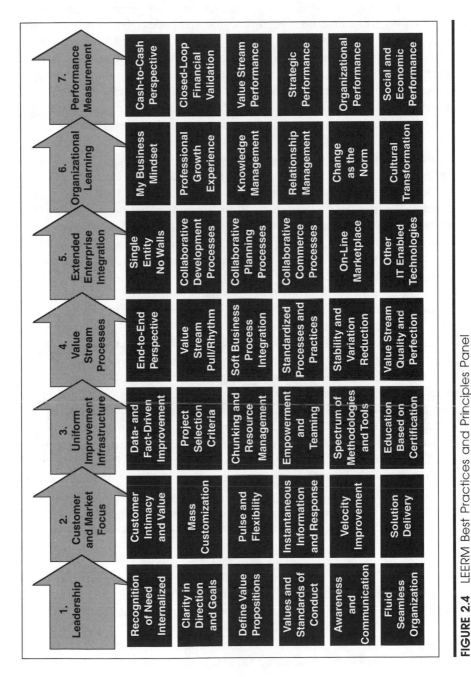

1. Leadership	2. Customer and Market Focus	3. Uniform Improvement Infrastructure	4. Value Stream Processes	5. Extended Enterprise Integration	6. Organizational Learning	7. Performance Measurement
Recognition of Need Internalized	Customer Intimacy and Value	Data- and Fact-Driven Improvement	End-to-End Perspective	Single Entity No Walls	My Business Mindset	Cash-to-Cash Perspective
Clarity in Direction and Goals	Mass Customization	Project Selection Criteria	Value Stream Pull/Rhythm	Collaborative Development Processes	Professional Growth Experience	Closed-Loop Financial Validation
Define Value Propositions	Pulse and Flexibility	Chunking and Resource Management	Soft Business Process Integration	Collaborative Planning Processes	Knowledge Management	Value Stream Performance
Values and Standards of Conduct	Instantaneous Information and Response	Empowerment and Teaming	Standardized Processes and Practices	Collaborative Commerce Processes	Relationship Management	Strategic Performance
Awareness and Communication	Velocity Improvement	Spectrum of Methodologies and Tools	Stability and Variation Reduction	On-Line Marketplace	Change as the Norm	Organizational Performance
Fluid Seamless Organization	Solution Delivery	Education Based on Certification	Value Stream Quality and Perfection	Other IT Enabled Technologies	Cultural Transformation	Social and Economic Performance

FIGURE 2.4 LEERM Best Practices and Principles Panel

it is not a discrete, sequential, left-to-right model with an end. Organizations need to move around and into the right cycle and pursue the correct activities in that cycle. If an organization is in the Execute stage and is either having implementation difficulties or running out of steam; it needs to go back into the Deploy and Plan stages to sustain momentum and then work its way back to the Execute stage. This is the characteristic of the model that makes it interactive and continuous, as in continuous improvement. These cycles also enable the organization to ultimately transition from an improvement program to culturally anchored, subconscious improvement. Figure 2.5 displays the Plan-Deploy-Execute stages in the Implementation Panel.

Many executives are not happy with the results versus investments from their lean, Six Sigma, ERP, and other improvement initiatives. In fact, many are skeptical about the return on investment based on previous experiences and are reluctant to pursue another program such as the Lean Extended Enterprise. The most frequently discussed reasons include lack of leadership, the wrong measures, and failure to communicate change, among others. However, a missing ingredient that is not discussed enough is the improvement strategy. Many organizations skip this step and jump right into applying the tools and techniques.

They may not realize it, but they are viewing the tools and techniques as the *ends* rather than the *means* (outcomes versus root causes). As a result, there is no formal linkage between the customer, the company's business plan, the day-to-day improvement activities, and financial objectives. At best, many organizations see only symptomatic fixes (firefighting) versus prevention and elimination of root causes. The most important stage of the Implementation Panel is the Plan cycle (Figure 2.5a). This is the foundation of the Lean Extended Enterprise or any other strategic improvement initiative. It provides a working road map to focus on the most significant opportunities with limited resources.

Figure 2.5a shows the Stage I: Plan cycle of the Implementation Panel. As we mentioned, this is the most important step in any improvement initiative because it does the up-front deep-core drilling to the organization's issues and root causes. The Plan stage of the Implementation Panel includes:

- Benchmarking best-in-class performance
- Conducting a self-assessment to understand current business performance
- Defining gaps between current and desired performance
- Developing an integrated business improvement strategy

The Plan stage lays out the vision, goals, and all of the details on how to implement lean across the total value stream. The Implementation Panel and in

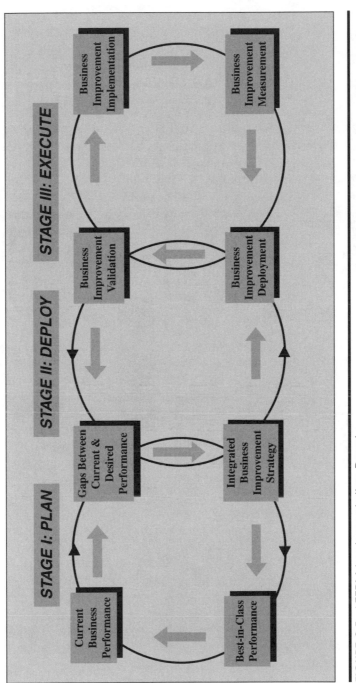

FIGURE 2.5   LEERM Implementation Panel

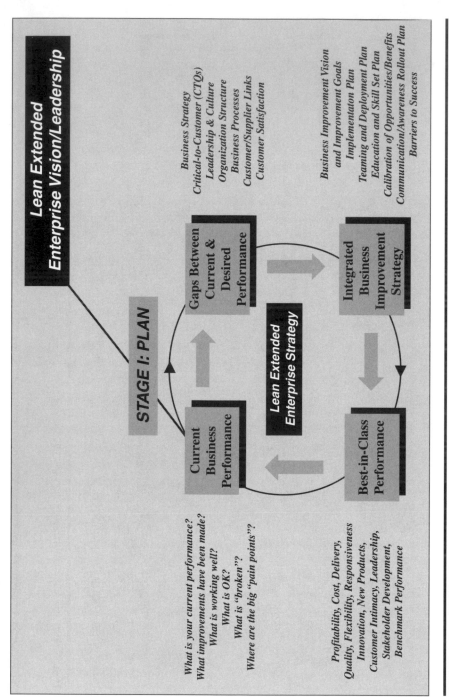

FIGURE 2.5a LEERM Plan subpanel

particular the Plan-Deploy-Execute methodology work well because the specific tools and methodologies are viewed as enablers, determined only after an organization defines its specific requirements, actions, and barriers for improvement. The focus is on facts and results, not on random application of the tools and techniques. We are no longer taking the *bag of tricks looking for a problem* approach. Rather, we are carefully sizing up value stream opportunities and then realizing those opportunities via deployment of the correct methodologies.

The following provides a quick snapshot of each of the elements of the Plan stage of the Implementation Panel.

Current business performance
- What is your current performance?
- Have you characterized current performance with data and facts?
- What are the key customer service issues?
- What improvements have been made?
- What is working well, what is okay, and what is severely "broken"?
- Where are the most significant "pain points"?

Best-in-class performance
- How are you doing vis-à-vis your strongest competitors in the areas of profitability, cost, delivery, quality, flexibility, responsiveness, innovation, new products, customer intimacy, leadership, stakeholder development, and benchmark industry performance?

Gaps between current and best-in-class performance
- Do you understand current performance?
- Do you understand best-in-class performance?
- Do you understand the gaps between current and best-in-class performance as they relate to business strategy, critical-to-customer (CTQs), leadership and culture, organization structure, key business processes, customer/supplier links, and customer satisfaction?
- What needs to change?

Integrated business improvement strategy
- What is your improvement strategy?
- What are the priorities and plans for improvement?
- How will the organization change and take care of day-to-day activities?
- Do you have all the skill sets internally?
- What do you expect to achieve and by when?
- Is there a shared vision of change?
- Are there any barriers to success?

The Plan stage of the Implementation Panel is necessary and works effectively because:

- Implementation of the Lean Extended Enterprise is based on quantified facts, not perceptions or opinions of what needs to change.
- The approach is integrated, focused, and addresses root causes of current performance. The methodology targets improvements in both "hard" and "soft" processes, both "inside" and "outside" of the bricks.
- The strategy and implementation plan are directly linked to gaps between current and desired performance, the business plan, and financial performance. Measurement is a critical element of implementation and results.
- The tools of change (e.g., Six Sigma, lean, kaizen, ERP, etc.) are determined after we define what needs to be done. These various techniques are the tools, the enablers of improvement.
- The strategy includes a clear road map for change (e.g., the vision, improvement goals, implementation plan, expected deliverables and timetable, teaming and deployment plan, and education/skill set needs).
- The improvement opportunities and expected benefits are realistically calibrated and linked to financial performance.
- The plan communicates a uniform approach to change, it matches problems to the right enablers (the right tools of improvement), and it makes people accountable for change.
- The barriers to success are identified and dealt with up front.

Developing a well-structured Lean Extended Enterprise strategy may not seem like such a big deal, but this deliberate, up-front planning process is missing in about 80% of the companies we walk into that are pursuing Six Sigma, lean, kaizen, supply chain, ERP, new product development, and other strategic improvement initiatives. An anxious executive once commented during a meeting, "We don't need a plan. We already know what we need and we're moving ahead. We're relocating the presses, putting up the cell signs, painting the kanban squares as we speak. And I need to remind them to get the new lean posters up." Two years later, when his company had been in the red for months, this same executive said, "We're going to continue on our same track because we know it's the right thing to do." Sorry, but there is a big difference between motion and progress, activity and results. If you want tangible progress, measurable results, and permanent cultural improvement in your Lean Extended Enterprise initiative, then don't skip the planning phase. It works well and makes a significant difference in your ultimate success.

There are examples all around us, like the company that began and ended its Six Sigma initiative by spending $350,000 to train 15 Black Belts...the organization that attempts to fix every problem in the company with its kaizen blitz consultants and is disappointed with the results...and all the IT groups around the globe that have spent billions on ERP implementations and are patiently waiting for the system to deliver the results.

The second stage of the Implementation Panel is the Deploy stage (Figure 2.5b). The objective of Deploy is to translate the activities of the Plan stage into initial actions and pilot successes. Sometimes there is some confusion between Deploy and Execute. Think of Deploy as the initial pilot successes and proveouts, the winning over of the skeptics, and think of Deploy as a larger scale migration of activities through cultural transformation.

The Deploy stage of the Implementation Panel includes both Business Improvement Deployment and Business Improvement Validation and typically includes the following activities:

- Formalizing the executive leadership, project management, and individual task teaming infrastructure.
- Developing and delivering "certification-based" education and training on the various methodologies, tools, and enabling technologies. Certification implies education based on attendance plus application plus achievement, not just attendance.
- Detailed implementation planning at the task/responsibility/due date/ deliverable level.
- Quick-strike containment actions. Remember that every improvement does not require a study or lengthy analysis. If the work area is a mess, clean it up. Don't do a design of experiments on the operators so you can get your Black Belt. Wrong tool!
- Contingency planning (e.g., do we have the right people on the right teams, are our plan and timetable realistic, how do we implement change without disrupting day-to-day activities, etc.).
- Chunking, which means the Paretoizing of opportunities (e.g., how do we manage resources so we do not make a stretched resource an ineffective resource at everything), and making sure we're not trying to boil the ocean or solve world hunger. Chunking implies slicing off manageable pieces of improvement that a team can get its hands around and achieve quick successes.
- Retrofitting the practices, principles, methodologies, tools, and enabling technologies to the realities and unique requirements of the business (i.e., lean means very different things to Keebler Cookies, Boeing Aircraft, Home Depot, or Celestica Electronics).

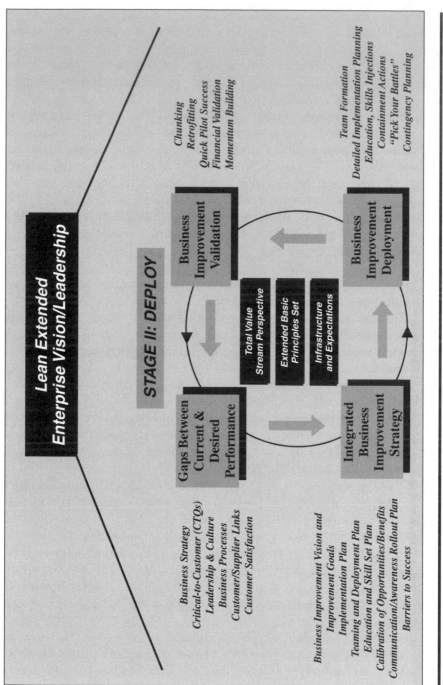

FIGURE 2.5b LEERM Deploy subpanel

- Quick successes, validation of initial improvements as real, linking of operational improvement to financial improvement.
- Internal selling, showcasing, and "show-me" efforts to the skeptics so we no longer need to deal with "Will it work here? We're different. We make big products. We have enormous configurations and options."

The third and final stage of the Implementation Panel is the Execute stage (Figure 2.5c). The objective of Execute is to transform the activities of the Plan and Deploy stages into broader migration opportunities and ultimately into natural everyday actions. Ideally, an organization would like a large critical mass of its organization making improvements every day without even thinking about whether it's a kaizen, lean, Six Sigma, or some other improvement program. The essence is transformation from a program to a way of life, thus institutionalizing the process of continuous improvement.

The Execute stage of the Implementation Panel includes both Business Improvement Implementation and Business Improvement Measurement and typically includes the following activities:

- Continuing to manage implementation efforts around focused hits that are directly related to the strategic plan. Over time, any improvement initiative becomes derailed without proper reinforcement and alignment.
- Establishing very structured and formal review processes so that improvement efforts do not break down into just activity for activity's sake.
- Celebrations, awareness and communication, and reinforcement of the Lean Extended Enterprise philosophy as the standard of daily conduct.
- Realignment of performance and reward systems.

METHODOLOGIES, TOOLS, AND ENABLING TECHNOLOGIES PANEL

This panel (Figure 2.6) includes the integration of kaizen, lean, Six Sigma, ERP, digitization, and other enabling technologies to achieve the "big bang" improvements of the Lean Extended Enterprise. The inner area outlines the kaizen, lean, and Six Sigma methodologies and provides guidance on the types of problems applicable to these tools. The outer area recognizes the importance of leadership and innovation, knowledge of the tools, focus of improvement, teaming and employee involvement, and closed-loop performance at the micro level. Finally, ERP, digitization, and other enabling technologies apply to all other spaces in the panel.

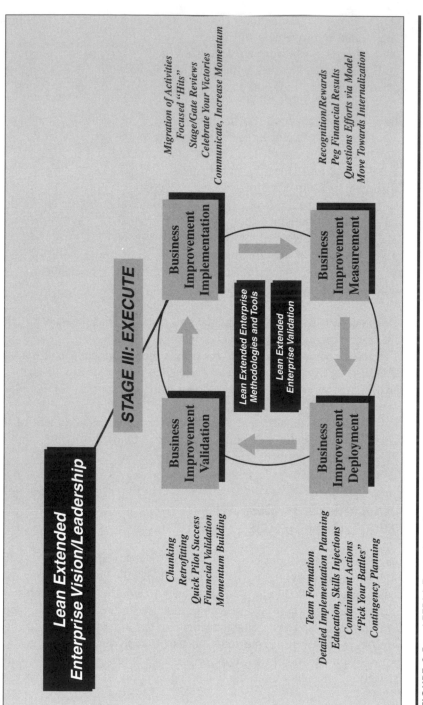

FIGURE 2.5c LEERM Execute subpanel

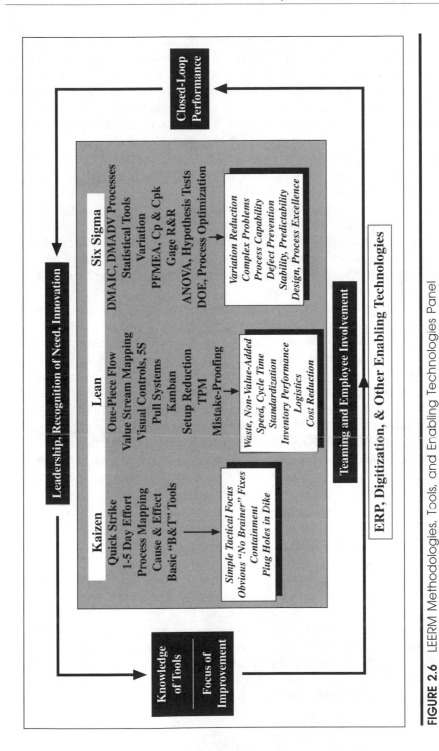

FIGURE 2.6 LEERM Methodologies, Tools, and Enabling Technologies Panel

A critical conclusion from the Methodologies, Tools, and Enabling Technologies Panel is that a single methodology by itself is not applicable to all of the operating issues of the total value stream. There is no such thing as a uniform set of lean tools that fixes every business problem. In this book we will help you to understand, integrate, and deploy the right tools to the right opportunities. Some of these opportunities are "no-brainers" and do not need a grand analysis. If you know the answer, kaizen blitz it and forget the analysis paralysis process. Some improvements require basic analysis and use of the basic blocking and tackling (B&T) tools such as checksheets, Pareto charts, process maps, or fishbone diagrams. Some of the larger improvement opportunities lie in the "soft process" areas. Some opportunities require understanding and eliminating complex process variation and require more advanced tools. Most will require instantaneous information and response. Our view is that no matter what you call the various tools and methodologies, they all have their place in the Lean Extended Enterprise. In Chapters 4 to 7 we will expand on the Methodologies, Tools, and Enabling Technologies in more detail.

One of the most familiar questions that we deal with is "We're not sure these methodologies apply to us because we're different." Some manufacturers bend and fabricate metal. Others assemble electronic boxes, automotive components, or consumer goods or process chemicals or blood plasma. Some build high-volume, low-volume/high-mix, mass-customized, or one-of-a-kind products. Others make microscopic widgets in a clean room environment or build large vessels. Some organizations design and sell their products and outsource their manufacturing needs. Others sell software and knowledge. Many have a variety of combinations of all of these modes and a lot more. All of these enterprises are held together with processes, and a closer look reveals that there are a lot more similarities than differences. In the final analysis, these are not legitimate reasons for postponing business improvement.

DOES THE LEERM APPLY TO SERVICE ORGANIZATIONS?

The Lean Extended Enterprise concept and the LEERM apply equally well to service organizations. The elements of each LEERM panel can be retrofitted to any process, be it in a manufacturer of commercial airplanes, a process industry, a health care institution, a bank, a retail or distribution/logistics business, a federal government agency, or post-sales service, installation, repair, or refurbishment depots. Any organization that has customers, suppliers, and a value stream of internal/external processes that consume resources, time, and cash and have variations in performance are candidates for the LEERM, and this includes just about everyone. Granted, we are not saying that the LEERM may be totally applicable to a two-person local hardware store or clam shack, but it is very applicable to organizations such as Home Depot, Houston Medical, J.P. Morgan, Citicorp, Best Buy, American Express, McDonald's, and government agencies. Many of these service organizations are well under way with their own versions of the Lean Extended Enterprise and are actually way ahead of the power curve. If we remove the labels and buzzwords, it's all about an unyielding customer and demand-driven Strategy of Improvement across the total value stream.

Organizations usually begin their lean or Six Sigma journeys in the *production* component of their value stream. However, the real opportunities lie in the soft process areas. Customer satisfaction, cash-to-cash cycle time reduction, damaged or warranteed goods, inventory and product availability, product and process quality, speed and accuracy of information, performance management, and other factors are all very relevant in soft process businesses. All of the organizations mentioned above have soft processes, and for some these processes comprise 100% of their value stream. Many of these soft processes have remained virtually untouched in terms of strategic improvement. As we take the total value stream perspective, manufacturing by itself is no longer the competitive weapon anyway. The largest value stream opportunities are in the soft process areas. This means that there are even more opportunities for service organizations that pursue the Lean Extended Enterprise as a business philosophy.

SUMMARY OF THE LEERM

The Lean Extended Enterprise and the LEERM are based on the premise of value stream integration. To reach this level, organizations must develop a solid strategy for their strategic improvement initiatives — one that recognizes gaps in current performance and truly addresses their customer, operational, and competitive needs. They must build the right infrastructure through well-connected activities similar to the Plan-Deploy-Execute process. They must understand the best practices and principles of a Lean Extended Enterprise and, most important, how these practices fit into the scheme of conducting their business. They must understand the methodologies, tools, and enabling technologies so they know how to apply the right solutions to the best improvement opportunities. Finally, organizations must develop the magic characteristic of *execution* — through the integration of strategy, infrastructure, improvement methodologies, financial results, and permanent culture change. They need to grow organizations of relentless indignant "doers." For many organizations, it will be a challenging process to grow and cultivate these core competencies.

The Lean Extended Enterprise means expanding the organization's vertical limit of manufacturing and aggressively going after the soft process areas, especially the previously untouchable areas. Organizations must also expand their horizontal limit and collaborate with suppliers and customers as part of their business improvement scope. Lastly, organizations need to continue the lateral journey by developing seamless organizations, building knowledge relationships, and creating that sense of "If this was your business, what would you do?"

The LEERM is not perfect, and there are certainly a number of other formulations and graphical displays we could think up for these concepts. We chose to use the component parts that we have been successfully using with our clients. It is our intent to package the critical components of success with your Lean Extended Enterprise journey into a working model, the LEERM.

CHAPTER 2 TAKE-AWAYS

- The LEERM is a structured framework for assisting companies, their customers, and suppliers in their transition to a total value stream conversion of lean.
- The LEERM consists of four distinct Panels of Value Stream Integration:
  - ☐ The Strategic Journey Panel, which includes the Seven Building Blocks of Value Stream Excellence
  - ☐ The Best Practices and Principles Panel, which includes criteria and categories of total value stream best practices
  - ☐ The Implementation Panel, which includes the Plan-Deploy-Execute model
  - ☐ The Methodologies, Tools, and Enabling Technologies Panel, which demonstrates how to integrate all of these approaches into an integrated solution set
- The Best Practices and Principles Panel incorporates the flow of categories and criteria for implementing a successful Lean Extended Enterprise and is organized somewhat similar to the Baldrige structure. Best practices categories include:
  - ☐ Leadership
  - ☐ Customer and market focus
  - ☐ Uniform improvement infrastructure
  - ☐ Value stream processes

- ☐ Extended enterprise integration
- ☐ Organizational learning
- ☐ Performance measurement
- ■ Within each of the seven best practices and principles categories are six specific criteria which serve as the underpinning practices and principles of value stream excellence. It is an expansion of the *five basic principles of lean* into 42 distinct criteria that cover the entire breadth and scope of improvement in an organization.
- ■ No matter what you call the various Methodologies, Tools, and Enabling Technologies, they all have their place in the Lean Extended Enterprise. Organizations must learn how to become great in all of these areas and deploy the right tools to the right opportunities.

SUGGESTED FURTHER READING

Bradford, Robert W., J. Peter Duncan, Peter Duncan, and Brian Tarcy, *Simplified Strategic Planning: A No-Nonsense Guide for Busy People Who Want Results Fast!* Chandler House Press, 1999.

Collins, James and Jerry Porras, *Built to Last: Successful Habits of Visionary Companies,* Harper, 1997.

Henderson, Bruce and Jorge Larco, *Lean Transformation,* Oaklea Press, 2000.

Jackson, Thomas, *Implementing a Lean Management System,* Productivity Press, 1996.

Lawton, Robin, *Creating a Customer-Centered Culture,* ASQ Press, 1993.

Murman, Earll, Thomas Allen, Kirkor Bozdogan, Joel Cutcher-Gershenfeld, Hugh McManus, Deborah Nightingale, Eric Rebentisch, Tom Shields, Fred Stahl, Myles Walton, Joyce Warmkessel, Stanley Weiss, and Sheila Widnall, *Lean Enterprise Value,* Palgrave Macmillan, 2002.

3

LEADERSHIP AND INFRASTRUCTURE DEVELOPMENT FOR THE LEAN EXTENDED ENTERPRISE

Here we go again. Another improvement program, another acronym, a different ribbon on the box, and another spin on improvement programs. The good news is that we're with you on this one. We think this issue is so important that we have devoted a whole chapter to it. Strategic improvement initiatives are now the norm for most organizations throughout the world today, but unfortunately, strategic results are less commonplace. Organizations recognize the need to reinvent themselves as superior competitors, dial in more precisely to customer and supplier needs, and increase their robustness to adverse changes in business conditions. These programs have been given different names over the years, but the heart of these programs is improving strategic and operating performance by fundamentally changing the way organizations conduct their business. In spite of the never-ending stream of improvement methodologies offering clear and consistent promises of improvement and return on investment (ROI), different organizations have achieved varying degrees of implementation success. In many cases, the real benefits have been part fact, but mostly delusionary.

STRATEGIC IMPROVEMENT IS A CORE COMPETENCY

Before we jump to conclusions about the Lean Extended Enterprise Reference Model (LEERM), this chapter will reflect on the critical leadership and *soft-side* infrastructure aspects of improvement. We need to answer some very tough questions about improvement programs before we go any further: Why is there variation in success among organizations implementing kaizen, lean, Six Sigma, enterprise resource planning (ERP), and other strategic improvement programs? What are the root causes of their successes and failures? How can we get beyond all the excuses and the enigma of these various situations and deal with the real facts about successful improvement?

We do not hold a monopoly on all the answers to these questions, but we do know from all of our experiences that strategic improvement is a core competency. What exactly do we mean by this core competency statement? It is a skill that most organizations do not have internally by osmosis, and they underestimate the difficulty of strategic improvement. Organizations must learn how to define, lead, and execute strategic improvement. You don't get there by developing a grand strategy and then delegating it off to a powerless organization. You don't go to a seminar or a plant tour and become an instant change master. You don't wake up one day, flip a switch, and have these competencies in place throughout your organization. And it certainly is not attached as an addendum to an organization's latest crisis situation. It takes a big commitment to define and organize a strategic improvement initiative and then integrate strategy, leadership, execution, the right methodologies, and permanent culture change. Those organizations that achieve impressive results from their improvement programs do so because they understand this fact. This is the essence of Chapter 3 — to discuss many of these factors in greater detail. Every executive knows about these factors, but *know-how* is much more prevalent than *practice* and *cultural norms*. Our objective in Chapter 3 is to reinforce the importance of these factors in the success of your strategic improvement efforts.

We were invited into a company recently to discuss Six Sigma. The CEO told us that one of their premier Fortune 100 customers was mandating that the company become involved with Six Sigma. We went through the normal discussions about how to implement Six Sigma as a business philosophy and the commitment and process required to get there. Near the end of the meeting the CEO said, "We're not ready for all of that. We just want you to give our management team a four-hour course on Six Sigma and then maybe you can certify our company, kind of like an ISO certification. Then we can put Six Sigma on our web site and be able to talk about it with our customers." He doesn't get it. He wants to become a Six Sigma organization with a two sigma approach! Some of the stories in this book must read like fiction, but we did not make this stuff up.

Executives who view strategic improvement as a punch list usually skip the most critical elements of change, and unfortunately their results show it. Another answer lies in the fact that although most methodologies offer steps and tools that are necessary to achieve success, they are neither sufficient nor exhaustive. Further, methodologies are ineffective without the right improvement strategy and infrastructure bundled around them. Methodologies, tools, and enabling technologies are the *means,* not the *ends.*

TOP TEN PITFALLS OF STRATEGIC BUSINESS IMPROVEMENT

Regardless of the buzzword — lean, kaizen, Six Sigma, ERP, reengineering, and so on — there is a common pattern of practices that result in performance above or below expectations. We have worked with hundreds of organizations, and regardless of the industry, there are a lot more similarities than differences in their successes. We have been benchmarking and studying these patterns for years and have summarized them into the Top Ten Pitfalls of Strategic Improvement, and they apply to any major strategic improvement initiative. These patterns allow us to reflect and learn from our mistakes, and it throws us back into the battle with renewed knowledge and skills.

Mistakes and learning are a part of any improvement effort. Early in my career, I (TB) was on an elevator with Dr. Land at Polaroid. I walked in, pushed a button for the wrong floor, and said, "Oops, I made a mistake." Dr. Land replied, "Son, a mistake is never a mistake if you learn something from it." The door opened and he walked out, but I never forgot that wisdom. Believe it. The benefits of learning and applying new knowledge far outweigh the cost of the mistake itself.

Ollie Wight used to talk about the definition of *insanity* and define it as doing the same things the same way with the same tools and expecting different results, and if that still didn't work, then redouble your efforts. We have never seen a plant or a business shut down because of a mistake in an improvement effort. "We'll shut down the place if we change" is a fallacy. In most cases, the mistake turns out to be an improvement over the current broken process. "I don't have time to change and do my regular job" is another familiar comment. It's funny how these individuals always find time to do things over. Leadership and infrastructure are the way we deal with these issues because, in all fairness, perception is reality and many of these realities must be modified to achieve success.

The Top Ten Pitfalls of Strategic Improvement are intended to be totally objective and eye-opening. Everyone knows these pitfalls, but they are preached more than they are practiced. They provide us with valuable insights about what

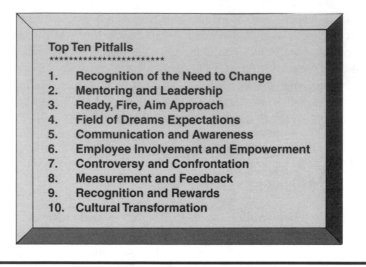

FIGURE 3.1   Top Ten Pitfalls of Strategic Improvement (Copyright 2000 by The Center for Excellence in Operations, Inc.)

went wrong with our previous improvement efforts. But more importantly, these practices will help us to understand and appreciate the LEERM and the new opportunities for improvement. The LEERM architecture incorporates the right sequence of activities necessary for successful strategic change. Skipping ahead without solid ground established in the prerequisite activities usually makes the improvement effort crumble or at least hit the wall. It's like framing a house before the concrete foundation is set. The remainder of this chapter addresses the Top Ten Pitfalls of Strategic Improvement (Figure 3.1) and specific issues that make the difference between successful improvement and failed improvement. Our purpose is to reinforce how these important factors are critical to success with the LEERM or any other strategic improvement program.

1. Recognition of the Need to Change

Many executives have a full plate of priorities, and often strategic improvement is lower down on the list than other more pressing needs. Some organizations postpone change and hope the economy will take care of things. Change is a reactive event rather than a proactive living event. For example, it was not uncommon to hear executives in the high-technology industry say things like "Just wait a while, things will change." That 30% compounded revenue growth covered up a lot of operating problems, but it also made these problems much larger over time. When the growth disappeared, those problems were cash flow dragons. It is very difficult to look reality in the face, and the first reaction is a string of denial thoughts and opinions. People waste a lot of time and energy looking for the exceptions. Another common occurrence is the continued debate about what needs to be done, which creates total confusion and conflicting directions about change. The front end of the LEERM architecture clarifies what needs to be done with data and facts.

The fact is, no matter where your current performance lies, it simply is not good enough beyond today. Just think about the hundreds or thousands of organizations that have been market leaders only to relinquish that position to a competitor within 12 to 24 months. The world is moving at clock speed, technology and product life cycle are very short, and everyone is involved in business improvement. The bar is rising at a much faster speed than many organizations can keep up with. However, this also provides the opportunity to leapfrog and surprise the competition with the right strategy. The best time to change is now, but it is unfortunate that it often requires a catastrophic event to prime the organizational pump for change. It is a lot easier to create urgency with catastrophe rather than leadership, but it often makes you late for the party. Catastrophe-driven improvement is also intermittent. The ratio of organizations that change by proactive leadership is much lower than organizations that change due to a catastrophic event. Without a solid recognition of the need to change, improvement programs are typically reactionary and short-lived, and the results are also disappointing.

2. Mentoring and Leadership

When executives fail to lead both intellectually and through daily actions, the organization suffers. They launch a lean effort and disappear or appear weekly to ask, "Are we done yet?" We have worked with several executives who try to justify their commitment by saying, "Sure I'm committed. Look how much money I'm spending on you guys!" We help them to understand the true meaning of commitment, and most rise to the occasion. Mentoring and leadership are things that people say they can and know how to do, but they fall down in actual practice. Why does this happen? They want to be effective leaders, but strategic improvement is a core competency that executives need to cultivate and develop because it is new to them.

The best leaders have the vision, conviction, confidence, and an amazing emotional resolve to prevail no matter what gets in the way. They live, breathe, and understand the details of lean, kaizen, Six Sigma, or whatever else they are doing. They have a passion to succeed, and their fire-in-the-belly commitment is very real. They make the effort to educate themselves like everyone else. They walk the talk, and many even take on a project like everyone else. They have a remarkable concern and interest in change and people. They put it all on the line and make it clear that success is the only option. They superglue their executive team together in unity of purpose with a consistent message of improvement. They calibrate and recalibrate their organizations and create a solid center of gravity. They know that "the most important thing is keeping the most important thing the most important thing."

We laugh at Jack Welch's comment about lunatic fringe, but that's an excellent adjective for the leadership style required for successful change. Recognize the difference between *knowing how to do something* and actually *doing it.* When everyone is running around saying they do not need help because they already *know how* to change, usually not much is changing. Recognize the organization's limitations and constraints, and seek outside help to deal with these issues from the get-go. You will achieve greater success.

Privately held family organizations are always a challenge, but it is possible to break the mold. On the first day of such a new client engagement, the president called me (TB) into his office and said, "I'm glad you're all here. Finally I will get these people to change to the way I want them to do things. I hope you realize that I'm not the one who needs to change, they [his staff] are. I want you turn these people around for me." Well, we met one on one with the other executives, and it took about a day before we called a meeting with the president and his staff to talk about a few serious show-stoppers. We took a chance on being thrown out on our ears, and things became very emotional. To make a long story short and leave out the details, the executive team recognized the need to adjust and get their mind-sets in sync for change or it would never happen. For the next ten months it was like watching your children grow up. These executives grew into a great mentoring and leadership team and achieved dramatic results with their lean effort. Mentoring and leadership create that level of strategic performance discussed in Chapters 1 and 8. They also provide the support structure for strategic improvement.

A brilliant example of mentoring and leadership is Secretary of Defense Donald Rumsfeld. Some time has passed since September 11, and, like most strategic improvement initiatives, people begin to get anxious about results. Where's Bin Laden? Are we done yet? They start to waver and drift away from the original vision and mission and start to question whether or not we're doing the right things to eliminate terrorism. Mr. Rumsfeld has kept the whole country on the bead of terrorism. He is sincere in his delivery and tells it as it is. He continues to reinforce the strategy of a new war on a new enemy and that weeding out terrorism is a very calculated and lengthy process. He has a great style of articulating the facts and progress, keeping people focused on the root causes, and communicating why the strategy of eliminating terrorism makes sense. Even under the most demanding of circumstances, he maintains his unbending core of values, beliefs, and priorities and brings the drifters back into the fold.

Rummy leadership style exemplifies the values of zero defects and zero tolerance. His brusque, hands-on management style frequently collides with the bureaucratic Pentagon culture. He always provokes open debate and doesn't like "yes people." He loves mavericks who enjoy poking sticks into the wheels of a bicycle. Mr. Rumsfeld's leadership is as solid as the Rock of Gibraltar. He's the type of individual people would follow anywhere. He's the author of *leaning forward.*

There is so much power and influence over change when executives send the right message and then align their actions to that message. On the flip side, it's just another fad program with discouraging results when they don't. Recently, one company decided to pursue Six Sigma, and the executive team delegated the effort to a middle-management committee. This organization had a track record for failed fad programs, and the committee began debating the applicability and benefits of Six Sigma. The majority of the team recognized the need to improve the business, but one individual wanted to calculate the ROIs and EBIT to five decimal places, then benchmark which competitors had implemented Six Sigma and what benefits they achieved. Another individual viewed Six Sigma as a personal challenge to his leadership ability and felt that no program could add to his engineers' performance. Another individual was fixated on limiting the number of candidates and was most concerned that the team addressed the internal politics of who to include and not include. These people were missing the point. They were in space looking for a planet with a scanning electron microscope. They could not envision the destination because they were too busy studying the particles in front of them at ×2,000 power. They were in denial and were looking for all the reasons why it won't work here, and their actions were proportional to their commitment. The committee was assigned an impossible task, and the end result was pretty obvious. Regardless of the label you assign to these programs, it is pretty ridiculous to debate whether or not an organization should improve its business. But the bigger point is that great intentions fail when executives fail to create a vision, lead, communicate, and align their actions with the message. With any strategic improvement initiative, actions definitely speak louder than words. When Rome is on fire, you don't allow your staff to hang around debating who lit the match.

3. Ready, Fire, Aim Approach

This is a pet peeve of ours. When you walk through organizations that practice this approach, all the managers have white boards with their own list of improvement projects they thought up in support of the program. They all have their own personalized checklist codes to monitor progress and little borders drawn around them. Sometimes there is so much stuff on their boards you wonder how they even notice the checklists. They look like one of those optical illusion posters: if you stare at it long enough, the 3D eagle and the American flag pop out at you. They all get together once a week to go through their lists. If you interview the management team and copy their lists, you find conflicts, redundancies, disagreement, finger-pointing, and pure going through the motions. There is this huge misconception that the volume of activity and the speed of *perceived* completion are proportional to the end results. People hurry up and launch dozens of activities, and soon their strategy resembles the little Dutch boy by the dike with a plethora of leaks and a shortage of fingers. Is this effective? What happens to a juggler who tries to juggle 100 pins at a time? There's your answer.

Another peeve of ours is the improvement silos and the "Hobson's choice" approach (i.e., all or nothing, my way or the highway). In this situation, organizations have their ERP/IT camp, their lean camp, their Six Sigma camp, their kaizen camp, and the like. Each of these improvement camps thinks it has all the answers to the organization's needs, and the primary focus is on *their* tools. They pump up their own achievements and downplay the other group's achievements. They view every problem as a problem that requires *their* camp's bag of tricks. They compete with each other rather than working together. In the process, they create a totally disconnected approach to improvement. These efforts begin with the right intent, but the combined results are disappointing. One of the strong messages in this book is that a single tool, a single methodology, a single program will not make you world class. It takes the integration of kaizen, lean, Six Sigma, ERP, and other enabling technologies.

Many organizations skip the most important element of improvement — the Strategy of Improvement. We covered this in detail in the LEERM in Chapter 2. Organizations tend to skim over a process like the Plan-Deploy-Execute model and dive into the methodologies and tools. People select and implement tools and techniques in an effort to get quick results. Their intentions are good because they are trying to make a quick impact. But their actions are bad because they end up chasing down outcomes and symptoms because they do not have a solid improvement plan. Their actions are "perception driven" versus "fact driven" and not focused on root causes of performance. This approach may produce a few short-term benefits, but it never becomes a sustaining process. A closer look, however, usually reveals the disconnects between customer requirements and the company's day-to-day improvement activities. The results are eventually very questionable and illusive, and before you know it they are victims of another "flavor-of-the-month" improvement program. For the employees of these organizations, another improvement program is about as popular as mononucleosis.

Again, we need to ask why. The answer is the same reason as above. Strategic improvement is a core competency that executives need to cultivate and develop because it is new to them. Dealing with change is ambiguous, even on a good day. Does this seem like bunk? Then why is this improvement plan missing in three-quarters of the organizations pursuing improvement programs? Another comment from a grinning executive comes to mind when thinking of this topic: "Of course we have a plan. It's not written down like you'd probably like to see it, but we all kinda know what needs to be done and we're doing it." Developing a solid improvement plan is complicated. It takes a lot of research, thought, and time to put a good workable improvement plan together. Most of the time there are tremendous pressures to make things happen now, so the plan goes out the window because people think they know what needs to be done. Speed can be an extremely harmful diversion, particularly if organizations choose to shortcut the most critical steps of improvement. After all, how long did it take you to get into your situation? Organizations will never realize the results they expect without this well-defined improvement plan.

The improvement plan becomes the vision, goals, and implementation instrument by which we can communicate why and what needs to change. A good improvement plan also answers many questions and concerns people may have about change and how we will deal with certain issues. Granted, it does not have all the answers contained within it, but it becomes a great target to shoot at, to embrace, to deploy and execute. And it sure prepares the organization for change better than the ad-hoc or mole-hole improvement approach. Improvements that begin at the tools and techniques level will produce some benefits because every organization has low-hanging fruit. These are the pennies and dimes. If you want to get at the sweet fruit on the tree, you need a solid improvement plan. The improvement plan will show you how to grow fruit and get you the hundred-dollar bills by comparison.

4. Field of Dreams Expectations

In this situation, organizations believe that "if you launch it, the results will come." Executives wish for change, but in their hearts they are not really committed to the tough work of change. Organizations have tended to embrace the latest buzzwords like fall or spring fashions. They hope the next coffee mug, tee shirt, or banner will make things better. The original goals are replaced by the mechanics of the improvement process itself. For example, countless people have told us they think Six Sigma is a big waste of time because they were assigned a certification project they knew the answer to on the first day but were told they had to go through the motions. Activity does not always translate into improvement.

The best example of this pitfall is the failure of most total quality management (TQM) programs a decade ago and, more recently, the thousands of ERP implementations that failed to deliver the expected results. The tough message here is that we cannot blame TQM, ERP, or any other acronym for the failure. You are in control of your improvement destiny. If you are not getting the results you expect, then stop the improvement process. Drill down into the root causes, confirm that everyone is pursuing the right opportunities, and recognize and remove the barriers. A painful but true message for some here is that all of these improvement methodologies and tools work very well when deployed correctly and to the right opportunities.

5. Communication and Awareness

A well-executed lean effort communicates the vision and need to change, builds employee awareness and commitment, and states the consequences of not changing. It addresses people's expectations and fears right up front and uses facts to win over people's hearts and minds. Remember, nothing changes until people are ready to change. Awareness and communication keep the interest level and momentum at a peak level. The strategic improvement plan, town meeting updates, and visual storyboarding are common approaches to facilitate communication and awareness.

Leadership behavior and actions must be consistent with the communication and awareness message. When leaders live the vision, people will follow. Similarly, when executives deliver one message and then act inconsistently with that message, it sends the wrong vision about change. In fact, it takes people backward at an exponential rate. One company had a layoff on a Friday. That afternoon, the president called an all-hands-on-deck meeting to discuss the reasons for the layoff and then told everyone that their salaries would be reduced by 10% to prevent further layoffs. Times were bad. About a week later, the president drove to work in his new $90,000 sports car. Someone let the cat out of the bag that he closed on a $2 million waterfront vacation property two days before the layoff. Do you think he won over people's minds and hearts? Executives must be very conscious about their selection of words, and then match their actions and behavior to the words.

6. Employee Involvement and Empowerment

This one is self-explanatory. "Empowerment" means "giving power away." There are two sides to this value proposition. Management must be willing to give up power because there is a level of trust in people's ability to perform. People must be given the correct education and skills to accept power. They also need to act responsibly with that new power and have the authority to act as process owners. They must have access to information and feedback so they can measure progress. Organizations have come a long way with teaming and employee involvement, but there are still many untapped opportunities in this area. This is probably one of the lesser pitfalls.

Although organizations are involved in teaming and employee involvement, there are a few common dilemmas with the mechanics of teaming. Sometimes the right people who can make a big difference are not involved in the right places, or they are spread too thin across too many teams. Another dilemma is the launching of teams and assignments before creating a solid improvement plan. This is not directly a teaming issue, but the point here is that we want to do everything in our power to set the teams up for success.

One of our clients implemented a pull system. When the team babysat the process, it worked great. When the team walked away, the system would fall apart. The team discovered that its supervisor, "Kanban Dan," was nervous about losing his supervisory power and began sabotaging the pull system. He would destroy kanban cards and make the replenishment requirement disappear. He would shuffle the kanban cards and change the replenishment priorities. He would remove kanban cards and replace them a few days later to create past dues. Dan understood pull systems and kanban for sure. The team also understood pull systems and kanban and caught on to his little games. This was only one of many games Kanban Dan played on his people involved in teams. News of the situation went all the way to the president of the company, who met with the team members and told them, "I have empowered you to make improvements to our business. I am also empowering you to decide what to do about this issue. Let me know what you decide to do and I will support your decision 100%." A human resources representative was added to the team, and the team decided to terminate Kanban Dan. That is as strong a message about empowerment as you can send. It also sent a clear message that you're either part of the solution or part of the problem. It's just like football — you're either on offense or you're on defense, and there's no in between.

7. Controversy and Confrontation

Change produces anxiety and controversy. Change in the absence of emotions is not change at all. Major strategic improvement creates a lot of emotions. We need to remove all the emotions and do a better job of managing change with data, facts, and analysis. Controversy and confrontation are extremely healthy when managed correctly.

It is not uncommon in controversy and confrontation situations where organizations are ready to make a change for someone to say that it will never work.

Denial is often the first step in recognizing the need to change. Rather than getting upset in these situations, listen to the other person's point of view. Don't be bull-headed about your position; resolve the situation with data and facts. Exhaust the nay-sayers, but be open-minded to the idea that some of their points may be very valuable things that you overlooked. One manager used to say something like, "SYMDTE (screw your mind down tight enough). Listen to the other person's point of view. Get in his or her mind. Get the facts. Put yourself in the other person's position and find the human drama. Draw a picture of it with facts. Reiterate the facts. Then you truly understand the situation."

Earlier we mentioned an example of a company whose Six Sigma decision became hung up in committee. The CEO delegated the leadership because he was too busy with other responsibilities. These organizations cannot understand why their results are illusive. Organizations are successful with change because they are strategically committed first and understand how to work through the issues of implementation together. When an organization begins its improvement journey, there's no answer to many of these issues— that's the challenge of improvement. But great leaders have this magic perseverance, faith, and confidence that the organization will figure out how to put it all together and succeed together.

Confrontation is a little stronger. When your recommendations are correct, supported by facts, and supported by the majority, then the organization needs to recognize and knock down the barriers, remove the prima donnas. Failure to do this sends a very strong message that it's okay not to change, plain and simple. Nothing undermines a major change process more than allowing the Kanban Dans to function against the tide of improvement.

The horse that refuses to drink or the dog that won't hunt are two analogies to describe this. You can offer education and training to a horse, you can provide a lot of hands-on coaching, you can pet and talk to the horse and tell him why its bad not to drink, you can lead the horse to water, you can hold the water to his mouth, you can hold his head in the water, but sometimes you cannot make him drink. Sometimes you have to send him to another ranch. It's the same with "that dog won't hunt." It's a fact of life with horses, dogs, and organizational life. Some people will never get it no matter what you do. It's not in their psyche to change or to be part of a team effort. Sometimes there is a place in the organization for these individuals, and sometimes the lights go on and they grow to be your champions. Occasionally, some of these individuals become hostile and attempt to undermine and sabotage change, like Kanban Dan. For an organization in this situation, looking the other way is not the answer. You can't pretend that bad performance is good performance. Leadership gets organizations through the barriers. Failure to deal strongly with inappropriate behaviors derails commitment and support.

8. Measurement and Feedback

This is another area where much progress has been made, but it is still an important factor of strategic improvement. In far too many cases, people either don't measure anything at all or they measure the wrong things. In other cases, the improvement activities are totally out of whack with customer and company requirements. The purpose of measurement is to provide a formal linkage between our improvement plan and our improvement actions. Measurement also closes the loop between our improvement actions and their corresponding results. Without measurement and feedback, there is no way to determine progress with facts. Often, when we visit plants and ask if things have improved, we get an overwhelming "Oh yeah, things are a lot better," especially from people on the shop floor. But they're not measuring anything!

Again, we hope you recognize the importance of the improvement plan by now. The Plan-Deploy-Execute model defines best-in-class, baseline, and goal performance right up front. As you work your way through the model, it defines performance at the individual team/project level and ensures that there is proper alignment between the plan and the day-to-day improvement activities. Recognize that a tight measurement and reconciliation process such as this does not exist in most strategic improvement initiatives. We will cover this performance measurement topic in more detail and provide specific tools for the LEERM in Chapter 8.

9. Recognition and Rewards

In a major improvement effort, recognition and rewards are often afterthoughts for most organizations. In the planning stages of improvement, recognition and reward are typically viewed as way out there in the scheme of things. We agree that there are many higher priority issues in the inertia stage of improvement, but eventually this is a topic that requires definition and thought. There are dozens of books and thousands of individual processes on this topic, but we want to share a few of our experiences in this area.

Many organizations have implemented a wide variety of recognition and reward practices ranging from free pizza coupons to formal gainsharing programs. Recognition is something that we view as a continuous process and non-financial in nature. Some companies showcase their top performers in town meetings or in featured articles on storyboards or in corporate newsletters. A key point of recognition is its genuineness. Recognition criteria should be somewhat formalized so people understand why a particular individual was recognized in the first place. We want to recognize our champions, but if we begin patting everyone on the back, then real recognition disappears. Rewards, on the other hand, tend to be financial in nature.

Many organizations conclude a wave of Six Sigma certification with a corporate project fair. Usually the corporate officers and vice-presidents attend, and each candidate has an opportunity to present his or her project and results to the group, followed by a dinner and formal certification ceremony. Some organizations go a step further and reward candidates with stock certificates or bonus checks for their effort and contribution. This is their standard recognition and rewards process for all waves of Six Sigma certification.

Recognition and rewards practices do not always come from the executive suite. A few years back, we had a client in a smaller community where almost everyone knew each other. This company heard the TQM religion and decided to implement a real quality improvement program. Recognition and rewards eventually became a topic of interest, and management asked employees for their input. One employee who had read about Toyota's suggestion system came up with the idea of "Greenbacks for Feedback." People would receive Greenbacks for Feedback points for their suggestions. They would receive points for any suggestion and bonus points if the suggestion was implemented. The improvement team visited with many local businesses and set up a redemption process between the company and the merchants. The quality improvement program spread into the community. Employees actually created a preferred list and blacklist of merchants and refused to redeem points at places of business with substandard quality practices (restaurants, dry cleaners, health clubs, etc.) or where they may have had a prior experience of being ripped off (tradespeople, auto repair shops, etc.). This recognition and rewards system received local and regional press coverage and became a speaking topic at a few local professional society meetings. It also made a lot of people in the community think about quality improvement.

10. Cultural Transformation

Cultural change and transformation occur at the far end of a strategic improvement program, the point where there is a transition from a program to a new operating philosophy. This happens when organizations are successful at behavioral change, and they have internalized and institutionalized the improvement process. Culture change occurs only when a new way of operating takes place without being constantly shored up by management, and for a reasonable period of time. It is the time when people no longer say, "I don't have time to change and do my regular job." Change is now viewed as part of their job, instead of in addition to it. It is the point where people identify and solve problems without giving a second thought to whether it's a kaizen, lean, or Six Sigma problem. It's a fascinating phenomenon when organizations cross over this magic line where strategic improvement is embedded in their cultural DNA. It's very rewarding to observe people seeking out and implementing improvements without giving a second thought to whether they're dealing with a kaizen, lean, ERP, or Six Sigma problem.

CULTURAL TRANSFORMATION — NOT STEADY-STATE

Let's talk reality for a moment. Ideally, improvement never ends once the transition from program to operating philosophy takes place and it becomes embedded in the culture. Picture a force field diagram of your strategic improvement program with its driving forces and restraining forces defined. For driving forces, you have all of these great improvement efforts in place. We are improving financial performance and competitiveness, and we may have been awarded a new chunk of business. People are enthusiastic, individual behaviors have changed, the culture is changing, and it's just a lot more fun to come to work every day. Now let's visit the restraining forces. First, there is a very grey area between behavioral change and cultural change, and you experience backslides occasionally. Second, people do not remain in their same positions forever. Sometimes new management comes in with a different twist on improvement. Sometimes people are promoted and their motivation/reward system changes. Critical resources may be on sick leave or retire and new people are hired. Third, people have human frailties. We get tired, we need reinforcement, we become complacent, our company relationships change, we drift and become unfocused, etc. And fourth, there are a *bejillion* other things tugging at us in the company, in our personal lives, and in the world that impact our continued progress — everything including new product launches, market shifts, your son's baseball game, a lot less low-hanging fruit, global competition, a hot customer complaint, tool wear, technology, pack-and-ship errors, the stock market, another new system or procedure, your temporary United Way assignment, incorrect drawings, and terrorism, among many others.

Cultural transformation is not steady-state. It's not like climbing a mountain, where you get to the top and then say you have arrived. It's a glacier without crampons! The best improvement paths are comprised of sawtooth curves characterized by successes, mistakes, breakthroughs, many smaller gains, backslides, and recoveries. The rate of improvement changes for many logical reasons, and organizations should not be disappointed about this fact of life. It's only a disappointment when organizations watch all of these things happen around them and then do not do anything about it. Strategic improvement programs require hard work, patience, and intellectual flexibility to achieve success. Transforming that program into the culture and maintaining the same rate of improvement are even tougher. Successful organizations make their improvement philosophy their business philosophy and live it every minute of every day. They make a conscious effort to reinforce this business philosophy and expect the same of others. They also have a very low tolerance level for those who are winging it.

IT'S NOT ALL MANAGEMENT'S FAULT

We wish to dispel the idea that everything is management's fault. If at this point in the chapter and are feeling that everything we discussed so far is management's problem, you have missed the point. Don't wait for these people to tell you what to do because they usually have 200 other items on their plates. Leadership can evolve from anywhere, not just from the executive suite. It's up to everyone to play a leadership role. When you take a closer look at innovative leaders, there's another factor that exists in their organizations — innovative people. What are the characteristics of their people?

- They have a passion for improvement and change.
- They have tremendous initiative to learn and develop new skills.
- They accept facts and waste little time on excuses and denial.
- They see the larger picture and think "process."
- They don't wait for opportunity to knock; they go out hunting for it.
- They take risks and understand that mistakes are part of the solution.
- They're team players who know their limitations and seek help from other sources.
- They get things done. They don't have the words "I can't" in their vocabulary.

Most CEOs and their executive teams are very bright people who can grasp concepts and understand very quickly what needs to be done. On the other hand, they have a culture that promotes idea generation like a tornado. Executives need help from their people in terms of upward information that can be easily assimilated and understood. It is the responsibility of everyone to help the organization synthesize information, draw the right conclusions, and take the right actions. Great executives build that ownership factor into the organization's culture. They promote the "What would I do if this were my company?" way of thinking, because if you take a hard look, it is your company. Great people pick up this opportunity and run with it; they don't sit around and suffer from the "ain't it awful" syndrome. These days, most people spend over one-third of their lives working, so you might as well use your brain, achieve your full potential, feel a sense of personal and professional accomplishment, and have fun! The need for strategic improvement is beyond your control. Remember that everyone has the opportunity to either make great contributions to change or hang around and become a victim of change.

GET BETTER OR GET WORSE

Another topic we wish to cover in this chapter is the *Get Better or Get Worse* concept (Figure 3.2). Earlier we discussed how the industrial world is moving at clock speed, technology and product life cycles are very short, and everyone is involved in business improvement. It's a fact that the bar is rising at a much faster speed than many organizations can keep up with. What this means is that organizations that have the Lean Extended Enterprise on their agendas do not have the luxury of putzing around with change for years and then realizing few results. Organizations need to adopt the perspective that every competitor is already pursuing strategic improvement and is out there ahead of you.

A Lean Extended Enterprise initiative and all strategic improvement programs follow a life cycle similar to the Get Better or Get Worse diagram. In the beginning there is a high degree of interest and enthusiasm for improvement; however, we get a waffling effect as we drop down from the 50,000-foot level and begin implementing improvements. The following provides a description of each element in the diagram:

- **Enthusiastic Beginner (C_1):** This is the point in the improvement process where many people are beginning to jump on the bandwagon of change. Individuals have a medium to high commitment and it is growing every day as the message of improvement spreads throughout the organization, the consultants are hired, and the education sessions are scheduled. People might also go through a formal education program to learn about the improvement methodologies.

- **Disillusioned Expert (C_2):** This is the point where people have learned enough about the improvement methodologies to become dangerous. They understand more about the improvement process but they may have doubts about applicability, so their commitment falls off. They go off and try something and it doesn't work. This is also the point where people begin to ask a lot of questions about whether these methodologies will work because they are different. In many cases, they bring up questions about situations which are really either what-if or exception conditions in the business. Some become baffled about how to proceed. Others outright give in to defeat and become the "I told you soers" of the organization. They begin to slide backwards into old habits.

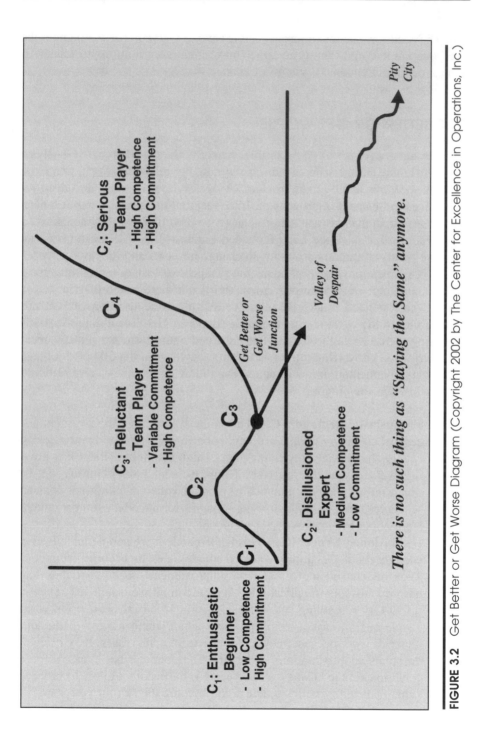

FIGURE 3.2 Get Better or Get Worse Diagram (Copyright 2002 by The Center for Excellence in Operations, Inc.)

- **Reluctant Team Player (C₃):** This is the crucial point in the improvement process where we reach the *Get Better or Get Worse Junction*. This segment of the diagram requires strong leadership and mentoring, TLC, and technical expertise to stop further backsliding and turn things around. If an organization allows itself to slide, it falls into the *Valley of Despair*. At this point, people retreat to the old practices, which continue to get worse. If organizations continue to slide, they reach *Pity City* and the improvement program fizzles.
- **Serious Team Player (C₄):** This is the point where we have made a successful turnaround and have implemented change with great results. Success breeds more success and we continue upward. People have both a high commitment and a high competence for change.

There is no such thing as staying the same anymore. Organizations either improve or they fall behind their competitors. We see more and more organizations doing a much better job with their improvement programs than we have in the past. We are seeing the interest and commitment levels rising in the LEERM area. When we discuss clock speed change, the reverse is also true. You can fall behind at clock speed. If your organization does not like change, then it will like being an irrelevant competitor and all the painful activities that often accompany this position even less.

The horrific tragedy of September 11, 2001 impacted every business, including ours. Proposals were put on hold, several projects were postponed or canceled, and the interest level for our services fell drastically. It seemed like almost every organization plunged into a huge industrial coma. A few months later, I (TB) was having dinner with the CEO of one of our clients. I had been in that CEO's office on 9/11, at which time we were just two weeks into his organization's Six Sigma program. I asked him why he didn't cancel or postpone our Six Sigma project after 9/11. His response: "Honestly, I thought about it. Then I realized that 9/11 has nothing to do with our problems. And if the economy gets better tomorrow, we would have worse problems if we did nothing. This is actually the best time to make changes. The risks are low and we have breathing room. Believe me, we will be much stronger than those who are doing nothing right now when things turn around."

Think about it, and then think about what your organization has been doing relative to strategic improvement. This is a great nugget of wisdom. If you're honest with yourself, you will admit that your delivery performance has nothing to do with bulls or bears. The design robustness of your new products has nothing to do with elephants or donkeys. Terrorism did not cause your billing errors, excess and obsolete inventory, or warranty/return problems. Those problems existed in 2000 and they will be much larger problems in 2004 if you stay in industrial coma mode. Think about it, then lead others to do the right things for your stakeholders, the economy, and society as a whole. A colleague of mine created a comical screen saver about this topic (Figure 3.3). Organizations that are heavily into strategic improvement will accelerate in the next economic upturn, gaining significant market share from those that do nothing and hobble out wondering what happened.

CHAPTER 3 TAKE-AWAYS

- Strategic improvement is a core competency. Organizations must learn how to define and organize a strategic improvement initiative and then integrate strategy, leadership, execution, the right methodologies, and permanent culture change. This skill is not automatically derived by osmosis or stature in the organization.
- Improvement methodologies by themselves are neither sufficient nor exhaustive. They are also ineffective and short-lived without the right improvement strategy and infrastructure bundled around them. Improvement methodologies, tools, and enabling technologies are the *means,* not the *ends.*
- Insanity is doing the same things the same way with the same tools and expecting different results, and then if that still doesn't work, redouble your efforts.
- The fact is, no matter where your current performance lies, it simply is not good enough beyond today. The world is moving at clock speed, technology and product life cycles are very short, and everyone is involved in business improvement. The bar is rising at a much faster speed than many organizations can keep up with.
- The best time to change is now, but it is unfortunate that it often requires a catastrophic event to prime the organizational pump for change. It is a lot easier to create urgency with catastrophe rather than leadership, but it often makes you late for the party.
- Speed can be an extremely harmful diversion, particularly if organizations choose to shortcut the most critical steps of improvement. Organizations will never realize the results they expect without a well-defined improvement plan.
- Leadership behavior and actions must be consistent with the communication and awareness message. When leaders live the vision, people will follow.
- Organizations are successful with change because they understand how to work through their implementation issues together. They help each

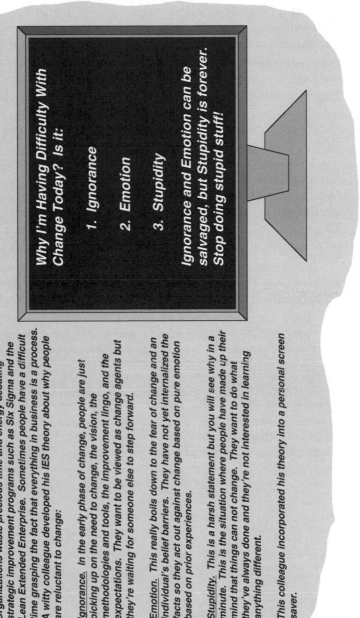

Is it Ignorance, Emotion, or Stupidity?

Organizations waste precious time and energy debating strategic improvement programs such as Six Sigma and the Lean Extended Enterprise. Sometimes people have a difficult time grasping the fact that everything in business is a process. A witty colleague developed his IES theory about why people are reluctant to change:

Ignorance. In the early phase of change, people are just picking up on the need to change, the vision, the methodologies and tools, the improvement lingo, and the expectations. They want to be viewed as change agents but they're waiting for someone else to step forward.

Emotion. This really boils down to the fear of change and an individual's belief barriers. They have not yet internalized the facts so they act out against change based on pure emotion based on prior experiences.

Stupidity. This is a harsh statement but you will see why in a minute. This is the situation where people have made up their mind that things can not change. They want to do what they've always done and they're not interested in learning anything different.

This colleague incorporated his theory into a personal screen saver.

FIGURE 3.3 Comical screen saver about change

other put the finishing touches and ownership on the change. They have this magic faith and confidence that they will figure out how to put it all together and succeed.

- The purpose of measurement is to provide a formal linkage between our improvement plan and our improvement actions. Measurement also closes the loop between improvement actions and the corresponding results. Without measurement and feedback, there is no way to determine progress with facts.

- Successful organizations make their improvement philosophy their business philosophy and live it every minute of every day. They make a conscious effort to reinforce this business philosophy and expect the same in others.

- Organizations need to adopt the perspective that every competitor is already pursuing strategic improvement and is out there ahead of them. There is no such thing as staying in the same position anymore. Organizations either improve or they fall behind their competitors.

SUGGESTED FURTHER READING

Burton, Terence and John Moran, *The Future-Focused Organization,* Prentice Hall, 1995.

Collins, James, *Good to Great: Why Some Companies Make the Leap...And Others Don't,* Harper-Collins, 2001.

Cotter, John, *The Heart of Change,* Harvard Business School Press, 2002.

Harris, Michael, *Value Leadership: Winning Competitive Advantage in the Information Age,* ASQ Press, 1998.

Rumsfeld, Donald, *The Rumsfeld Way: The Leadership Wisdom of a Battle-Hardened Maverick,* McGraw-Hill, 2002.

VonOech, Roger, *Expect the Unexpected or You Won't Find It,* Berrett-Koehler Publishers, 2002.

4

KAIZEN: QUICK-STRIKE OPPORTUNITIES IN THE LEAN EXTENDED ENTERPRISE

In this chapter we will explore the process of kaizen and its relationship to the Lean Extended Enterprise Reference Model (LEERM). There has been a great deal of confusion surrounding kaizen and misapplication of the technique. Many companies claim they have implemented lean manufacturing, and the basis for this claim is that they conducted kaizen events. Their intent is noble, as they want to institutionalize a continuous improvement philosophy and believe the process of kaizen is the correct tool for accomplishing this objective. The broader perspective of kaizen is that it is a process, not a tool, and as a process can be applied to various activities within the LEERM. Kaizen in itself should not be considered lean, as it is only one of several processes, as noted in the Methodologies, Tools, and Enabling Technologies Panel of the LEERM. Kaizen is not a one-time project; it is a process and a state of mind for continuous improvement that supports waste elimination.

The use of kaizen events for eliminating waste in manufacturing operations has been well documented. Unfortunately, the application of kaizen events in the soft processes of the organization has not kept pace with achievements as accomplished by the manufacturing areas of the business. The opportunities that

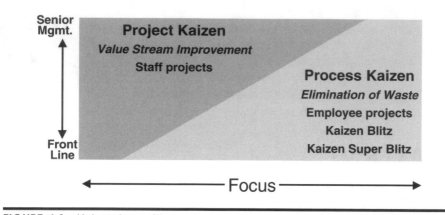

FIGURE 4.1   Kaizen breadth and scope

exist for continuous improvement and elimination of waste in the soft areas of the enterprise are the next significant frontier for creating competitive advantage for the enterprise (Figure 4.1). Think about the abundance of opportunities that exist in the human resources, sales, marketing, customer service, order entry, sales support, purchasing, accounting, legal, engineering, quality, information systems, environmental, health and safety, and research and development areas of the enterprise for eliminating visible and non-visible waste. One example that quickly comes to mind is use of procurement credit cards for conducting purchases for non-manufacturing expenses. In this example, the cost savings and waste elimination are significant for procurement activities of authorization, documentation, communication, receiving, and invoicing.

KAIZEN DEFINED

If you ask ten individuals to define kaizen, you will most likely get ten differing definitions. The various names used to describe kaizen include gemba kaizen, kaizen blitz, kaizen supper blitz and just plain kaizen. The roots of kaizen are derived from the Japanese words *kai,* meaning "to take apart," and *zen,* meaning "to make good." Kaizen is the gradual, incremental, and continual "improvement" of activities so as to create more value and less non-value-adding waste. The following definitions should help clarify terms associated with kaizen.

Continuous improvement means improvement in *small, incremental, continuous steps* that can be placed in the context of a number of tactical initiatives. Daily improvement in small amounts carried out in every job and function of the business eventually accumulates into very large gains.

Gemba is a Japanese word, the literal translation of which is "the real place." In the manufacturing field, gemba means the shop floor, where the actual product is being made, as contrasted with the office, where support services are provided. The term "gemba kaizen" refers to kaizen events that take place on the shop floor.

Kaikaku is a Japanese term that means the "radical improvement of an activity" to eliminate non-value-adding waste. It is also called *breakthrough kaizen, flow kaizen,* and *system kaizen.*

Kaizen is composed of the Japanese *kai,* meaning "to take apart," and *zen,* meaning "to make good." It is the gradual, incremental, and continual "improvement" of activities so as to create more value and less non-value-adding waste. Its success depends on the total commitment of the workforce to increase efficiency and reduce costs. It is also called *point kaizen* and *process kaizen.*

Kaizen blitz is a planned kaizen event that is conducted over a period of three to five days that utilizes the kaizen process to achieve value enhancement and eliminate non-value-adding waste.

Kaizen event is a planned and structured event that enables a group of associates to improve some aspect of their business. Prior to the actual event, an area is chosen and prepared, a problem is selected, leaders and teams are chosen, the problem is baselined, an improvement target is set, measurements are selected, and a time frame is set for the event. The actual kaizen event aims for the quick, focused discovery of root causes and quick, focused implementation of solutions.

Kaizen super blitz is a kaizen event that takes place immediately upon detection of a defect for a process, piece of equipment, or product and is of limited durations (hours).

APPLICATION OF KAIZEN WITH THE LEERM

Let's refer back to the Methodologies, Tools, and Enabling Technologies Panel of the LEERM to understand how the process of kaizen integrates with the process of becoming lean. The fourth panel of the LEERM identifies the methodologies, tools, and enabling technologies that are utilized as a set of tools applied to focused opportunities to enhance the value stream to achieve lean. We can use the analogy of an apple tree (Figure 4.2) to describe the form-fit-function characteristics of these various improvement tools. Kaizen should be used as a process that is applied to achieve event-specific continuous improvement that is focused across several levels of the organization. Thus the process of kaizen events is used as a basis for application of lean and Six Sigma activities, such as setup reduction, 5S, daily corrective action activities, design

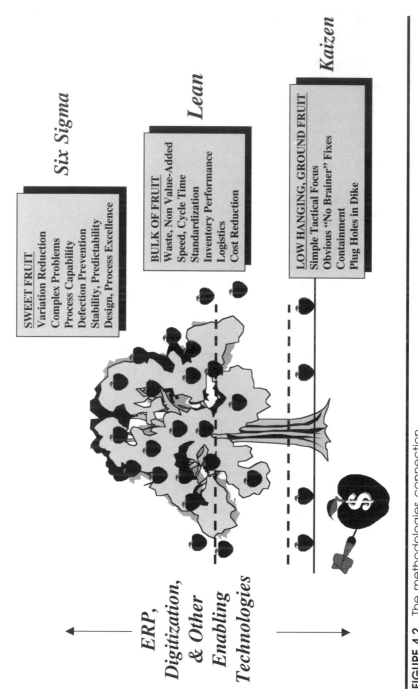

SWEET FRUIT
Variation Reduction
Complex Problems
Process Capability
Defection Prevention
Stability, Predictability
Design, Process Excellence

Six Sigma

BULK OF FRUIT
Waste, Non Value-Added
Speed, Cycle Time
Standardization
Inventory Performance
Logistics
Cost Reduction

Lean

LOW HANGING, GROUND FRUIT
Simple Tactical Focus
Obvious "No Brainer" Fixes
Containment
Plug Holes in Dike

Kaizen

ERP,
Digitization,
& Other
Enabling
Technologies

FIGURE 4.2 The methodologies connection

of experiments, one-piece flow, visual controls, housekeeping, and other lean tools. Kaizen is a low-cost common sense approach of incremental improvement and is a low-risk approach for value stream improvements. Kaizen is about going after the obvious low-hanging fruit or the fruit on the ground. Within the soft process areas and support activities, there is enormous potential for improvement with the simple kaizen approach. In many cases, this is the first structured "look-see" at these business processes.

The benefits of applying kaizen have been well documented across many organizations. Process improvements resulting from kaizen events are realized from conducting both planned kaizen events as well as daily kaizen super blitz events. Application of kaizen to daily quality defects in processes, equipment, and products results in a sustainable continuous improvement process focused on both corrective action and prevention activities. The long-term impact of conducting kaizen super blitz activities is exponential when viewed over sustainable periods of time. For example, think about the impact several 1% improvements conducted each day would yield over a one-year period of time. A secondary benefit of conducting daily events is the impact it has on employees and their willingness to contribute to continuous improvement initiatives. A wise and experienced plant manager once noted, "If you can teach a person to fish, they will be able to feed themselves for their entire lives." The key benefits of institutionalizing kaizen include the following:

- Workers are always thinking about all kinds of problems and solutions in their daily activities.
- The process of continual adjustments is institutionalized into the daily fabric of the organization.
- Process/departmental needs are more easily identified by the people working in the area, as they are the most knowledgeable about their processes.
- Resistance to change is minimized, as individuals are now included in the improvement process.
- Solutions are grounded in reality based on the knowledge of individuals who are closest to the processes they use on a daily basis.
- Solutions emphasize common sense and low-cost approaches.
- Workers begin to accept and enjoy continuous improvement activities.
- Suggestions increase overnight as people feel that they can impact change.
- Upper management approval is not always necessary now to cause change. Responsibility for change will be primarily acted on by those involved in the process.
- Efficiency improvements of 20 to 50% realized.
- Inventory reductions of 20 to 80% realized.

- Distance traveled reduced up to 40 to 90%.
- Setup times reduced 50 to 80%.
- Process time reduction of 40 to 80%.

CATEGORIES OF WASTE

Kaizen events are conducted to eliminate waste in both manufacturing and administrative areas within the organization. Waste is defined as any process that adds time or cost but does not add value. The primary focus of kaizen events is identifying and driving out wastes from the processes. So often, kaizen events are limited to only production areas within the organization. Those organizations that choose to conduct kaizen events for production and administrative functions enjoy greater benefits in terms of waste elimination.

Eight waste categories	Sample opportunities for improvement
Overproduction	Reduce lot size/batch size Reduce setup time Reduce start-up rejects Simplify the process Shorten search time Eliminate unnecessary data
Waiting	Synchronize work Combine work Balance workloads Cross-train employees One-touch information access Implement visible cues
Transport	Create work cells Create one-stop workstations Create paperless processes Fewer suppliers and closer Minimize number of moves Point of use storage
Processing	Redesign the part/process to eliminate components/tasks Redesign the part/process to simplify Fail-safe the process Establish standard work

Eight waste categories	Sample opportunities for improvement
Inventory	Reduce batch size
	Reduce lead time
	Synchronize work flows
	Add capacity to handle peak loads
	Minimize checks and reviews
Motion	Every-move-counts philosophy
	Combine multiple steps into one
	Eliminate searching activities
	Organize layout through 5S
	Create visible systems
Defects	Quality standards
	Standard documentation
	Standard work
	Process capability
	Fail-safe processes
Information	Decrease process waste
	Easy-to-understand information
	Visible systems
	Accuracy of data

KAIZEN TYPES

Kaizen is a confusing methodology, and the term itself is often used interchangeably to mean different things, which increases the confusion factor even more. Figure 4.3 provides a *kaizen hierarchy* to help clarify the different applications of terminology. Most often, individuals associate kaizen with short-duration continuous improvement projects that are conducted over a one- to five-day duration. The term most often associated with this type of event is *kaizen blitz*. Unfortunately, this limited view of kaizen excludes additional opportunities for applying the kaizen methodology to longer duration or shorter duration events. Two types of focus can define kaizen activities. These two types of events are defined as either *project kaizen* or *process kaizen* events. Both types of kaizen events can be applied to administrative or manufacturing areas.

Project kaizen events are events that focus on value stream improvement activities. These types of events are characterized as improvement activities that

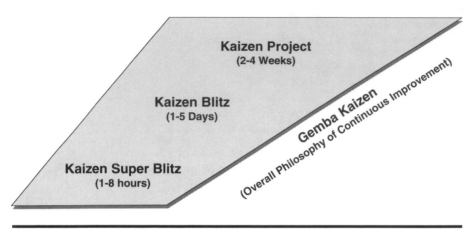

FIGURE 4.3 The kaizen hierarchy

enhance value across multiple functions within a value stream. Typically, these project kaizen events are composed of cross-functional teams (internal and/or external) and are project-based continuous improvement activities. Most often, these events are sanctioned by senior-level management and have strategic importance to the organization, suppliers, and customers. Careful selection of a project-based kaizen event is critical because the organization has limited resources that can be deployed for work on time-consuming projects. Project kaizen events span a duration of many weeks to complete the continuous improvement initiative. Redesigning a quotation process to shorten the lead time from inquiry through generating a formal quote to the customer is an example of a project-based kaizen event.

Process kaizen events, on the other hand, are focused on elimination of waste for activities that are of limited definition. The main emphasis is on waste elimination, workplace effectiveness, or standardization. Waste elimination is defined by the main waste categories of overproduction, inventory, rejects, motion, processing, waiting, transport, information, and human potential. These kaizen events are initiated as employee projects for the purpose of quick-hitting process improvements. The range of time to complete process kaizen events can be as little as hours or up to days. The terms used to describe these types of events are either *kaizen blitz* or *kaizen super blitz.*

Kaizen blitz events can typically be completed in a one- to five-day timeframe. In a typical kaizen blitz project, a cross-functional multilevel team of 6 to 12 members works intensely, 8 to 12 hours a day, to rapidly develop, test, and refine solutions to problems and leave a new process in place in just a few days.

They don't plan, they don't propose, they *do*. An example of a kaizen blitz event would be conducting a setup reduction project for a specific product on a specific machine.

Kaizen super blitz events are completed in one to eight hours. Typically, the occurrence of a defect, failure, or safety issue immediately authorizes a kaizen super blitz event to take place. Similar to the kaizen blitz event, a cross-functional team of three to six individuals works intensely to determine the root cause and implement short-term corrective action. Commonly, a kaizen blitz event occurs after corrective action has been initiated to implement long-term prevention activities. An example of a kaizen super blitz event would be determining the root cause of a safety incident or determining the root cause and adjustment of startup rejects for a manufacturing process.

SELECTING THE RIGHT KAIZEN EVENTS

Choosing the correct kaizen events to conduct is critical to leveraging the limited resources available for carrying out continuous improvement initiatives. The last thing you want is an environment where individuals act like kaizen cowboys by choosing kaizen events for their own personal gain or selecting events of low strategic importance. One of our clients had asked us to come to their rescue to fix their kaizen process. They had good intentions when they first initiated their kaizen events, but they had not followed a structured approach to selecting and coordinating kaizen events. Without considering how to sanction events, they just started identifying kaizen events without considering the consumption of resources. Eventually they had over 30 kaizen events in process within several weeks of beginning their kaizen initiatives. The success of the kaizen events was dismal at best. The success of their kaizen events could have followed a different path had they followed a structured process for selecting kaizen events and coordinating kaizen events.

Utilizing a *priority matrix* (Figure 4.4) to select kaizen events provides a structured approach to sanction events. The priority matrix has four quadrants that are used to qualify kaizen events. Axis one identifies the impact a kaizen event has on improving efficiency, either high or low. Axis two identifies the effort required to coordinate the kaizen event, either low effort or high effort. The best kaizen events to approve are those that have a high impact on improving efficiency and require low effort to complete. The worst events are those that have low impact on improving efficiency and require high effort to complete. Events that have a high impact on improving efficiency and require high effort to complete should be "chunked out" into several smaller kaizen events.

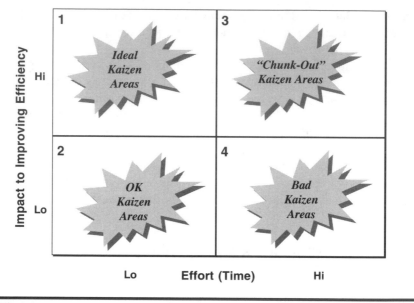

FIGURE 4.4   Kaizen priority matrix

THE KAIZEN FRAMEWORK

A kaizen event must be carefully prepared, effectively coordinated, and thoroughly followed up in order to be considered a successful kaizen event. No matter what type of kaizen events are conducted, they follow a standardized framework for completing the continuous improvement activity. Figure 4.5 provides a *structured kaizen framework* adopted from the Six Sigma methodology. People often gravitate toward solutions without properly conducting fact-finding activities to identify the root causes of the problem. Thus, they prescribe solutions out of sequence. You would not expect a doctor to prescribe a treatment without first understanding your symptoms and then diagnosing the causes so that the proper treatment can be prescribed. Thus, both project kaizen and process kaizen events must follow a definite framework so that a standard methodology is institutionalized for kaizen events. The failure to create a standard methodology and apply it universally creates confusion in determining when to apply or not apply a set of standards for conducting the kaizen event. Time spent on a kaizen event can be categorized as having three main components: preparation, the event itself, and follow-up. To successfully conduct an event, approximately 40% of the time should be spent on preparation, 40% on conducting the event, and 20% on follow-up activities.

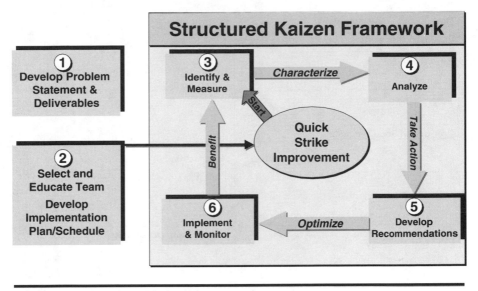

FIGURE 4.5 Structured kaizen framework

Our kaizen model has six cornerstones. One might see the familiar Six Sigma DMAIC (Define Measure Analyze Improve Control) process embedded within it. That's because it is. Although kaizen is not concerned with the application of complex statistical tools, the problem-solving process (thought process) itself works well. We prefer this approach because it provides a consistent problem-solving model for all problem-solving methodologies and tools. The time frame for completing this six-step process varies based on the type of kaizen event (project or process) being conducted. For example, the steps in a kaizen super blitz event are conducted in rapid succession, where some steps may take minutes or hours to complete.

1. Develop the Problem Statement and Deliverables

During this step, a concise statement is created to qualify the problem, objectives, and deliverables. This is the "what is it" and "why is it important" step. The purpose of conducting this step is to make sure that all individuals involved clearly understand the problem and clearly identify the desired outcomes. In order for a problem to be correctly understood and solved, the problem must first be recognized and the relevant data gathered and analyzed. Without this understanding of the problem and the desired outcomes, the group will not be focused properly on the remaining cornerstones. This step should be carried out very quickly.

Date:	Project Area:	Current Situation & Problems:
Kaizen Team:		
Production Requirements:		
Process Information:		**Kaizen Team Objectives:**

FIGURE 4.6 Kaizen activity worksheet

Identifying the kaizen event
- Identify an "open-ended" question.
- How can we improve our efficiency?
- How can we eliminate waste?
- How can we make our workplace safer?
- How can we fail-safe the process?
- How can we organize the work area?
- How can we reduce scrap?
- How can we reduce cycle time?
- How can we reduce setup time?
- Question should be keyed to business objectives.
- Question should be related to team members.

A *kaizen activity worksheet* (Figure 4.6) should be completed to identify team members, production requirements, process information, statement of the current situation and problems, and the kaizen objectives. The worksheet is one of the elements in a kaizen event storyboard, which provides a visual representation to exhibit the activities of a lean project team and the key information it has discovered. Storyboards serve to inform, educate, and motivate other workers and teams.

2. Select and Educate Team, Develop Implementation Schedule

Stakeholders are identified during this step to make sure that the team has representation from all areas that have ties to the problem. Stakeholders should not be limited to only internal company employees. Selection of the team members is important, so individuals are chosen based on their ability to work together cohesively and support the kaizen event. Education of the team members is paramount to properly conducting steps 3, 4, and 5. Team members need training regarding specific tools that will be used during the identifying, measuring, and analyzing steps. Think of it this way: If the only tool in the toolbox is a hammer, then every problem looks like a nail. Finally, an implementation schedule is developed to guide the team in execution so that the key milestones are accomplished in a timely manner.

When selecting team members, you should consider the following. Team members should:

- Be cross-functional and represent different areas
- Be employees
- Know the process they are addressing
- Be interested in improvement
- Be different from previous teams
- Have an impartial facilitator
- Be willing to contribute
- Be team players who value improvement of the process versus their own personal gain

Training opportunities for consideration might include:

- How to set the targets
- How to select the team leader
- How to evaluate the area in advance
- How to explain the purpose of the project
- How to manage the change process
- How to run a project
- What tools are to be utilized and how are they used
- How to instruct operators in the new processes or changes that are to be implemented

- How to prepare standards
- How to prepare a summary report
- How to use the spreadsheet tool for managing the project

3. Identify and Measure

During this step, the team conducts activities to manage the actual kaizen event. Team roles are assigned for the kaizen event. Event objectives, implementation schedule, and procedures are reviewed. The team decides which tools will be used throughout the event to collect data. Baseline metrics must be determined so that the current process can be evaluated based on facts. Baseline metrics might include process lead time, throughput rate, value-added content, etc. Without fact-driven data, the next step, analyze, cannot be conducted effectively.

Examples of tools for gathering baseline metrics
- Cycle time flowchart
- Time study sheet
- Analysis of variance
- Control charts: C, P, X-R
- Cost of quality
- Process capability ratios
- Variance analysis
- Pareto chart
- Defect map
- Multivariable chart
- Line chart
- Frequency distribution
- Time observation sheets
- Process capacity table

Too often, teams want to jump to implementing recommendations without properly understanding the current state. As mentioned earlier, you cannot prescribe solutions until diagnosis has been properly completed. Finally, the current process is mapped through use of various techniques. Mapping techniques might include cycle time flowchart, value stream map, process flowchart, facility layout diagram, workflow analysis, 5S map, top-down flowchart, and activity analysis.

Benefits of mapping
- Helps to visualize the process so that you can see the flow
- Identifies sources of waste in the value stream

- Provides a common language for talking about the processes being analyzed
- Makes decisions about the flow apparent
- Shows linkage between information flow and material flow
- Forms the basis of an implementation plan
- Provides tally of non-value-added steps, lead time, distance traveled, and amount of inventory

4. Analyze

Upon completion of identifying and measuring the process, based on thoroughly observing the current state, you now are able to understand how things could be improved to eliminate waste. The team can now begin to identify improvement ideas, evaluate the improvements, and prioritize the improvements. This requires that the team drill down to the root cause of key pain points. By understanding the root causes, you are able to prescribe solutions that not merely correct but, most importantly, prevent waste. The baseline metrics that were collected during step 3 are now reviewed to understand the major wastes for the process. The use of a fishbone diagram will aid the group in determining the root cause of the observed wastes that were documented during collection of the baseline metrics. Generating alternative solutions can be accomplished through one of the standard methods for conducting brainstorming. Do not accept "boil the ocean" items such as improve communication between X and Y or improve training. It is important to demand "doable" items such as clean up and organize the workplace through use of 5S, implement visual controls x and y, create an operations/methods sheet, or relocate operations into a logical assembly flow.

A *kaizen action plan worksheet* (Figure 4.7) can be used to document the brainstorming ideas. The worksheet serves as a project management tool so that all ideas are documented in writing. The kaizen action plan worksheet will be used during the remaining two steps of the kaizen event to track implementation activities. The worksheet is completed during this step to identify the action item and the originator of the improvement suggestion.

5. Develop Recommendations

Now that improvement suggestions have been identified, the kaizen team needs to evaluate and select improvement suggestions for implementation. The evaluation process includes estimating the financial savings for each suggestion. Additionally, each suggestion should be classified as to the waste category that is impacted.

When evaluating and prioritizing the improvement suggestions, analyze each

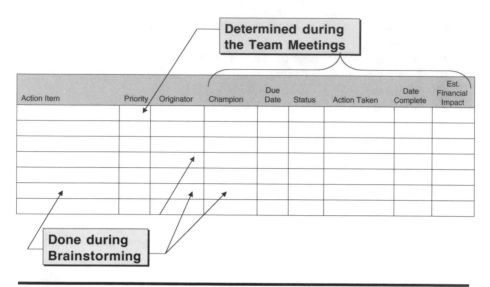

FIGURE 4.7   Kaizen action plan worksheet

suggestion based on the ability to impact efficiency and the resources required to implement the suggestion. Each suggestion is then assigned a priority for implementation. Each of the highest priority suggestions is assigned a kaizen champion to coordinate its implementation. The champion should be "passionate" about seeing that the item is completed. The champion may or may not actually work on the solution for the suggestion. It is the champion's responsibility to verify the solution with the originator of the item to ensure that the solution and deliverable reflect the original intent of the item. For each suggestion that is implemented the following tasks must be completed:

- Determine a due date
- Document the new solution
- Define roles and responsibilities for the revised process
- Create tools, templates, and job aids for the improvement
- Establish metrics for the improvement
- Establish the measurement process

6. Implement and Monitor

During this step, the assigned champion coordinates implementation of a suggestion. The champion may enlist additional employees to assist in implementation of the specific suggestion. This may include members from the original team or other individuals from within the company. Update meetings, known as council meetings, are held with the core team to review progress on the prioritized improvements that were selected. The team should discuss business priorities during these council meetings and adjust its efforts accordingly. The champion for each improvement item should report progress at the council meetings. Any requests for assistance should be brought to the group for discussion and approval. Reassignments may be necessary based on lack of progress for a specific item. Progress may be impeded by lack of resources or roadblocks that are uncovered during the implementation activities.

The champion for each suggestion creates a rollout plan. The rollout plan includes development of training and education activities, identification of cutover elements necessary to implement the improvement, determination of whether migration of the improvement is applicable to other areas, identification of implementation support resources, and finalization of measurements to determine benefits from the baselines metrics. The implementation process utilizes the documentation of standard operating procedures, templates, and job aids that were developed during the previous step. During the rollout process you may discover further improvements that are related to the original improvement that make good sense to also implement.

It is critical for employees from the area where the improvement is being implemented to be part of the implementation process. One overzealous champion was so caught up in the improvement tasks for his area that he took it upon himself to carry out all of the tasks for the rollout plan. The improvement implemented involved sort and set-in-order activities for visual management. The champion was quite proud of what was accomplished, but the staff in the area where the improvements were implemented did not accept the improvements because they were not involved in the process. One of the improvements involved painting lines to visually identify walkways, operation areas, and work in process, raw materials, and finished goods. The employees commented to the project champion, "You must think that we are stupid little children who need to have outlines painted around everything so we know where everything is." Don't underestimate the change process when implementing improvements.

Closing the loop is an important step once the improvement has been successfully implemented. This is accomplished by publishing and communicating results of the improvement to all employees within the organization. This information is beneficial, as it provides consistent communication to the organization regarding continuous improvement initiatives. One of the best tools to utilize to easily share the results is a *kaizen storyboard* (Figure 4.8). The storyboard is a visual summary of key information from the project. Components of the storyboard include the kaizen activity worksheet, metrics before and after the improvement, 5S map before and after the improvement, listing of improvements implemented, and categories of waste eliminated or reduced during the

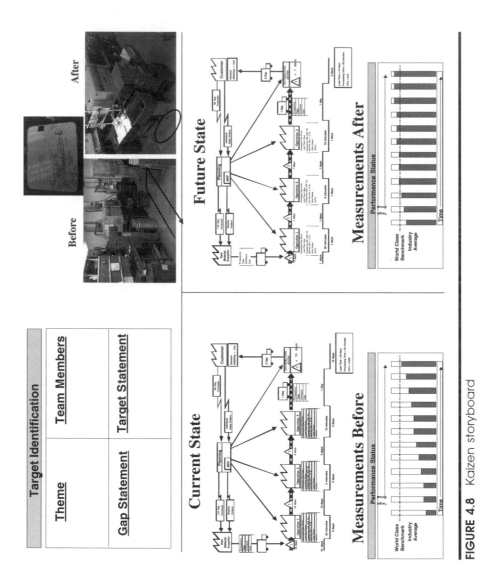

FIGURE 4.8 Kaizen storyboard

kaizen event. The information presented in the storyboard may spark application of similar improvements in other areas of the organization.

KAIZEN BLITZ

A kaizen blitz event differs from a kaizen event, as it is a focused, short-term project to improve processes within a short duration of time. A kaizen blitz event (Figure 4.9) follows the same six-step methodology as noted previously. The typical duration of a kaizen blitz event is three to five days. The process is an accelerated kaizen event that includes training, quick analysis, and process design improvements. It is important to focus the kaizen blitz event improvement activity on a narrow and specific objective so that it can be completed quickly and effectively. If the event is not narrowly focused, the outcome improvements will not be optimum. When selecting an event for a kaizen blitz, it is important to understand dangers associated with kaizen blitz events. Events should not be chosen if it is anticipated that essential lean elements will be ignored, it fails to integrate with chosen strategies, training and learning are superficial, and the process is complex. A kaizen blitz event has value, but substituting a blitz event for sound fundamentals is not good management practice.

Sample Format for a Five-Day Kaizen Blitz Event
Day One

The project kickoff meeting begins with the team reaching a common understanding of the team's purpose for the kaizen blitz event. This helps establish

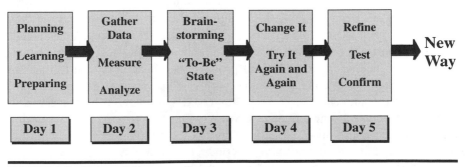

FIGURE 4.9 Kaizen blitz overview

boundaries for conducting the event. The team needs to be trained how to conduct a successful event. A concise statement is created to qualify the problem, objectives, and deliverables for the event. It is important to identify the limits and expectations with the team members. Examples of limits and expectations include deadlines, workload, priorities, resources, training, and process boundaries, as well as what will not be included in this event. Next the group should agree on ground rules for conducting the kaizen event. The purpose for agreeing on ground rules is to set expectations and avoid conflict during the event. A work plan is created to identify the main activities, estimate time and resources, and identify measures of progress for the event. This serves as a tool for management of the activities that will be carried out during the five-day event. As part of the work plan, the kaizen activity worksheet is completed. Data-gathering tools are explained to the group and selected for utilization during day two of the event. Explanation of high-level concepts/techniques is conducted with the team: takt time, 5S, one-piece flow, value stream mapping, kanban, setup reduction, mistake-proofing, etc.

Day Two

The second day begins with an early morning review of the previous day. This is followed by a debriefing on day two activities based on the work plan developed during day one. A muda walk is conducted for the process or area. The purpose of the muda walk is to videotape the current state and identify wastes based on the eight categories of waste. The group then reconvenes to discuss observations and develop a process map of the current area or process. Data are gathered for the current state based on the measurements that were determined to be relevant during development of the work plan. The collection and use of data are critical to identify issues, develop focus, understand the nature and extent of wastes, resolve conflicts and differences of opinion, and make better decisions during brainstorming. Examples of metrics include measuring space and distance traveled, throughput rates, lead times for each step in the process, value-added content, first-pass quality, and variances. A cause-and-effect diagram is a useful tool to focus the team on root causes versus symptoms. Either the dispersion analysis or process classification type of format can be used when constructing a cause-and-effect diagram. The finding are presented to the team. The data are now reviewed and analyzed by the group to agree on the current state and process wastes. Day two may include a working dinner to accomplish all of the tasks. Day two is completed by reviewing the work plan and critiquing the activities conducted during the day. Any changes to the work plan are discussed and approved by the team.

Day Three

The main thrust of day three is to conduct brainstorming to generate improvement ideas aimed at eliminating wastes that were identified by the team. A structured approach is necessary to allow the team to creatively and efficiently generate a high volume of ideas. It is critical that all team members be involved and enthusiastic to eliminate a few people from dominating the process. Either the structured approach or the unstructured approach can be utilized as a format for conducting the brainstorming session. Another approach that can be used is an affinity diagram. This technique also allows a team to creatively generate a large number of ideas for improvement and summarize ideas in natural groupings. The groupings can be organized around the eight categories of waste. Each of the improvement ideas should be evaluated for appropriateness, and each should be evaluated against the measurement data to determine effectiveness in eliminating waste and the resources required to carry it out. Strengths and weakness of each improvement should be considered. A great tool to use is a solution checklist. The solution checklist identifies the following information: improvement idea, cost, benefits, potential problems, and how hard or easy it is to implement. Once consensus is reached regarding the improvements to implement, each improvement idea is thoroughly documented. This requires construction of tools, templates, standards, and visual systems required to properly carry out the improvement.

Day Four

The fourth day begins with an early morning review of the previous day's selected improvement ideas. The main emphasis for day four is implementation and evaluation of the improvement ideas. The team assigns responsibility for each improvement and develops a work plan for sequentially implementing the improvements throughout the day. The team meets with operators to explain changes and new procedures that will be implemented. The improvements are then implemented in sequence as identified in the work plan. The new processes are videotaped and then evaluated for effectiveness. Changes are recommended, evaluated, implemented, and reevaluated throughout the day.

Day Five

The main purpose for day five is to prove out, refine, and document the new process to establish standard operating procedures. The only way to prove out the improvements is to conduct the actual process activities and observe the changes to confirm that the intended effect is accomplished. It is important to realize that there is a learning curve for new processes. This should be taken into account when confirming that the outcomes are as intended. Measurements are now taken on the new process and compared to the baselines established during day two. Refinements are made as necessary, and the final process is documented. Examples of documentation are a revised 5S map, visual diagrams, standard work instructions, metrics, charting, digital pictures, and checklists. The final activity is to conduct a final project presentation for management and those impacted by the new processes. The presentation should include a storyboard that is posted on the improvement bulletin board after completion of the presentation.

KAIZEN SUPER BLITZ

A kaizen super blitz event is an activity that takes place immediately upon detection of any type of waste. Waste can defined based on the eight main categories identified previously. The kaizen super blitz event should not be limited to just the standard areas such as product rejects or equipment failures. The process can be applied to other non-standard applications such as safety incidents and human errors. Typical kaizen blitz events range anywhere from 30 minutes to 8 hours. The overall objective of conducting a kaizen super blitz event is to apply a structured approach to daily problem solving to eliminate waste through creation of standards to prevent recurrence. All too often organizations take immediate corrective action but do little to implement prevention activities to eliminate waste from occurring in the future. The Japanese are well known for applying the concept of immediate line stoppage to correct quality errors. By using a structured tool that is applied consistently, the process of problem solving is institutionalized throughout the organization and becomes part of the daily standards for conducting continuous improvement. Think about the long-term impact of achieving 1% improvements many times throughout the day. In a year's time these improvements have a significant positive financial impact on the profitability of the organization.

Many of the steps utilized in project kaizen and kaizen blitz events are also used to conduct a kaizen super blitz. Each organization must determine which elements are important to effectively and efficiently conduct the kaizen super blitz event. Oftentimes the process of conducting a kaizen super blitz event identifies opportunities for conducting either a project kaizen event or kaizen blitz event, which are more thorough and of longer duration. An example of a kaizen super blitz technique is conducting a daily routine that involves examining rejects made the previous day or previous shift, so that countermeasures can be adopted immediately. This is accomplished by having an operator tag and place all rejects in a central area for each shift of production. A summary listing of all the rejects is generated at the end of the shift. In the summary listing, the rejects are classified as Type A, Type B, or Type C. Type A rejects are defined as causes are clear and countermeasures can be implemented immediately. Type B rejects are defined as causes are known but countermeasures cannot be adopted immediately. Type C rejects are defined as unidentified causes. At the beginning of the next shift or the next day, supervision visits the central area to view the rejects and the report listing. Supervision and staff then review the rejects to discuss countermeasures that need to be implemented.

Another example of a kaizen super blitz technique is use of an *after action report* (AAR). Once an incident has been identified, an AAR (Figure 4.10) is completed to identify what happened, the root causes, corrective action to take in the near term, and preventive action recommended to mistake-proof the process in order to eliminate recurrence. The employee who was involved and his or her immediate supervisor complete the AAR. By involving the employee in the process of completing the form, he or she is now committed to understanding the root causes and problem solving to generate solutions. It is critical that the AAR process be a positive experience and not administered to demoralize the employee. The AAR is typically submitted to the supervisor's manager for review.

CHANGE MANAGEMENT

When creating and deploying a kaizen system, it is important to consider change management issues. Your ability to achieve either success or failure is greatly dependent on how change is managed when establishing the kaizen structure for continuous improvement. Successful change depends on the integration of both formal and informal change techniques. Formal change is intentional, deliberately initiated, and managed with respect to the strategic application of kaizen within the organization. Non-directed change, on the other hand, is informal, reactive, and has little linkage to the goal of deploying kaizen. Change is not a one-time event and must be managed during the deployment phase as well as throughout the kaizen life cycle. The application of several principles will aid in the change process.

Kaizen principles
- Be open-minded to continuous improvement.
- Maintain a positive attitude.
- Waste elimination is everyone's responsibility.

INCIDENT
After Action Report (AAR)

> **Purpose:** To provide a means to communicate incidents, their causes and recommendations for corrective action to prevent future incidents.

This report is to be completed and turned into the Manufacturing Manager within 8 hours of the incident.

Date of incident: _____ Shift of incident: _____ Time of incident: _____

Person completing report: _____ DMR # if applicable: _____ Date of report: _____

What happened? (describe the incident and quantify the cost of quality):

_____
_____
_____
_____
_____
_____

Why? (causes leading to the incident):

_____
_____
_____
_____
_____

Corrective action to resolve the problem near term:

_____
_____
_____
_____
_____

Preventive action recommendations (short term and long term) to mistake-proof the process (prevent it from happening again):

_____
_____
_____
_____
_____
_____
_____
_____
_____
_____

_____	__/__/__	_____	__/__/__
EMPLOYEE	**DATE**	**SUPERVISOR**	**DATE**

FIGURE 4.10 Kaizen after action report

- Reject excuses and be driven to seek solutions.
- Ask why, why, why, why, why...
- Do not wait to be asked to intervene.
- Take action and implement countermeasures immediately.
- Use all of the team's knowledge during all phases of the kaizen event.
- Disregard rank.
- When waste occurs, ask whether it occurred because a standard does not exist, was not followed, or is not adequate.
- Creating a sense of mission and pride is an integral part of management's responsibility for kaizen. Beginning with the strategic view, senior management leadership is critical.
- Will the kaizen event create results that are consistent with the lean strategy?
- Is the organization culturally ready for the event?
- All levels of management must serve as team members for a kaizen event.
- Be careful when choosing the first kaizen events to conduct.

When choosing the first kaizen events to conduct, it is important to select events that are clear and unambiguous, are supported by management, satisfy a business need, are highly visible, are simple projects, have stable repeatable processes, and will involve worker contribution. You should avoid as first events processes that are significantly out of control and are unnecessary improvement areas. Save the more difficult kaizen targets for when you are confident the kaizen process has reached the end of the learning curve.

CHAPTER 4 TAKE-AWAYS

- The broader perspective of kaizen is that it is a process, not a tool, and as a process can be applied to various activities within the LEERM.
- Kaizen should be used as a process that is applied to achieve event-specific continuous improvement that is focused across several levels of the organization. Thus the process of kaizen events is used as a basis for application of lean and Six Sigma activities.
- Within the soft process areas and support activities, there is enormous potential for improvement with the simple kaizen methodology.
- Process improvements resulting from kaizen events are realized by conducting kaizen projects, kaizen blitz events, and daily kaizen super blitz events.

- Choosing the correct kaizen events to conduct is critical to leveraging the limited resources available for carrying out continuous improvement initiatives. The best kaizen events to approve are those that have a high impact on improving efficiency and require low effort to complete.
- When choosing the first kaizen events to conduct, it is important to select events that are clear and unambiguous, are supported by management, satisfy a business need, are highly visible, are simple projects, have stable repeatable processes, and will involve worker contribution.
- It is important to focus the kaizen blitz event improvement activity on a narrow and specific objective so that it can be completed quickly and effectively.
- The overall objective of conducting a kaizen super blitz event is to apply a structured approach to daily problem solving in order to eliminate waste through the creation of standards to prevent recurrence.
- The kaizen model has six cornerstones: (1) develop the problem statement and deliverables, (2) select and educate the team and develop the implementation schedule, (3) identify and measure, (4) analyze, (5) develop recommendations, and (6) implement and monitor.
- Proper and consistent usage of the tools separates those companies that make a short-term, unsustainable improvement from those that institutionalize their new improved process.
- Closing the loop is an important step once the improvement has been successfully implemented. This is accomplished by publishing and communicating results of the improvement to all employees within the organization. The kaizen storyboard is shared with everyone in the organization so they have the opportunity to learn and possibly apply the continuous improvement to other areas within the value stream.
- Kaizen needs long-term direction; people need a sense of direction to avoid playing cowboy with a process without accomplishing anything. Management should establish clear targets to guide everyone and be certain to provide leadership for all kaizen activities directed toward achieving the targets.

SUGGESTED FURTHER READING

Imai, Masaaki, *Kaizen: The Key To Japan's Competitive Success,* Random House, 1986.
Imai, Masaaki, *Gemba Kaizen: A Common Sense, Low-Cost Approach to Management,* McGraw-Hill, 1997.
Kaizen for the Shop Floor, Productivity Press, 2002.
Laraia, Anthony C., Patricia E. Moody, and Robert W. Hall, *The Kaizen Blitz: Accelerating Breakthroughs in Productivity and Performance,* Wiley, 1999.

Lareau, William, *Office Kaizen: Transforming Office Operations into a Strategic Competitive Advantage,* ASQ Quality Press, 2003.
Mika, G.L., *Kaizen: Event Implementation Manual,* Kaizen Sensei, 2002.
The Memory Jogger, GOAL/QPC, 1994.
The Team Memory Jogger, GOAL/QPC, 1995.

5

THE NEW GENERATIONS OF LEAN

U.S. companies have always been enamored with strategies to reduce waste, create competitive advantage, increase throughput, and gain market share. Mass production manufacturing methods have been replaced by results-oriented lean production systems that focus on waste elimination throughout the enterprise. The concepts, definitions, and methodologies of lean have been present in American industry for decades. Probably the most well-known example of lean is Toyota, when it developed its Toyota Production System (TPS) after World War II; it finally caught the Western world's attention after the 1973 oil crisis. For over 20 years before anyone knew it, Toyota pursued the TPS primarily to eliminate waste and reduce costs in its production system — it was the obvious solution to manage the constraints of space, people, and limited resources. But the reality is that many of the basic concepts of lean have been applied in business for the past 100 years. As we mentioned in Chapter 1, the book *Lean Thinking* by James P. Womack and Daniel T. Jones brought a more focused and disciplined approach to lean with the *five key lean principles*: (1) specify value, (2) create the value stream, (3) flow, (4) pull, and (5) perfection. However, it has been our experience that 80% of organizations have, for the most part, "dabbled" in lean, and the remaining 20% have adopted lean as a business philosophy and have real substance to show for their efforts.

Lean deals with the elimination and reduction of many types of non-value-added activities, often referred to as waste. The driving force for waste elimi-

TABLE 5.1   Eight waste categories

Waste	Description
Overproduction	Producing more than is demanded by the customer
Waiting	Waiting for the next process step to occur
Transportation	The unnecessary movement of materials or information
Processing	Excessive processing because of poor product or process design
Inventory	Storing more than the bare minimum
Motion	Excess or unnecessary motion for anything: people, machine, or materials
Defects	Creating scrap, rework, or paperwork errors
Human potential	Failure to utilize the skills of people

nation is improved customer value and increased profitability in the products and services offered by the organization. The seven types of waste that were identified by Taiichi Ohno as part of the TPS provide the areas for emphasis within the extended enterprise for waste elimination. We have added "human potential" as an eighth category of waste because we feel this is one of the most important types of waste within an organization. Table 5.1 lists the eight waste categories. The systematic focus on waste creates a culture that eliminates existing waste and prevents additional waste from being built into new processes. Once people are trained to identify waste, they are able to eliminate it. The eight categories of waste are applicable to both manufacturing and non-manufacturing activities. Too often, organizations fail to focus on waste elimination opportunities in the soft areas that are non-manufacturing.

BEYOND THE FIVE KEY LEAN PRINCIPLES

James Womack and Daniel Jones identified the five key principles of lean in their landmark text *Lean Thinking — Banish Waste and Create Wealth in Your Corporation.* This book provides a vision for organizations to implement lean thinking across the enterprise in both manufacturing and soft areas of an organization. The following is an expanded version of our earlier discussion about the five principles of lean:

- **Principle 1:** Accurately specify value from the customer's perspective for both products and services.

- **Principle 2:** Identify the value stream for products and services and remove non-value-adding waste along the value stream.
- **Principle 3:** Make the product and services flow without interruption across the value stream.
- **Principle 4:** Authorize production of products and services based on the pull by the customer.
- **Principle 5:** Strive for perfection by constantly removing layers of waste.

These principles are fundamental to the elimination of waste and must be embraced across all functions within the organization and also applied up and down the value chain by suppliers and customers. It is important to get the entire organization focused on understanding the value streams so that waste can be identified and eliminated from the value streams. Most often, organizations fail to realize the importance of identifying value from the customer's perspective and thus fail to set direction for the organization on elimination of wastes that are non-value-adding for the value chains. Rather, they focus inwardly on the obvious waste on the shop floor. Thus the organization believes that implementing several of the lean tools is all that is necessary to claim it has embraced lean thinking. Lean strategy and structure is about alignment of the organization's lean initiative to customer requirements. The Strategy of Improvement enables organizations to deploy the right methodologies to the right opportunities and eliminate the non-value-adding waste. In time, lean becomes part of the DNA of the business so that the lean methodologies and tools are institutionalized across the value streams.

The word *lean* means different things to different people. At the strategic level, lean is a business philosophy. Lean is also used to refer to a set of practices and principles to eliminate waste. Finally, lean is used to describe specific lean tools. Some people use the word lean interchangeably, but it really has several different meanings depending upon your particular perspective. Figure 5.1 displays the lean transformation journey and the three distinct generations of lean. The first generation of lean is *Lean Manufacturing*. This has been presented as an enterprise-wide approach to eliminate waste, increase value, and reduce cycle time. However, most of the efforts in this generation of lean have been limited to the manufacturing floor. This is the logical place for an organization to begin its lean journey because people can *see, touch, and feel* tangible things such as equipment, scrap parts, downtime, setups, bottlenecks, and excess inventory. Most begin by applying the five key principles and kaizen events and harvesting the low-hanging fruit. Most of the benefits achieved in this area include reductions in space, workplace organization, cycle time, work

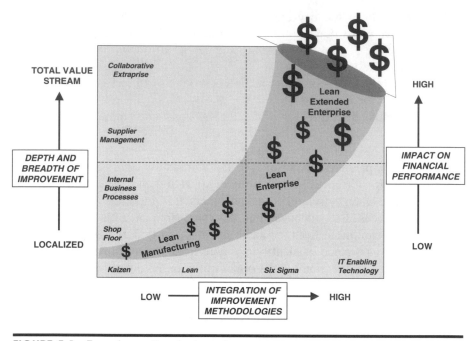

FIGURE 5.1   Transformation to lean journey

in process, and scrap. The five key lean principles can carry you a long way toward localized shop floor improvements.

The next generation of lean is the *Lean Enterprise*. This is where organizations migrate from the production line to the support areas and pursue the "soft process" areas such as new product development, sales and marketing, purchasing and material planning, distribution and logistics, customer/field service, and finance. Organizations find themselves dealing more with information flows than product flows, and these soft processes are the drivers of why things operate the way they do at the plant level. The further upstream we apply lean, the more significant the benefits, and they rise exponentially. For example, the opportunities for most organizations in the excess/obsolete inventory, warranty/ returns, and product development areas alone are in the millions of dollars. However, we need to expand our methodologies and tools beyond the five key principles because we are dealing with more complex, cross-functional business processes and unexplainable variation. Six Sigma, enterprise resource planning (ERP), and other enabling technologies become very important in this transition. There is also a need for stronger leadership to facilitate improvements across the traditional boundaries.

The highest generation of lean is the *Lean Extended Enterprise*. This is where an organization views all the entities in the total value stream (e.g., suppliers, subcontractors, your enterprise, and customers) as if they were a single entity. The Lean Extended Enterprise is an expansion of our traditional notion of lean to improve velocity, flexibility, responsiveness, quality, and cost across the total value stream. The speed and effectiveness of each partner in the total value chain determine how successful the overall value chain will be among competing value chains. This is a gold mine of opportunity because 70 to 95% of many organizations' product cost, lead time, design, supply chain planning, and manufacturing are outside of their four walls. However, it requires deployment and integration of various improvement methodologies to the broader nature of process improvement opportunities. It also requires migrating beyond ERP to other enabling technologies such as customer relationship management, supply chain management, product life cycle management, supplier relationship management, and other Internet-based applications. Many organizations are years into implementation, but for the industry as a whole it is the new frontier of improvement — a frontier with order-of-magnitude opportunities and larger benefits than any single improvement initiative that preceded it. Manufacturing is no longer a competitive weapon; the total value stream is more important. Organizations such as Daimler Benz, Dell, Ford, Lockheed Martin, Timken, and many others have already discovered the power of the Lean Extended Enterprise even though they might not call it that exact name.

There are very distinct trends with respect to lean. First, many organizations are well on their way to integrating lean beyond the production floor to the high-impact soft process areas. Many others are integrating lean beyond the four walls to capitalize on the larger value stream opportunities. Others recognize the importance of integrating kaizen, lean, Six Sigma, ERP, and other enabling technologies. Moving from one generation of lean to the next generation requires a broader toolbox and integration of improvement methodologies, a higher focus on the soft business processes, and the right applications of enabling technology. Many elements of the Lean Extended Enterprise will become the accepted norms for how customers and suppliers conduct their business.

BENEFITS OF LEAN THINKING

A majority of organizations are either in the process of applying lean thinking or considering making the leap to embracing lean thinking. What is it about this infatuation with lean thinking that has such a powerful influence on organizations? In short, the benefits of eliminating non-value-added waste across value streams are significant as it positively impacts profitability and creates value for

TABLE 5.2 Lean benefits

Element	Benefit
Capacity	10 to 20% gains in capacity by optimizing bottlenecks
Inventory	Reductions of 30 to 40% in inventory
Cycle time	Throughput time reduced by 50 to 75%
Lead time	Reduction of 50% in order fulfillment
Product development time	Reductions of 35 to 50% in development time
Space	35 to 50% space reduction
First-pass yield	5 to 15% increase in first-pass yield
Service	Delivery performance of 99%

customers, which in turn leads to competitive advantage. Financial performance for an organization can be impacted from both a cost perspective and a growth perspective. The ability to create double-digit growth in sales has slowed for most organizations in today's economy. Thus the emphasis has shifted to improving gross margins through cost reduction. There is such a large untapped amount of cost reduction that can be generated by eliminating waste across value streams. It is not uncommon to have ratios of 5 to 30% value-added content in many value stream components. That means there is the opportunity to eliminate 70 to 95% of waste in the value stream.

What can an organization expect as bottom-line results of applying lean thinking to eliminate waste? Documented results across various industries indicate the results in Table 5.2 can be achieved.

The key internal and external benefits for the organization include the following:

External
- Creates an environment that anticipates customer needs and positions the organization to respond through a "deliberate" operating philosophy.
- Establishes organizational strengths that set customer expectations and are difficult for competitors to replicate.
- Establishes benchmark performance and best practices against which competitors will be judged.
- Yields higher profitability, product margins, and stock prices.
- Reduces waste in inventory, cost, quality, flexibility, and response time.
- Facilitates intimate customer and supplier involvement from design to production to delivery.

Internal

- Views customers, suppliers, and the internal organization as a single enterprise model.
- Aligns people and systems to build vision and strategy into daily operations.
- Provides an integrated framework for improving the total business.
- Simplifies organizational structures by linking people together across key business processes.
- Provides a means of correlating day-to-day improvement activities with the overall business strategy.
- Drives information across and within functions via simple visual practices.
- Leverages productive capability of all employees, and expands organizational knowledge.

It is important to note that the benefits are attainable for both convergent and divergent types of organizations. Convergent organizations are defined as typical discrete manufacturing infrastructures where many parts are assembled into few end items. Divergent organizations are defined as process infrastructures where few raw materials are processed through standard steps to produce a wide variety of finished items. Most often, divergent organizations reject lean thinking because they get hung up on the concept of one-piece flow and base their ability to apply lean thinking to the organization on only the lean tool of one-piece flow. Thus they reject lean thinking because they confirm in their minds that they cannot create work cells where one-piece flow can be achieved.

Consider the financial impact of one dollar of cost savings compared to one dollar of sales growth. For example, suppose an organization is able to generate 10% profit from each increase of a dollar in sales. Compare this 10% bottom-line sales impact to a dollar of cost savings. For each dollar savings in cost the profitability of the company is impacted favorably by one dollar. Thus the ratio in this example is 10 to 1 in favor of cost savings over sales growth. As lean producers improve their value stream through systematic waste elimination, their costs go down. This is the rationale behind applying lean thinking to remove waste both inside and outside of the organization. This does not mean the organization should abandon initiatives for sales growth; that would be shortsighted as it relates to long-term viability of the organization. But instead it is critical to focus efforts on both sales growth and waste elimination. The fact is, one feeds the other: as an organization reduces waste and increases velocity, it becomes more competitive and opens up new opportunities for growth. We want to be very clear here that lean does not stand for *Less Employees Are Needed.* Many organizations that have mastered the Lean Extended Enterprise have revenue growth, higher market share, increased profitability, and higher employment to show for it.

LEAN TOOLS FOR THE LEAN EXTENDED ENTERPRISE

Many organizations are familiar with the traditional lean tools in Figure 5.2. It is our intent to provide a brief refresher on the tools in this book and focus on the more critical elements of success. We discussed the need to develop a Strategy of Improvement (Chapter 2) as a prerequisite to deploying these tools. Yet many people become too anxious about results and jump right into the tools. This mentality leads to "flavor-of-the-month" types of programs where tools search for problems. For example, an executive in an organization reads an article on kanban and decides that it must be implemented in every single part of the organization in order to "implement the savings of inventory reduction."

FIGURE 5.2 Traditional lean tools

The organization falls into the outcome trap and fails to address the root causes of poor inventory performance. We all know conceptually that opportunities require many different tools to properly eliminate waste, and these tools must be implemented in an integrated methodology to maximize results. The correct approach is to identify the opportunities and then select the lean tools, rather than first selecting the tool and then looking for opportunities.

Many companies have failed at institutionalizing lean methodology in their daily functions across the enterprise because they struggle with making the transition from understanding the five key principles of lean to application of the lean tools in a structured manner. The five key principles of lean by themselves do not cut it. They must be integrated with the Lean Extended Enterprise Reference Model (LEERM) because the process of transforming the enterprise addresses a broader spectrum of issues. You must set direction to establish a framework to create value for your customers by establishing a vision, strategy, and structure within your organization and then execute a strategic improvement process that cascades the strategy into actionable initiatives in the departmental plans across all functions within the organization. The strategic improvement cycle is defined by three phases as outlined in the LEERM Strategic Journey Panel: Plan-Deploy-Execute.

Companies often underestimate the time frame required to successfully implement lean thinking within their extended enterprise. Most often, executives want the quick fix that can be accomplished in less than a 12-month time frame. Many organizations that have made the journey to application of lean thinking have fallen prey to ingrained cultures that consumed the revised vision and strategy to apply lean thinking throughout the organization, thus disabling the lean initiatives. Realistically, transferring an organization to the successful application of lean thinking requires a three- to five-year implementation commitment. Executives *wish* and *hope* for quicker sustaining results, but three to five years or more is the norm for best-in-class lean organizations. Any time frame less than this will not create an infrastructure that is sustainable for the long term. An important function of leadership is to bring about needed change by identifying a vision, aligning employees to that vision, and then motivating them to achieve that vision. Creating the vision and strategy and then transferring the strategy into actionable initiatives are the foundation of success. But it is just the foundation; you still must execute and measure improvements. The LEERM is a dynamic cycle of improvement.

Selection of the appropriate lean tools is based on priorities established in Stage I activities of understanding the current business performance, recognizing gaps in current and desired performance, and developing an integrated business improvement strategy to obtain best-in-class performance for the enterprise. Application of the lean tools is conducted at three levels for the enterprise. It is critical that all three levels be conducted concurrently to institution-alize the application of the tools. Failure to institutionalize application of the tools will result in continued waste in existing processes, products, and equipment and will result in these wastes carrying over into new processes, products, and equipment. Level 1 is application of the tools to existing products, processes, and equipment. This is required to eliminate wastes that already exist within the enterprise on a daily basis. The elimination of waste that already exists has a significant favorable impact on profitability, as it directly impacts current operations as the wastes are identified and eliminated. Level 2 is application of the tools to new processes, products, and equipment. This prevents wastes from increasing and further eroding profitability. Level 3 is application of tools to existing and new processes and products for customers and suppliers. This allows waste to be eliminated throughout the entire value stream for all stakeholders. So often, companies focus on existing processes, products, and equipment and miss the opportunity to prevent new waste from occurring. We have heard many companies comment that they made significant gains in waste elimination only to experience backsliding and wonder why. The root cause for the backsliding is they did not institutionalize the tools into the culture of the enterprise because they failed to understand the importance for prevention and only focused initiatives on correction.

Ask yourself the following question: Are there any problems with waste, bottlenecks, speed, flexibility, quality, and inefficient use of resources in your materials, customer service, accounting, engineering, sales, marketing, and other areas? Confidently, you will respond with a resounding *yes*! The lean tools that have traditionally been applied in manufacturing can also be easily extended to non-manufacturing administrative functions to eliminate process waste in the value stream. In the Lean Extended Enterprise there is a strong relationship between all functions to drive out non-value-added waste (Table 5.3). The relationships between functions require total integration to leverage opportunities for waste elimination and create processes that are sustainable.

We have found a few basic *blocking and tackling* tools to be very useful for improving soft process areas. We can spend a lot of time debating how kanban, pull systems, quick changeover, and other traditional lean tools apply to soft process areas. But we might find ourselves in that familiar trap of a tool looking for a problem. When you migrate lean to the enterprise level, you will be focused on knowledge and information-based business processes. There is typically lots of low-hanging fruit here, and the lean process improvement tools that you will find most useful at the enterprise level include the following:

- Value stream mapping
- Value analysis (value-added versus value-consuming)

TABLE 5.3 Examples of administrative opportunities for waste elimination

Reduce work batch size	One-stop workstations
Easy access to information	Online to suppliers
Eliminate unnecessary data	Eliminate unnecessary work
Simplify the process	Establish standard work documentation
Shorter search time	Apply fail-safe mechanism
Combine work tasks	Reduce batch sizes
Cross-train workers	Minimize checks and reviews
One-touch information access	Synchronize work flows
Paperless processes	Eliminate searching
5S applications	Record accuracy
Create visible systems	Establish quality standards

- Cause-and-effect analysis, fishbone charts
- Pareto analysis, basic statistical data analysis
- Failure mode and effects analysis

These will not address every issue of improvement, but they will take you a long way quickly. Many organizations deploy the more advanced Six Sigma tools to understand complex variation in soft process area such as inventory pipelines, warranty/return and failure analysis, distribution and logistics, cash-to-cash analysis, and other applications. Examples of some of these soft process improvements are included in Chapter 6.

Value Stream Mapping

Toyota developed value stream mapping in the 1950s. It has gained widespread attention during the last several years. Value stream management and value stream mapping are key foundation principles for creating the lean enterprise. It is important to acknowledge that improvement initiatives begin with constructing a map of the current process that is based on facts. Value stream is defined as the activities that occur to produce a product or service through the design, source, make, and deliver functions.

A value stream map has two main components. The first component is the flow of materials through transformation processes to produce the finished goods or services. The second component is the flow of information to support the transformation process for the finished goods or services.

The benefits of value stream mapping are limited if information flows are not included in constructing the value stream map. It is important to note that there are ranges of wastes that are not accounted for in the value stream map, and these wastes should not be ignored as opportunities. An enterprise has several core value streams that comprise the key functions of the organization. It is important to recognize that the value stream includes both internal and external activities for the enterprise. The external activities include both direct and indirect suppliers and customers.

Value stream mapping (Figure 5.3) is the tool that is utilized to graphically represent the current state of a value stream. Icons are used to show the sequence of materials, processes, and information for the specific value stream. Creating a value stream map is the first step required in any lean improvement initiative. It is critical that the current value stream be documented so that waste can be correctly identified in the value stream and a future state determined to eliminate non-value-adding wastes.

Developing a visual high-level map of a value stream by itself is not enough to minimize waste. It must be combined with the lean principles and lean tools to truly transform the enterprise and achieve improvement in the value-added content of specific core value streams for the enterprise. Value stream mapping is only a tool, and the objective is to enhance the value stream by identifying a future state and creating an implementation road map that can be executed to achieve the future state. It is not uncommon for a specific value stream to yield 5% value-added content to 95% non-value-added content. Think about the opportunities that exist to drive out waste for a value stream and the significant positive impact on the financial performance for the enterprise and all stakeholders.

Benefits of creating a value stream map

- Allows a graphic visualization of the entire material and information flow for the current-state value stream.
- Shows linkages and connections between information flow and material flow.
- Identifies sources of waste in the value stream.
- Provides common language for talking about the processes.
- Makes decisions about the flow apparent.
- Forms the basis of an implementation plan to identify and eliminate wastes.
- Allows identification of non-value-added steps, lead time, distances traveled, and amount of inventory for a process.
- Provides a common language for discussing the future-state value stream and identifying gaps between the current state and future state.

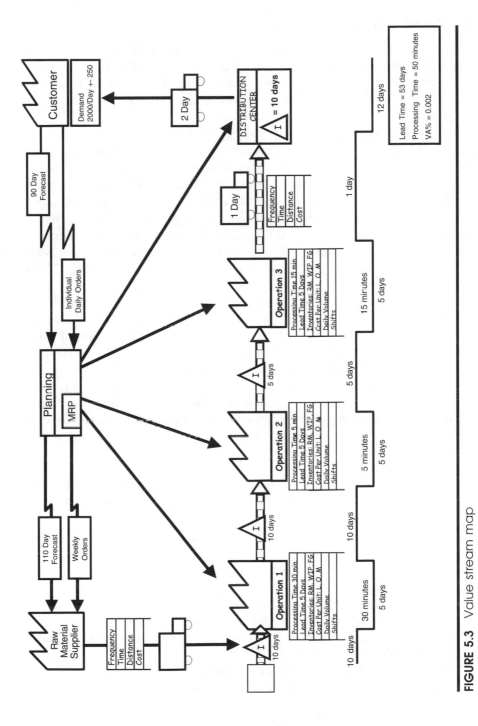

FIGURE 5.3 Value stream map

5S Visual Management

Honda and Toyota acknowledge that 25 to 30% of all quality defects are related to safety, orderliness, and cleanliness. Clean, safe, and efficient must become the expectation for conducting daily processes. Why implement the five pillars of the visual workplace? Because it is a good starting point for all improvement programs.

The techniques for 5S were originally applied to production operations and have recently been extended to safety and office activities. 5S visual management is a key foundation principle for creating the lean enterprise because the concepts of organization and orderliness are focused on achieving cost reductions, waste elimination, zero defects, safety improvements, and accident reductions. The savings that can be generated by small incremental improvements on a daily basis add up to significant savings on an annual basis. For example, if every employee in a company of 100 employees could eliminate $5 of waste each day during the year, the company could realize a cost savings of $125,000 on an annual basis.

The techniques used for 5S activities are useful during implementation of various lean techniques. For example, many of the techniques for sort, set-in-order, shine, and standardize are also applicable to the lean tools of quick changeover, one-piece flow, standard work, point-of-use storage, autonomous maintenance, kanban pull, and mistake-proofing.

5S visual management is defined as an improvement process originated by the Japanese to create a workplace that supports company-wide integration of workplace organization, standardization, visual control, visual display, and visual metrics. The five principles of 5S are sort, set in order, shine, standardize, and sustain (Figure 5.4):

1. *Seiri* (sort) means to separate needed tools, parts, and instructions from the unneeded. The goal is to keep only what is required and eliminate everything else.
2. *Seiton* (set in order) means to neatly arrange and identify parts, processes, and tools for ease of use.
3. *Seiso* (shine) means to clean, shine, and inspect the workplace by eliminating contamination.
4. *Seiketsu* (standardize) means to require as the norm sort, set in order, and shine activities daily to keep the workplace in perfect condition and also to make use of visual control systems to maintain compliance with the established standards.
5. *Shitsuke* (sustain) means to maintain the 5S gains by training and encouraging workers to form the habit of always following the first four S's.

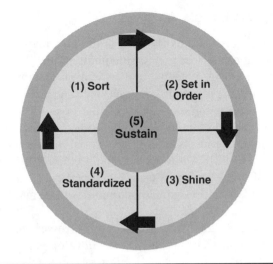

FIGURE 5.4 5S principles

Benefits of applying 5S

- Communication with a shared perspective and with total visibility, as well as improved communication between shifts, work areas, and organizational levels.
- Reduces workflow problems, increases product quality and productivity, as well as improves communication.
- Improves workplace safety by eliminating hazards and establishing compliance to work standards.
- Aligns employee efforts with goals and strategies for eliminating waste.
- Improved appearance of the facility and expectation for compliance to maintain that condition.
- Establishes standards for operating equipment and conducting processes.
- Training time significantly reduced for new employees.
- Quality improvements of 10 to 20% by preventing defects and errors from occurring.
- Reduced changeover time by 20 to 50%.
- Reduced search time by 50%.
- Increased floor space by 20 to 40%.
- Reduced lead time and cycle time by 10 to 25%.
- Improved morale and pride in the workplace.
- Reduction in materials handling of 70%.
- Decrease in flow distance of 80%.
- Reduced equipment breakdowns yields better equipment utilization.

Failure Mode and Effects Analysis

Failure mode and effects analysis (FMEA) is the systematic method of identifying and preventing product or process problems in the planning, design, and production stages to ensure potential and logical failures are minimized. The purpose of a FMEA is to prevent defects, enhance safety, and increase customer satisfaction by identifying the root causes behind potential failures and implementing preventive measures to eliminate occurrence. FMEA can and should be conducted for existing products and processes as well as new products and processes. The point of FMEA is to foresee and predict. A key input to successfully conducting a FMEA process is team-based participation to identify potential failures and brainstorm prevention opportunities that can be implemented to reduce risks.

FMEA used in the design of new products or processes substantially reduces costs by identifying improvements early in the development process. Thus you have a more robust product or process that prevents after-the-fact correction and prevention activities. A system FMEA is used to analyze systems and subsystems in the early concept and design stages. A design FMEA is used to analyze products before they are released to production. A process FMEA is used to analyze manufacturing, assembly, and service processes.

Benefits of applying FMEA

- Quantifies process problems, outcomes, root causes, actions, and improvements.
- Improves the quality, reliability, and safety of products/processes.
- Increases customer satisfaction.
- Prevents accidents and safety incidents.
- Reduces process cycle time and cost.
- Prevents process and product problems before they occur.
- Creates a more robust product, process, or service.
- Establishes standards for conducting process improvements.
- Documents and tracks actions taken to improve products/processes and their impact.
- Cost reductions through elimination of failures and warranty.

Standard Work

Standard work is defined as a set of work procedures that effectively combine people, materials, processes, technology, and machines to maintain quality, efficiency, safety, and predictability. It establishes the best methods and sequence steps to optimize performance and minimize waste. The most efficient method is then documented and people are trained to follow the established standard. Thus a process is completed the same way every time no matter who completes the tasks. High quality is a direct output of a repeatable process. Standard work must be applied throughout the enterprise to gain consistency in administrative and manufacturing processes. Standard work is not just a lean tool for manufacturing. Our experience with clients indicates there is a wealth of opportunities for applying the lean tool of standard work to administrative processes. Be sure to integrate the lean tool of 5S visual management, quick changeover, and mistake-proofing when conducting standardized work improvements.

Benefits of applying standard work

- Creates repeatable processes that are consistently executed.
- Identifies the most efficient method for a process.
- Effective and productive training for employees.
- Established documentation for each process.
- Higher process and product quality.
- Lowers cost associated with scrap and rework.
- Reduces excessive processing due to poor process design.
- Eliminates excessive and unnecessary motion for a process.
- Identifies waste in a process.

Total Equipment Reliability

Lean cannot result without dependable and effective equipment, as optimum machine uptime is necessary to support one-piece flow production. Equipment breakdowns, poor equipment performance, and process rejects are waste thieves that can be controlled through total productive maintenance systems. Total productive maintenance (TPM) is defined as a comprehensive, team-based approach that utilizes a series of methods for the design, selection, correction, and maintenance of equipment to ensure that every machine or process is always able to perform its required tasks of defect-free production without interrupting or slowing down. TPM is required as a prerequisite of quick changeover, one-piece flow, and kanban lean tools. The major components of a TPM system include predictive maintenance, preventive maintenance, autonomous maintenance, early equipment management, and focused equipment improvement. The integration of 5S techniques is integral to total equipment reliability through application of the 5S techniques for the major components of TPM. Additionally, the lean tools of FMEA, mistake-proofing, and quick changeover are utilized by TPM activities. The principal performance measure of TPM is overall equipment effectiveness (OEE).

The autonomous maintenance component of TPM is defined as use of equipment operators for step-by-step activities to ensure optimum conditions of machine operation. The steps of autonomous maintenance include initial cleaning and inspection, eliminating contamination, establishing standards for ongoing equipment care, skills training in equipment operation, conducting general inspections, and managing and controlling the production process. The main theme of autonomous maintenance is the transfer of basic, unskilled maintenance activities to machine operators.

The preventive maintenance component of TPM is based on the critical operating characteristics of the equipment and the acceptable operating ranges for those characteristics. Machine maintenance is planned at predetermined intervals to achieve smooth, continuous operation based on equipment inspections and equipment diagnosis. Restoration of equipment is conducted to correct deterioration of equipment operation.

The predictive maintenance component of TPM is based on equipment history and data-acquisition-based equipment knowledge. Measured key equipment parameters are compared to engineering limits to trigger replacing or servicing of components so that breakdown and malfunction are prevented. Maintenance tasks are tied to hours run, pieces produced, or cycles performed. Focused equipment improvement is defined as the identification of equipment enhancement for parameters or capabilities to improve OEE. Early equipment management is focused on obtaining optimal value-adding contributions for new equipment, which includes all phases of equipment management from design through start-up and obsolescence.

Benefits of applying TPM

- Elimination of minor, medium, and major stoppages due to chronic and sporadic breakdowns.
- Reduction of lengthy setup times and excessive adjustments.
- Prevention of chronic defects due to equipment abnormalities.
- Elimination of dangerous and unnecessary activities.
- Effective and consistent ongoing operation of equipment by all employees.
- Shortened training time for new employees.
- Product rework, defects, faulty products, and low yields are prevented.
- Reduction in the amount of planned downtime because of increased equipment availability.
- Reduces equipment problems at production start-up and eliminates start-up rejects.
- Provides early detection of poor machine performance.
- Increased employee skill and knowledge.

- Establishes team-based design, maintenance, and operation of equipment.
- Increases the performance of OEE.

Quick Changeover

Quick change is critical to any company wishing to implement one-piece flow and apply waste-eliminating techniques for all types of service, administrative, manufacturing, and assembly processes. Significant waste can be eliminated from changeover activities with very little investment in resources. Many companies produce large lot sizes because of the excessive resources required to change over from one process to a subsequent process. When the process or machine is down because of a changeover, value-added activity ceases. Scrap generated from a start-up can be significant when a trial-and-error approach is used to adjust for process capability during the changeover.

Single-minute exchange of die (SMED) is a series of operator techniques developed by Shigeo Shingo that target changeovers of production equipment, fixtures, or processes in less than ten minutes. Even though the target of SMED is ten minutes, the long-term goal is always zero changeover time so that changeovers are instantaneous and do not interfere in any way with one-piece flow.

Companies often take a narrow view of changeover as only the time required to pull an existing tool or fixture and set the new tool or fixture. Changeover in the true sense is defined as the time between the last good piece off one production or process run and the first good piece off the next run (Table 5.4). Physical changeover includes managing both internal and external changeover tasks. Internal activities are those that can only be performed while the machine or process is shut down or idles, whereas external activities are those that can be performed while the machine or process is running. Making changeover times quicker and simpler allows companies to produce in smaller lot sizes. Significant waste can be eliminated from the steps of preparation, sample, test, and adjustment.

TABLE 5.4 Changeover Time

Basic steps in a changeover activity	Average proportion of time
Preparation activities	30%
Mounting and removing tasks	5%
Measurements, settings, and calibration	15%
Sample, test, adjust activities	50%

Benefits of applying quick changeover
- Increased flexibility to react to changes in customer demand.
- Improved quality based on reduction in start-up rejects and reduced setup errors.
- Capacity gains based on fewer resources required to conduct changeover activities.
- Simpler setups for employees who conduct the changeovers.
- Safer setups for employees who conduct the changeovers.
- Consistency in changeover activities for employees from shift to shift and over time.
- Reduced inventory because of fewer rejects and smaller lot sizes.
- Less clutter.
- Setup tools and methodologies are standardized.
- Reduced searching waste during changeover activities.
- Reduced motion waste during changeover activities.
- Reduction in lead times and quicker deliveries based on shorter changeover times.

Mistake-Proofing (Poka-Yoke)

The concept of mistake-proofing (poka-yoke) is critical to reducing variation. Mistake-proofing is applicable to the design of products, operation of equipment, and design of processes. Most often, mistake-proofing is limited to existing processes. It is important to stress utilization of mistake-proofing during the design phases of products and processes to eliminate the potential for variation to ever occur.

Mistake-proofing is defined as an improvement technology that uses a device or procedure, also called a poka-yoke, to prevent defects or equipment malfunction during operation of equipment or processes. Mistake-proofing devices are important as they enforce correct operations by eliminating choices that lead to incorrect actions, signal or stop a process if an error is made or a defect created, and prevent machine and product damage. Mistake-proofing activities can be integrated with the lean tools of quick changeover, 5S visual management, one-piece flow production, and standard work. The possibilities for mistake-proofing are endless and typically involve very little investment in resources.

Benefits of applying mistake-proofing (poka-yoke)
- Promotes individual responsibility for quality ownership.
- Poka-yokes are analogous to 100% inspection, but with little investment.
- Detect and eliminate defects as early in the process as possible.
- Provides immediate feedback, thus reducing the time for corrective action.

- Establishes a system of successive checks for each operation.
- Provides for self-check activities, which gives quicker feedback than successive checks.
- Ensures that proper conditions exist prior to actual production, and prevents mistakes from occurring in the first place.
- Focuses on elimination of causes for errors rather than just identification.
- Enhances customer satisfaction through the elimination of defects.
- Focuses on waste reduction in defects and processing.
- Improves first-pass yield.

Level Mix Model Production

The transition to producing daily quantities of all products produces a facility that overall has common rhythm and is synchronized to market demand. Leveling production is a method of scheduling daily production of various types of products in a sequence that evens out the peaks and valleys of quantities produced. Those companies that can achieve level mix model production are better able to respond to customer shifts in demand quantity and mix.

The existence of inventory at any stage causes waste and ties up enterprise resources. Level mix model production allows the enterprise to build the variety of products demanded by customers in a smooth, repetitive, mixed sequence that minimizes inventory and the wastes associated with it. During a week if customers order 500 of product A, 500 of product B, and 1,000 of product C, level mix model production would sequence those products to run in the progression A, C, B, C, A, C, B, C, A, C, etc. The target would be to produce a total of 400 pieces per day over a five-day week to level the production requirements for the work cell.

Level mix model production is a prerequisite to support the lean tools one-piece flow production and kanban. Key objectives of level mix model production are schedule attainment and production linearity. Level mix model production is integrated with the lean tools of quick changeover, kanban, mistake-proofing, 5S visual management, standard work, total productive maintenance, and one-piece flow production.

Benefits of applying level mix model production
- Transition from large lot production to small lot production.
- Provides better distribution of inventory to meet customer demand.
- Allows quicker response to market demand changes.
- Supports kanban and one-piece flow production.
- Reduction in inventory for raw materials, subassemblies, finished goods, and work in process.

- Improves performance for schedule linearity.
- Provides linkage between cycle time of demand and cycle time of production.
- Supports the ultimate objective to make small quantities of every product, every day, in ratios that match incoming demand.
- Daily level production synchronized plant-wide.
- Improves return on assets.

Kanban

Kanban is a Japanese word that means "card" or "signal." At the core of pull production, a kanban signals upstream operations to deliver what is needed, in the quantity needed, and when needed. For a pull system to work effectively, demand variations must be smoothed. Distributing both the volume and mix of total customer orders evenly over sequential time periods through load leveling can satisfy variable demand. This achieves a steady and consistent work flow. With erratic demand patterns, higher inventory levels must be utilized, and this is accomplished by applying a policy variable to modify the kanban calculation.

Takt time is an important element used to determine the rate at which product must be produced to satisfy market demand. It is determined by dividing the available production time by the rate of customer demand. For example, if customer demand is 240 parts per day and the factory operates 480 minutes per day, takt time is 2 minutes. It sets the pace of production to match the rate of customer demand.

Success for kanban is best achieved when a company has committed implementation for the lean tools of level mix model production, quick changeover, one-piece flow, mistake-proofing, 5S visual management, TPM, and point-of-use storage. The integration of these lean tools is required to allow rapid response to customer demand.

There is a role for use of MRP in a pull scheduling system. MRP should be used for the purpose of planning to forecast material and capacity requirements within the enterprise and for suppliers.

A kanban system can be manual or automated. The various methods to trigger replenishment are physical kanban, min/max kanban, "things" kanban, electronic kanban, interplant kanban, and single enterprise kanban (Table 5.5 and Figure 5.5).

Benefits of applying kanban

- Production priorities are determined dynamically and directly linked to customer demand.
- Integrates all processes to one another and connects the value stream to customer demand.

TABLE 5.5 Types of kanban

Type of kanban	Description
Transport kanban	Permission for material to be moved from the upstream supplying work cell to the downstream consuming work cell
Withdrawal kanban	Requests that material stored in one inventory location be delivered to a process step or other inventory location
Replenishment kanban	A request from an inventory location or a process step that the goods it has used up need to be replaced
Production kanban	Authorizes a process step to produce the needed replacement material
Supplier kanban	Requests material external to the enterprise, such as from another division, plant, or a supplier
Emergency kanban	Is used to designate that defective parts have occurred and need to be replaced immediately
Express kanban	Generated when an unexpected shortage has occurred and authorizes expediting for production replenishment

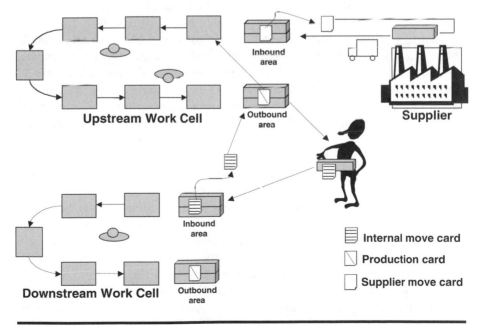

FIGURE 5.5 Kanban example

- Improves flexibility to respond to customer demand.
- Simplifies the procurement process.
- Uncovers hidden waste in processes.
- Employees are empowered to sequence work based on current conditions.
- Execution-based scheduling.
- Unnecessary paperwork is eliminated.
- Supports waste elimination of overproduction.
- Inventory reduction for finished goods, raw materials, and subassemblies.

One-Piece Flow

Continuous flow production results in the most efficient production method by the elimination of many wasteful activities. Normal queues and backlogs associated with a batch-and-queue manufacturing approach are eliminated. In one-piece flow layouts, operations are sequential. Operators understand the total process. Products move singularly. Buffer socks are not required because lines are balanced. The flow path is predefined. Equipment is right-sized. Emphasis is on faster flows.

A work cell is completely different compared to traditional batch manufacturing. Manufacturing departments in a traditional plant environment perform a specific task (i.e., grinding, welding, fabrication, drilling, assembly) utilizing workers who have developed a single skill. Manufacturing cells, however, are designed to provide complete products to an internal work cell or an external customer. Work cells perform several operations or tasks and require multi-skilled, flexible workers. The most common obstacle to implementing one-piece flow production is that old beliefs and habits need to be discarded and replaced by new ones. For years, producing parts in large batches has been the rule. Major inhibitors to flow in a production environment or business process include process variability, product defects, material shortages, and equipment failure.

In a one-piece flow environment, each part is pulled through one piece at a time. This greatly reduces the manufacturing lead time. The ultimate goal is to have each activity task producing in a one-piece flow methodology. The key to one-piece flow is to connect and synchronize each individual activity process to eliminate the eight categories of waste. This requires improved layouts to minimize travel distance between successive operations. Thus, u-shaped work cells are created and linked to complete all process activities in the minimal amount of physical space. Principles of good work cell layout include arranging the work sequentially, using a counterclockwise flow, locating machines and processes close together, and locating the last operation close to the first operation.

The work cell is designed to accomplish line balance with respect to takt time, and authorization for production is triggered by kanban.

Work cell employees are responsible for the daily production of products to meet internal and external customer needs. The typical work cell employee is empowered to take all actions necessary to meet customer needs, as long as that action is not in conflict with the work cell principles.

Benefits of applying one-piece flow

- Reduces throughput time and increases velocity for customer orders from order receipt through production and shipment.
- Improves value-added ratio through elimination of non-value-added activities which reduces operating costs.
- Allows the company higher degrees of flexibility to accommodate changes in customer demand.
- Saves space in the factory.
- Promotes continuous improvement as problems are exposed.
- Reduces transportation, waiting, overproduction, processing, inventory, and motion waste that occurs with batch processing.
- Lowers the risks of product damage, deterioration, and obsolescence.
- Simplifies scheduling.
- Supports high-variety production.
- Reduces cycle time through increased production velocity.
- Supports quality production.
- Enhances the employee's productive capability through multi-skilled multi-machine operators.

REMINDER: LEARN BEFORE YOU LEAN

In Chapter 1 we included a section with this title. We gave a brief overview of the lean concepts and tools used most frequently to support a Lean Extended Enterprise in this chapter. In Chapter 7 we will provide a discussion of ERP and other *super booster* enabling technologies such as supply chain management, customer relationship management, product life cycle management, and others that make the Lean Extended Enterprise possible.

Organizations must think through the specific application of these lean methodologies and tools and how it will improve the business (e.g., Strategy of Improvement). The two familiar questions are asked: How will this tool improve the business? How do we apply the methodology to the unique characteristics of our business? There are huge differences in how you apply these tools to high-volume/repetitive, low-volume/high-mix, process, engineered products, clean room environments, service and repair centers, and other diverse environments. There is also a great chance to misapply the concepts if one jumps right into tool demonstrations. We have observed a few organizations that placed kanbans between every single operation in their plants and then wondered why work in process grew overnight. We have observed a few companies that kept adding kanbans (instead of shutting down and fixing problems) and wondered why the place gets logjammed. We have observed companies that set up duplicate point-of-use material for common parts, only to expedite shortages and part mismatches across dozens of work cells. We have observed an organization that ran lean Monday through Thursday and reserved Fridays for re-work, repair, and buffer replenishments. We have seen organizations set up cells only to be destroyed by mix changes and external cross-flows. All of these organizations had the very best of intentions. But they had a poor strategy and execution process. It all looks so simple and easy, but it is not.

Finally, the lean tools discussed in this chapter by themselves are static in nature. They are also totally ineffective without a Strategy of Improvement. Many organizations begin their lean journey by test-driving these tools manually. While this may be a good approach to increase familiarity and knowledge, implementation becomes very static as the dynamics of demand, supply, and value stream variation throw our lean efforts in tilt. An organization may begin with manual kanban cards or visual replenishment systems, and in fact, it's a good idea to begin with designing the process before one goes searching for the "lean screens" in ERP. Organizations must integrate these concepts with the appropriate enabling technology or the lean processes gain waste very quickly. New product introductions, ECNs, shifts in demand and mix, supplier issues, and other value stream variation alter the design characteristics of the lean strategy significantly. Many organizations make the mistake of implementing the tools, watching the process for a few days, and then walking away claiming to be lean. The philosophy and tools of lean work only within a limited design bandwidth, and the critical characteristics of the value stream must be constantly monitored so we can make dynamic adjustments to our lean value stream. As organizations focus more on velocity improvement, variation reduction, and value stream optimization, the enabling technologies will actually enhance the execution and dynamic maintenance of our Lean Extended Enterprise strategy.

CHAPTER 5 TAKE-AWAYS

- The five principles of lean are
  - Principle 1: Accurately *specify value* from the customer's perspective for both products and services.

- Principle 2: Identify the *value stream* for products and services and remove non-value-adding waste along the value stream.
- Principle 3: Make the product and services *flow* without interruption across the value stream.
- Principle 4: Authorize production of products and services based on the *pull* by the customer.
- Principle 5: Strive for *perfection* by constantly removing layers of waste.

■ Moving from one generation of lean to the next generation requires a broader toolbox and integration of improvement methodologies, a higher focus on the soft business processes, and the right applications of enabling technology.

■ It is important to get the entire organization focused on understanding the value streams so that waste can be identified and eliminated beyond the shop floor.

■ Organizations struggle with implementation as they focus their lean initiatives as a tools-based approach. The tools-based approach is short-sighted, as it limits the lean initiatives to a few selected lean tools that are applied without properly conducting a lean assessment of their current extended enterprise.

■ Application of lean tools should be conducted for both *existing* and *new* processes, products, and equipment across the entire supply chain (internal and external to the enterprise) to institutionalize application of the tools into daily operations.

■ In the Lean Extended Enterprise, there is a strong relationship between all stakeholders to drive out non-value-added waste.

■ Developing a visual high-level map of a value stream by itself is not enough to minimize waste. It must be populated with data and facts about the process and combined with the lean principles and lean tools to truly transform the enterprise.

■ Applying the lean tools individually provides value, but when the tools are combined, the result creates sustainable competitive advantage at a significantly higher value.

SUGGESTED FURTHER READING

Henderson, Bruce A. and Jorge L. Larco, *Lean Transformation — How to Change Your Business into a Lean Enterprise,* The Oaklea Press, 2000.

Hirano, Hiroyuki, *5 Pillars of the Visual Workplace — The Sourcebook for 5S Implementation,* Productivity Press, 1995.

Jackson, Thomas L. with Karen R. Jones, *Implementing a Lean Management System,* Productivity Press, 1996.

Liker, Jeffrey K., *Inside Stories of U.S. Manufacturers Becoming Lean,* Productivity Press, 1997.

Louis, Raymond S., *Integrating Kanban with MRPII — Automating a Pull System for Enhanced JIT Inventory Management,* Productivity Press, 1997.

MacInnes, Richard L., *The Lean Enterprise Memory Jogger — Create Value and Eliminate Waste Throughout Your Company,* GOAL/QPC, 2002.

Monden, Yasuhiro, *Toyota Production System — An Integrated Approach to Just-in-Time,* Engineering & Management Press, 1998.

Rother, Mike and John Shook, *Learning to See — Value Stream Mapping to Add Value and Eliminate MUDA,* The Lean Enterprise Institute, 1999.

Sekine, Ken'ichi, *One-Piece Flow — Cell Design for Transforming the Production Process,* Productivity Press, 1992.

Sekine, Ken'ichi and Keisuke Arai, *TPM for the Lean Factory — Innovative Methods and Worksheets for Equipment Management,* Productivity Press, 1998.

Shingo, Shigeo, *Zero Quality Control: Source Inspection and the Poka-Yoke System,* Productivity Press, 1985.

Smith, Wayne, *Time Out — Using Visible Pull Systems to Drive Process Improvement,* John Wiley & Sons, 1998.

Swartz, James B., *The Hunter and the Hunted — A Non-Linear Solution for Reengineering the Workplace,* Productivity Press, 1994.

Tapping, Don, Tom Luyster, and Tom Shuker, *Value Stream Management — Eight Steps to Planning, Mapping, and Sustaining Lean Improvements,* Productivity Press, 2002.

Womack, James P. and Daniel T. Jones, *Lean Thinking — Banish Waste and Create Wealth in Your Corporation,* Simon & Schuster, 1996.

6

SIX SIGMA: A MANAGEMENT REVOLUTION WELL UNDER WAY

The original roots of Six Sigma (6σ) can be traced back to Carl Frederick Gauss (1777–1885), who introduced the concept of the normal curve. Six Sigma as a measurement standard in product variation was used in the 1920s when Walter Shewhart showed that three sigma from the mean is the point where a process requires correction. The real credit for 6σ as we know it today goes to Motorola in the late 1970s and specifically an engineer named Bill Smith. Motorola developed the 6σ methodology and documented over $16 billion in savings. More recently, hundreds of organizations around the globe are pursuing 6σ as a critical component of their business strategy. More recent pioneers such as Mikel Harry, Rich Schroeder, Bill Ross, Gary Cone, Steve Zinkgraf, John Lupienski, and several others deserve honorable mention for further development and implementation of the 6σ methodology in places like GE, Allied Signal, Whirlpool, and other highly publicized successes.

Six Sigma is rapidly becoming the new metaphor shift in today's industrial society and the new world standard for customer satisfaction and profitability improvement. Almost every organization is either implementing, contemplating, or busy learning more about 6σ. Notwithstanding its 20-plus-year history beginning at Motorola and the usual hype of any new management concept promising organizations huge bottom-line benefits, 6σ is paying off big time.

127

Benchmarking information obtained from industry sources such as the American Society for Quality, iSixSigma.com, consultants, and many other company sources indicates that organizations are saving millions from their 6σ efforts. But beyond the initial savings, organizations are building a solid foundation for growth and cash generation through common analysis tools and a global improvement language. In this chapter we will highlight many of the important aspects of 6σ and how it supports the Lean Extended Enterprise Reference Model.

WHAT IS SIX SIGMA?

Put simply, 6σ is a data-driven methodology that strives for perfection in the organization's entire value chain. The 6σ methodology goes well beyond the qualitative eradication of customer-perceptible defects and is deep-rooted in statistical engineering techniques. The statistical objective of 6σ is to drive down process variation so that ± 6 standard deviations (6σ) lie between both the upper and lower specification limits and the target value in a process. The practical explanation equates to just 3.4 defects per million opportunities.

The 6σ process is a highly disciplined effort that closely examines variation and root causes of current performance, with a focus not only on the production floor but on all *key* business processes. Six Sigma puts the entire value stream under the microscope — new product development, manufacturing, engineering, configuration management, quality, sales/order management, customer service, finance, and suppliers.

Six Sigma uses a deliberate structure commonly referred to as DMAIC, which stands for Define Measure Analyze Improve Control (Figure 6.1). The DMAIC process is the needle and thread that string 6σ together. Within each phase are specific 6σ process requirements and the deployment of various statistical problem-solving techniques. Individuals are educated in how to follow the 6σ process, as well as the appropriate analytical tools to use at each step of the process. DMAIC is the heart of the 6σ process. It provides the structure, discipline, and logical progression for achieving breakthrough improvements.

PERFECTION, DEEP CORE DRILLING, AND HIGH IMPACT

Six Sigma strives for perfection and value-added in every aspect of the total value chain. Most importantly, 6σ begins and ends with financial performance, one project at a time. The average company spends about 10 to 20% of revenues on Cost of Poor Quality (COPQ). A company that has a few years of 6σ under

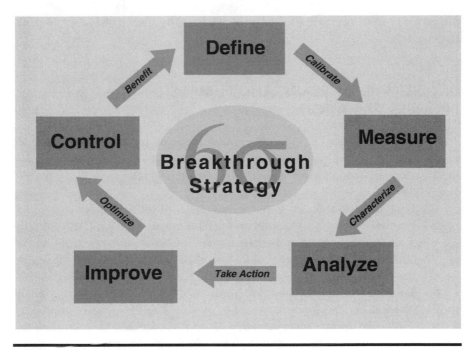

FIGURE 6.1   The Six Sigma DMAIC road map

its belt can knock this down to 1 to 2% of revenues. Beyond the financial savings, imagine the additional benefits involved in having only 3.4 defects per million products shipped, 3.4 bugs per million lines of code written, 3.4 defects per million drawings released, $3.40 of excess/obsolete inventory per million dollars of total inventory, or 3.4 unhappy customers per million customer service calls received.

Unlike many previous quality improvement initiatives, 6σ focuses on all aspects of the total value stream. Many organizations are having tremendous success with 6σ in the professional and soft process support areas such as product development, design for manufacturability, customer service, materials/ purchasing, distribution/logistics, invoicing, and other "soft" transactional processes. Customers take product quality for granted these days. A big differentiator in today's marketplace is total value-added services. Customer satisfaction can be improved significantly by paying attention to the soft processes inside and outside the four walls of the organization. These are the "hidden costs" where prevention and containment up front can improve the bottom line very quickly. Think about how many organizations deal with excess/obsolete inventory and warranty/returns. They create financial reserves to cover it. If you can prevent the problem from occurring in the first place, that's instant megabucks to the bottom line.

UNDERSTAND, EXPLAIN, AND ELIMINATE PROCESS VARIATION

The key to the success of 6σ is the extreme focus on process variation. Some of the variation in a process is pure inherent noise and is uncontrollable. But most variation is controllable and comes in many flavors:

- **Part variation:** Piece to piece, raw material lot to lot, etc.
- **Human variation:** Operator to operator, supervisor to supervisor, differences between setup people, number of tasks performed in a procedure/practice, ergonomic conditions, skill and experience levels, information accuracy, etc.
- **Tool variation:** Tool wear over time, mold cavity to mold cavity, spindle position, tool to tool, etc.
- **Time variation:** Hour to hour, shift to shift, sample time to time, day to day, week to week, month to month, season to season, etc.
- **Location variation:** Plant to plant, state to state, machine to machine, line location to line location, building to building, country to country, etc.

To improve any process, we need to chase down and understand variation, and the first step is to baseline current capability. Process capability indices (Cp and Cpk) are used to measure the spread and non-centering characteristics of a process. The next step is to understand the components of variation and the associated factors and root causes that create this variation in the first place. Every process includes both common causes (inherent noise) and special causes (explainable variation). The common causes create a 1.5σ shift over time, but the special causes can be categorized and eliminated. With a 3σ-capable process, there is a built-in scrap rate of 6.68% at best.

Figure 6.2 provides a graphical representation of process variation. As we understand the key process inputs and outputs statistically, we can begin to make changes that reduce/eliminate variation. As we reduce variation, we improve process capability by reducing the spread (Cp) and centering (Cpk). The diagram on the left says, "The garage door is equal in width to the car," which is the same as saying that our process is equal to the specification limits. Any shift will produce a dented fender and defective parts, respectively. The diagram

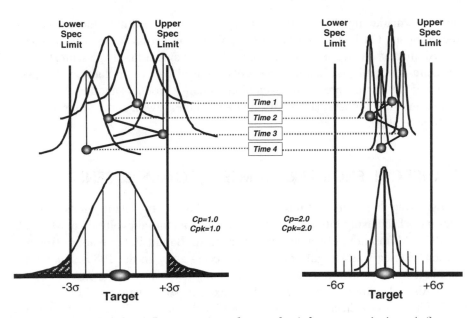

Processes shift by 1.5σ over time due to the inherent variation. A 3σ process generates a long-term defect rate of about 66,807 PPM. By contrast, a 6σ process generates only 3.4 PPM.

FIGURE 6.2 Variation and effect on process capability

on the right says, "The garage door is twice as wide as the car," which is the same as saying that our process capability is twice the specification limits. A process shift will still produce good parts. Hence, we improve quality exponentially. Even better, we reduce the COPQ exponentially. This is a dynamic process. If we begin storing garden tools, bicycles, and other things in the free space (if we don't have the right metrics in place to identify and eliminate creeping variation), we lose some of that capability.

3M: A RAPID ADOPTER OF SIX SIGMA

3M is one of many great examples of 6σ. 3M introduced 6σ in February 2001 as a business improvement methodology. Currently, over 4,000 people have participated in 6σ training and over 100 projects have been completed worldwide — from manufacturing to new product development to customer service and sales/marketing. As with most strategic initiatives, 3M introduced 6σ across the company but is now migrating the philosophy across its total value chain. Six Sigma has created a uniform business improvement language with standard measurement and problem-solving tools focused on cost reduction and asset turnover. Customers are seeing even higher quality products and faster response times, and shareholders see a company focused on growth, competitiveness, and cash generation.

STATISTICAL ENGINEERING MEETS COMMON SENSE

Considering its history, 6σ has seen a slow adoption in organizations. Companies have been using bits and pieces of 6σ since its initial evolution at Motorola in 1978. Motorola has been at this for years. Its Bandit Pager plant in Boynton Beach, Florida was a highly publicized success story in the 1980s. Like many strategic improvement programs, the only thing that is new is the execution. The 6σ statistical techniques have existed for decades, some dating as far back as the 1930s at Western Electric and Pareto's 80/20 rule in the 19th century. The new element is the structured 6σ process and methodology.

About 26% of organizations today either have a formal 6σ program implemented and in place or are pursuing 6σ as a strategic improvement program. It is our opinion that this slow adoption over the past 20 years is due largely to four major factors:

1. The approaches of previous total quality management (TQM) programs placed much of the emphasis on education about the philosophy and individual tools, but little on implementation, application, and results. As we mentioned in Chapter 3, it was *Field of Dreams* quality at its best. If you keep up the activity, the results will come. People equipped with a bag of religion and tools looking for a problem. Quality for quality's sake. Hence, organizations saw little return on investment for their TQM efforts.

2. Many of our previous quality improvement initiatives focused on process control with statistical tools as a first step without understanding process variation. Quality gurus such as Deming, Crosby, and Juran professed their views about quality, but many initiatives in organizations fizzled after the training. The programs that survived were often limited to measuring defects on the shop floor. Many organizations relied on statistical process control charts and symptomatic fixes and took all the underlying process variation for granted. Finally, many statistical engineering efforts were not much more than an exercise in "techniques

looking for data." The underlying root causes were left unsolved, and the anticipated benefits never arrived at the bottom line. In contrast, 6σ is a highly structured problem-solving methodology that focuses first on understanding explainable process variation and root causes followed by reengineering the process, preventing future defects, and then controlling the process.

3. The availability of user-friendly statistical applications software such as MiniTab did not exist. Twenty years ago, it took a statistician three months to conduct a Design of Experiments (DOE) manually. When the statistician was done, nobody could understand the analysis, so many improvements were never implemented. In today's 6σ environments, engineers, maintenance technicians, and team leads can perform several DOEs in a day. MiniTab automates the analysis and simplifies the intimidating statistics. More emphasis is placed on fact-driven interpretation of the results versus statistical theory and derivations.

4. The 6σ process and methodology are very new. This was the main missing ingredient up to now, an application road map for a complex set of statistical tools. Six Sigma also has a much stronger project and measurement focus. The 6σ methodology provides a highly disciplined and structured DMAIC approach. The methodology is powerful because it strings together the application of appropriate 6σ problem-solving tools to use for different stages of the problem-solving process. It guides you to use the right tools at the right time and to avoid "using a sledgehammer for a plumbing problem."

Benchmarking data illustrate that this slow adoption trend is changing rapidly. Larger organizations such as Motorola, GE, Allied Signal, Texas Instruments, Ford, DuPont, John Deere, American Express, Honeywell, 3M, Kodak, and NCR, to name a few, have led their 6σ charges with great success (their reported combined savings are in the billions of dollars). These organizations *live and breathe* 6σ daily and are assisting their suppliers with 6σ as a condition of doing business with them. This is creating both a renewed interest and motivation for other organizations to jump on board.

Although 26% of companies surveyed have a 6σ program in place, almost 70% of these companies began their 6σ efforts just within the last 24 months. This trend suggests that at least 60 to 70% or more of organizations will be actively involved in a 6σ effort by 2003–2004. Postponement of 6σ as an operating philosophy is a risky business option.

Bucking up against this trend is this naive market perception that 6σ is only for large corporations and that smaller organizations will have a more difficult time implementing a 6σ program. This is true only if the small organization attempts to implement 6σ like a large organization, but executives in the smaller organizations recognize that the implementation process must be retrofitted to the realities of their environments, and many have done so with great success. On a scale of magnitude the $50 million to $200 million clients that we have worked with have actually achieved 6σ results quicker and much greater than larger organizations.

Bottom line: The 6σ process works well at GE, and it works well at Brazeway, Stewart Warner, Atlantic Research, Acadia Polymers, Thomas & Betts, and many other small and mid-sized facilities. There's a powerful message in this: "We're too small for 6σ" and "We can't implement 6σ right now because the economy is bad" are poor excuses for not removing millions of dollars of waste from your business. Organizations with these mind-sets may find themselves well behind their competitors when the economy rebounds. An overwhelming majority of respondents agree that now is the best time to implement major change because the risks are low, and 6σ self-funds itself with the savings.

THE PROOF IS IN THE PROCESS

There are a number of reasons why 6σ is so successful, but two factors at the top of the list are leadership involvement and the structured problem-solving methodology. First, leadership involvement is a requirement, and most executives go through Champion, Black Belt, or Green Belt certification as part of the implementation process. They are not only providing strong leadership and mentoring, but they are conducting their own projects. They understand 6σ on the two critical planes: They live 6σ as a philosophy of conducting business every minute of every day. On the technical plane, don't try to fool these people because they understand the methodology and statistical tools. These executives may not debate with a candidate about their p-values or correlation coefficients, but they're much more willing to accept the results when they know that people worked their way through the 6σ process and have the facts to support their recommendations.

The structured 6σ methodology becomes a common problem-solving language for organizations. The 6σ methodology is a very deliberate process of:

- Defining and calibrating a problem
- Baselining current and goal performance
- Understanding process variation component by component
- Quantifying root causes and their magnitude on the resulting effects
- Exploring options with a scientific approach of data and facts
- Making calculated improvements and measuring the impact of changes

- Experimental designs and replications to predict process performance
- Implementation, verification, mistake-proofing, and transition to process owners

Figure 6.3 provides one of the project tracking instruments we use in Black Belt and Green Belt certification. The 6σ process prevents people from jumping right to the answers before they understand the problem and root causes. It discourages "band-aiding" and symptomatic fixes by focusing on elimination of root causes and the associated process variation. It strings together the appropriate tools to apply at various stages of the problem-solving process. It makes people validate that their changes are, in fact, effective rather than chance. Finally, it makes people super problem-solvers.

HOW TO BECOME A SIX SIGMA BELIEVER

Everything new has its skeptics, and 6σ is no exception. A four-month experience through Black Belt training removes the skepticism very quickly. For many candidates, 6σ is almost a religious experience where they see their previous thinking shattered and replaced by a whole new set of feature-rich methodologies and tools. For four months, candidates are placed in a 6σ bootcamp-like experience. They receive intensive training in the 6σ methodology/tools and statistical software, and then they apply this new knowledge to a real business problem.

For some, that project might be fixing an automated assembly line that every engineer in the place has failed to fix in the last two years. But those "it can't be done" projects really make a candidate appreciate the power of 6σ and become a strong advocate of the methodology. The skeptics snicker as the candidate deploys the 6σ process and tools religiously. Then, one day the root causes of variation are understood using facts and real data, and the answer becomes obvious. The right changes/adjustments are implemented (often at $0 capital investment we might add) and yields improve tenfold! The company saves $500,000 to $1 million a year from that one project alone. The skeptics stand around thinking about their misguided energies as an inexperienced Black Belt candidate fixes their problem.

These candidates grow and become the Masters and Champions, leading and supporting dozens of similar projects, making 6σ a way of life in their organizations. They convert many skeptics by putting them through their own 6σ experience. They recognize that 6σ is very powerful, impressionable stuff. They begin to use the 6σ process and methodologies without even thinking about it. They develop others on 6σ tools and methodologies and expand their own

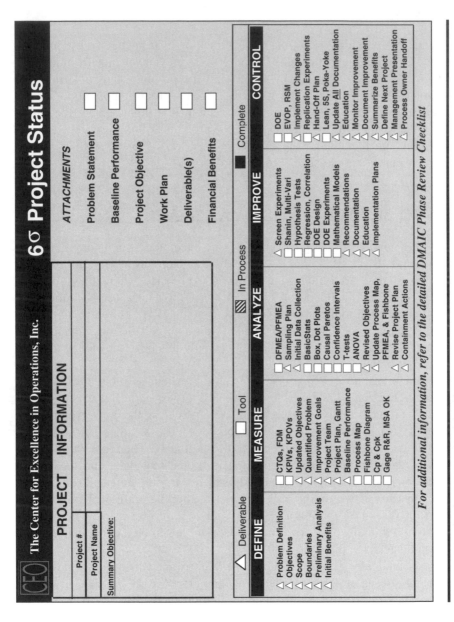

FIGURE 6.3 Six Sigma project tracker

knowledge and beliefs. They become very intolerant of those who insist on "winging it" and creating even more problems for the organization.

PROJECT SELECTION: THE KEY TO SUCCESS

Organizations must fully understand the underlying principles of 6σ if they hope to do a good job of project selection. Like all the methodologies and techniques, 6σ is not applicable to everything. Although the benefits are impressive for almost every organization pursuing 6σ, project selection is often a challenge. Why? You know the answer by now (strategic improvement is a core competency). By comparison, 6σ promotes proactive leadership involvement and the equivalent of a good Plan-Deploy-Execute process in its methodology, and this is why organizations are seeing higher results than previous improvement programs. At the wave level, however, sometimes candidates are assigned to projects that really are not 6σ projects. We probably sound like a broken record by now, but if you understand the importance of these things, we have accomplished one of our objectives with this book.

Project selection should be a formal process that is aligned to the improvement strategy. At a very minimum, projects "in the queue" should be defined by the following parameters:

1. **Problem statement, supported by quantitative data:** Background, magnitude of problem, likely root causes, current performance and gaps
2. **Project objective:** Purpose and expectations
3. **Project scope:** "Chunk" boundaries and timing
4. **Deliverable(s):** What will be different, how will we know we accomplished the objective
5. **Financial benefits:** Rough-cut goal performance

Many organizations have an effective process at the executive leadership level, and they maintain a prioritized and categorized pool of "ready-to-go" projects based on their business strategy and improvement needs. They use a formal prioritization and ranking process such as function deployment analysis, transition trees, and other analytical assessment tools to make sure that their limited resources are working on the most important opportunities. After these projects are assigned, the drill-down details of team formation, project timelines, detailed work plans, and expected benefits are flushed out in the D stage of DMAIC. What happens when projects are assigned randomly so candidates can meet their certification requirements? It becomes a disappointing experience and accomplishes the exact opposite of developing believers. It becomes a "going through the motions" project rather than a critical project where candidates discover the 6σ experience. One of the comments you hear from these candidates goes something like this: "Six Sigma was a big waste. I fixed the problem in the first week, but they made me go through the rest of the process." These individuals never get to experience the power of 6σ because their project was not a 6σ project. It was probably a kaizen blitz. The organization makes a significant investment in these individuals and then loses them. Project selection is important on two fronts: real tangible improvement and behavioral alignment.

One of the things we hear in industry is this casual "you win some, you lose some" approach to 6σ. We disagree adamantly! When you go into 6σ or any other improvement initiative with a casual mind-set, you will get poor results. We cannot stress enough the importance of project selection. You must set people up for success. If they're not moving in that direction, then change the objective, the scope, change the project if you need to. You don't want people going through the motions and feeling like it was a big waste of their time. You want to equip people with new knowledge and tools and let them experience the emotions of solving a problem that nobody else could solve. Let them internalize their victories. These are the little things that turn people into winners, modify perspectives, and ultimately transform culture.

DESIGN FOR SIX SIGMA

Six Sigma has also found great applications in the area of new product development. This makes sense because we are attacking variation upstream, where the process truly begins, not in the middle of the process or further downstream. If a product or process design includes a high level of performance unpredictability and inherent variation in the first place, organizations can only get so far with 6σ unless they expand their efforts upstream. Six Sigma is a methodology that helps organizations understand and remove variation in a process — in essence, fix a broken process. By contrast, Design for Six Sigma (DFSS) helps organizations develop products and processes that are flawless. They don't break in the first place, at least as the theory goes. Figure 6.4 displays the degree of influence that the development process has on total cost. For many companies, they have committed 80% or more to the product's ultimate cost when they write the functional specification. The further you progress in the development process, the less of an impact you have on cost or performance. In a nutsheil, this diagram says that you have a higher degree of influence up front in the product development process. While 6σ may achieve benefits after launch, the real opportunity is upstream through prevention, robustness, and perfection in product/process design.

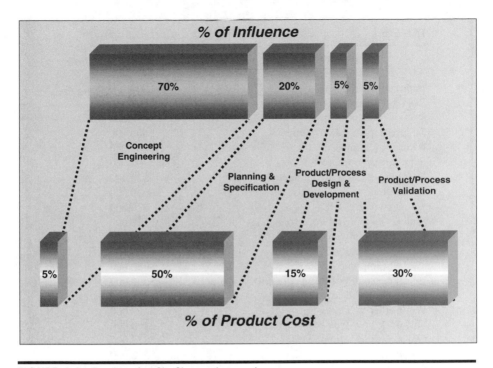

FIGURE 6.4   Design for Six Sigma impact

Organizations can never achieve 6σ if they bypass the development process. Changing the design after a product is introduced is a very costly value proposition. Worse yet, it is too late or cost prohibitive to make many of the changes you would like to make. DFSS is all about eliminating defects and variation before product launch, which results in a tremendous cost savings in the total value stream, a significant reduction in time to market, and superior products in the marketplace. DFSS also employs the voice of the customer and many other statistical tools that result in higher market share and increased profitability. DFSS is all about a flawless design and development process and a flawless rollout.

HOW SIX SIGMA ENABLES
THE LEAN EXTENDED ENTERPRISE

The most compelling aspect of 6σ is that it replaces perceptions and opinions with data and facts. Benchmarking information also tells us that 84% of companies pursuing 6σ achieve significant improvements and documented savings

TABLE 6.1   Partial summary of individual 6σ project benefits

Benefit reported	Annualized hard $ savings
Improve on-time delivery to 99%	$3,000,000
Reduce unplanned maintenance	$867,000
Reduce process waste	$58,000
Reduce unplanned downtime	$560,000
Reduce cycle time	$1,600,000
Paint adhesion improvement	$500,000
MRO inventory usage, 1 item	$22,000
Reduce fuels, oils, solvents	$420,000
Screw machine DOE	$36,000
Reduce shipping/billing errors	$238,000
Reduce warranty/repair	$4,200,000
Improve inventory performance	$1,800,000
Tool life improvement	$450,000
Injection molding DOE	$396,000
Eliminate mixed parts	$120,000
Work order variances	$360,000
Fast-track prototype design	$2,200,000
Order fulfillment improvement	$872,000
Automated weld line DOE	$382,000
Scrap reduction	$1,400,000

Note: Each Black Belt and Green Belt candidate must complete a successful project similar to the above, using the 6σ methodology and appropriate analytical tools. This is a requirement for certification.

(the remaining 16% are just beginning their 6σ efforts, 0% of the respondents reported failure). Typically, a single Black Belt or Green Belt certification wave has saved well over $1 million alone. The big difference with 6σ is its focus on tracking bottom-line improvements, project by project. Table 6.1 provides a partial summary of individual 6σ project benefits from various companies.

So how does 6σ support the notion of a Lean Extended Enterprise? Six Sigma is applicable to any process that has problems due to complex unexplainable variation. While many projects begin with hard processes (i.e., machines and equipment), soft knowledge processes inside and outside the four walls are ripe target areas for 6σ projects. The methodology is very appropriate for these end-to-end business processes because it is often the first time someone has looked at these processes with a scientific approach. These processes contain a high level of complex, unexplainable variation. Opportunities such as new product development, inventory pipeline management, logistics and distribution, shipping/billing errors, forecasting and demand management, quick response delivery, etc. are typically significant pain points and significant wins. Simple 6σ techniques such as Pareto analysis, confidence intervals, and basic statistical distributions can reveal a lot about these processes. The more complex tools such as hypothesis tests, ANOVA, Multi-vari analysis, and DOE help to understand the critical factors of these processes and to test whether or not the improvements are, in fact, real improvements versus chance. It is common for organizations to find that 50% or more of their 6σ projects are within the soft process areas. One of our Black Belt friends summed up his experience: "A 6σ project on a welder saves you 2 to 3 points of yield, but a 6σ project in warranty/returns or new product development saves you millions." The following are some examples of 6σ projects in soft process areas.

- **New product strategy and creation:** Transition a company from a "me-too" supplier to a market leader; deploy 6σ methodologies for market/technology scanning, Voice of the Customer and requirements definition, business feasibility, pro-forma profit-and-loss analysis, etc.
- **Customer service:** Reduce shipping, credit, invoicing, warranty/returns, invoicing and receivables errors, customer complaint resolution cycle time, and cash-to-cash cycle time.
- **Engineering change:** Reengineer the ECN process into a streamlined, total business-oriented process (e.g., variation reduction, obsolescence, commonality, etc.).
- **Forecasting/demand management:** Eliminate mismatches in supply and demand, excessive inventory, poor customer service, premium freight costs, and other supply chain inefficiencies.
- **Inventory rationalization:** Eliminate root causes of poor inventory performance, simplify business processes between multiple ERP platforms, and implement both quick-strike and strategic actions (the inventory dashboard) to improve asset utilization.
- **Accounting:** Reduce accounts receivable days outstanding, simplify the monthly close process, reduce billing and reconciliation errors, and the process of foreign currency conversion and exchange.
- **Supply chain management:** Improve product management/rationalization, inventory versus service levels, quick-response stocking strategies, value stream synchronization, product consolidation and pruning, and large-dollar-services procurement.
- **New product development:** Reduce time to market, formalize stage/gate process design, design and phase review processes, integrated product/process design, test strategy and reliability engineering, and other DFSS tools.

- **Software development:** Design for value and ease of integration, design for scalability and ease of configuration, design for high usability (quick, simple, easy to learn, look and feel, assimilate environment, etc.).

THE FUTURE OF SIX SIGMA

Is 6σ worth the effort? The answer is a resounding *yes*. Like any new management technique, there is much debate about the newness or mechanics, but benchmarking data speaks for itself. TQM proponents say that TQM would have accomplished the same results if management supported it. Others call it a slick marketing ploy and a new twist on an old topic. One vice-president of quality who completed Black Belt certification commented, "I've been in quality for 25 years and I thought I knew it all. Six Sigma certification was a real eye-opener. It makes you realize all the hidden opportunities you've been missing."

Six Sigma is not the silver bullet, nor is it the panacea for all of management's challenges. But make no mistake about it — 6σ is here to stay because its demonstrated success is proven in the numbers. Six Sigma is a highly "customer-centric" improvement process that focuses on tangible results — one project at a time. Many organizations are well into 6σ and are migrating the methodology upstream to new product development and suppliers. Many smaller and mid-sized companies that are suppliers to these larger organizations recognize this trend and are proactively implementing 6σ before they are told to do so. These organizations are the early beneficiaries of 6σ.

If you are implementing 6σ, there is a good chance that you will see millions of dollars added to your company's bottom line this year. Congratulations to you, your employees, and your stakeholders! If you are not currently implementing 6σ or have not heard about it yet, chances are you will — especially if you do business with any Fortune 1000 company. If you wait until one of these organizations mandates 6σ as a condition for doing business with them in the future, you have given away a lot of ground to your competition.

For many organizations, 6σ is an arduous task but not a totally overwhelming task. In fact, the heart of the 6σ process is a lot closer to arithmetic than integral calculus, particularly through the user-friendly MiniTab software application. For practitioners, 6σ is about perfection, deep core drilling to root causes, logical reduction of variation, and driving significant cost reductions out of all processes. It's about deploying indignant people who get upset about bad processes, with the right technical and people skills to make a big difference. It's about developing "relentless hunters" versus becoming a hunted organization.

The remainder of this chapter will provide a few case studies to demonstrate how 6σ enables a Lean Extended Enterprise.

CASE STUDY 1: PROCESS CAPABILITY IMPROVES INVENTORY PERFORMANCE

To improve any process, one must recognize and appreciate the concept of process variation. Some of this variation is natural: It results from the normal expected variations in people, equipment, setups, suppliers, and other types of process variation. However, most variation is unnatural: It can be eliminated by detecting and studying the significant cause-and-effect relationships. One useful 6σ tool that companies use to support this effort is called *process capability index,* or Cpk.

What Is Cpk?

Cpk is a measure of process capability, which statistically describes how centered or dispersed the variation is in a process. The Cpk goal is expressed as an index of at least 1.33, which equates to a defect rate of 63 parts per million (ppm). However, the actual Cpk will most likely be much lower for organizations that have not used this Black Belt tool in the past. The 6σ equivalent of Cpk is 1.5 long term or 2.0 short term, which means almost zero process shift, which equates to a defect rate of 3.4 ppm. For production runs of 20,000 units or less, normal process defects will make meeting a Cpk of 1.33 challenging. For larger production runs of 300,000 or more, the same level of random defects may make 6σ performance more achievable. Whatever your production run or Cpk goal, chances are your organization will be busy trying to improve processes that are substantially below your Cpk goal.

Organizations should not get hung up on the goal, but instead just get going on improving process capability. This means making processes very predictable and "centered" around a desired performance goal. Many organizations and their suppliers are not even close to 100 ppm, never mind a Cpk of 1.33 or 6σ performance. On the other hand, great organizations are beginning to talk about parts per billion. The objective of Cpk analysis is to predict and eliminate as many sources of product/process variation as possible via preventive measures, not after something goes wrong.

This is a good time to revisit the first paragraph of this chapter for the benefit of our 6σ purists. Walter Shewhart was really focusing more on product quality than process quality. He showed that 3σ from the mean is the point where a process requires correction. In the early part of the 20th century, he was viewing quality from the goalpost perspective where anything inside the specification was acceptable. In the world of 6σ, this is no longer true because we are more concerned with variation from a target value. So Shewhart's comment about "three sigma from the mean is the point where a process requires correction " is no longer true. Why? Because a 1σ or 2σ shift could make a big difference in our stack-up tolerance situation. With 6σ, we attempt to understand, quantify, and reduce as much process variation as possible because any deviation from the desired target value has an exponential effect on COPQ.

Figure 6.5 shows an example of using 6σ to improve inventory performance. Working through the DMAIC process, the entire inventory pipeline was mapped and quantified using current and historical data. One of the objectives was to understand the root causes of inventory performance so that preventive measures could be installed to keep inventory within a desired performance bandwidth (turns, days of supply). The company also wanted to quantify the capability of its inventory management process to perform within this bandwidth. The 6σ team defined the major and minor inventory drivers with live data and Pareto analysis. Team members could correlate inventory performance to a number of factors including scheduling practices and changes, shortages, supplier defects, late or early deliveries, ECNs, etc. They began implementing improvements to the process and validated that their actions were improving the capability of their inventory management process.

CASE STUDY 2: GAGE R&R REDUCES SUPPLY CHAIN COSTS

Another useful 6σ tool is called Gage R&R. This tool helps to distinguish between the variation within the process itself and the variation caused by the measurement system. In any process, the variation is explained by the formula

$$V_t = V_p + V_m + V_o$$

The total variation is equal to the part-to-part variation in the process itself plus the measurement system variation plus the normal noise. Measurement system variation can be broken down further into reproducibility and repeatability. *Reproducibility* is the variation due to different operators, and *repeatability* is the variation due to the gage itself. Why is this an important issue? It is important because in many cases we provide measurement systems to people that are bad, and fixing the measurement system itself results in quality improvement. Companies such as Allied Signal have achieved enormous success by eliminating measurement system variation.

A team took on a cost reduction project for a newly released product with

FIGURE 6.5a
In the beginning of the project there is significant variation in the process and a log Cpk

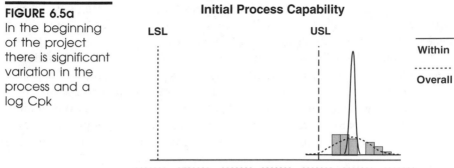

FIGURE 6.5b
During the project many improvements are implemented; variation is reduced and the Cpk improves, validating that our actions are correct

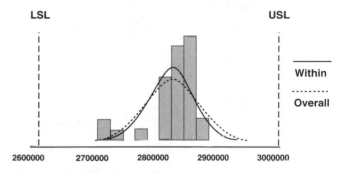

FIGURE 6.5c
The Cpk Improves further as additional improvements are implemented

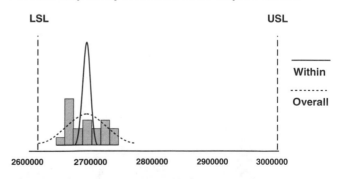

low yields, a high material content, and excessive manufacturing costs. Team members went through the DMAIC process and used Gage R&R on their final inspection equipment (refer to Figure 6.6a and b).

They found that the test equipment had a 72% Gage R&R, and a minimum acceptable level is 30%. The process was not the source of variation; the source was a poor measurement system. Without getting into the statistical details, they were rejecting good product and sending defective product to the next operation. Further, this part was not repairable, so they were always expediting additional material and paying premium freight costs, not to mention the constant chaos to

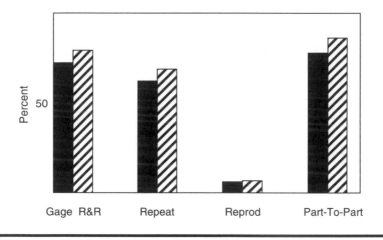

FIGURE 6.6a Initial Gage R&R results

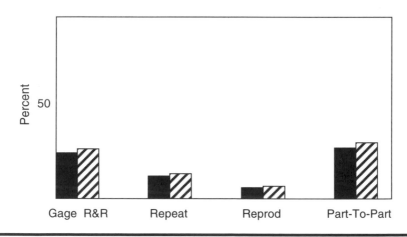

FIGURE 6.6b Gage R&R results after improvement

the suppliers for unplanned demands. This is why Gage R&R is important. The gage was not capable of doing what it was intended to do. The variation was due to the bad gage, not the process itself. If they replaced the test equipment with a toss of a fair coin, they would eliminate 22% of the measurement system variation instantly! The manufacturing process was fine, it was the measurement system. The measurement system was redesigned and recalibrated and they realized a big cost reduction.

Six Sigma Improves Warranty and Returns

Another 6σ team was assigned the task of reducing warranty and returns. The team went through the DMAIC process and conducted multi-level Pareto analysis on the data. The objective was to isolate the root cause, so team members analyzed warranty/return issue by product, by customer, by dollar volume, by quantity, by time period, and many other dimensions. They used many of the other 6σ tools like Multi-vari analysis to categorize root causes and their impact on various warranty/return outcomes. It was much more difficult for the team than we make it sound. This analysis does not seem technically impressive, but keep in mind that this kind of analysis is a first for many organizations. A major opportunity surfaced when the team isolated warranty/returns to a particular customer and the agreements in place from 20 years ago (i.e., the customer does not have to physically send back the defective return). Further analysis proved with data and facts that the problem was an installation problem, not a product problem. The returns policy was revised and one of the segments of warranty/returns dropped immediately. The installation process was also revised, and it was a win–win for everyone. The big lesson here is that most of the time the perceived problem is not the real problem; the real problem is something else. Only data and facts get you to the real truth.

CHAPTER 6 TAKE-AWAYS

- The statistical objective of 6σ is to drive down process variation so that ±6 standard deviations (6σ) lie between both the upper and lower specification limits and the target value in a process. The practical explanation equates to just 3.4 defects per million opportunities.
- The most compelling aspect of 6σ is that it replaces perceptions and opinions with data and facts. Six Sigma uses a deliberate structure commonly referred to as DMAIC, which stands for Define Measure Analyze Improve Control. The key to 6σ's success is the extreme focus on eliminating process variation.

- Every process includes both common cause variation (inherent noise) and special cause variation (explainable variation). The common causes create a 1.5σ shift over time, but the special causes can be categorized and eliminated. With a 3σ-capable process, there is a built-in scrap rate of 6.68% at best. The objective is to understand variation and the associated root causes and then eliminate it.
- Organizations must fully understand the underlying principles of 6σ if they hope to do a good job of project selection because 6σ is not applicable to everything. Project selection should be a formal process that is aligned to the improvement strategy. Project selection is important on two fronts: real tangible improvement and behavioral alignment.
- Six Sigma is a highly "customer-centric" improvement process that focuses on tangible results, one project at a time. Many organizations are well into 6σ and are migrating the methodology across their extended enterprise. Typically 50% or more of open 6σ projects are targeted at soft process areas.
- Process capability is a methodology that statistically describes how centered or dispersed the variation is in a process. Process capability uses two statistical measurements: Cp describes the overall sample dispersion, and Cpk describes how well the sample is centered around a nominal or target value.
- Total variation is equal to the part-to-part variation in the process itself, plus the measurement system variation, plus the normal noise. Measurement system variation can be broken down further into reproducibility and repeatability. Reproducibility is the variation due to different operators, and repeatability is the variation due to the gage itself.

SUGGESTED FURTHER READING

Bhote, Keki and Bhote, Adi, *The Ultimate Six Sigma: Beyond Quality Excellence,* AMACOM, 2001.

Breyfogle, Forrest, *Implementing Six Sigma,* John Wiley & Sons, 1999.

Chowdhury, Subir, *Design for Six Sigma,* Dearborn Trade Publishing, 2002.

Montgomery, Douglas, *Design and Analysis of Experiments,* John Wiley & Sons, 1997.

Taguchi, Genichi, Subir Chowdhury, and Shin Taguchi, *Robust Engineering,* McGraw-Hill, 1999.

Tennant, Geoff, *Design for Six Sigma: Launching New Products and Services without Failure,* Gower Publishing, 2002.

www.isixsigma.com.

www.minitab.com.

BEYOND ERP: DEPLOYING THE RIGHT ENABLING TECHNOLOGIES

It has been a few years now since many companies implemented their enterprise resource planning (ERP) systems. For many organizations, this is a topic they would rather not talk about, because of their prior Y2K implementation experiences. However, we need to revisit this area in the context of the Lean Extended Enterprise. For the most part, organizations were successful in integrating core business processes and achieving Y2K compliance, including:

- Sharing common data and practices across the organization
- Producing and accessing information in real time
- Leveraging best practices available within the ERP package
- Avoiding and eliminating costly legacy system development, customization, and maintenance
- Speeding up consolidation of financial and operating information in a multiple-site business environment

Although ERP has received bad press, many organizations have been working diligently to make their ERP experience a success. Unfortunately, the great expectations of ERP were tempered by the desire to minimize the cost and time associated with getting the new system up and running. When an organization lives for many years with a poorly implemented ERP system, the hidden costs of poor quality continue to escalate and the benefits get further away. The good news is that there are hundreds of "quick-strike" improvements that we can make in this arena. Like everything else we've discussed, the money is still on the table.

Technology is the easy part of improvement. Information technology (IT) solutions do not solve strategic and organizational problems, and they are not plug-and-play solutions to achieve the company's mission. Like any other strategic improvement initiative, it takes an enormous level of commitment and effort to be successful. Changing people and processes is much more difficult and time consuming. But it's the only way to get the full value out of that enormous IT investment. This is not a new concept, but it is finally taking on a higher urgency. People are beginning to pay more attention to process because organizations have made huge investments in ERP and Internet technology. In addition, the Lean Extended Enterprise concept is demanding more real-time accurate information and tighter collaboration among trading partners, to address the grueling pressures to cut costs in a down economy. The interconnected world of the Lean Extended Enterprise requires business partners to analyze and understand each other's core business processes, then apply the right methodologies to simplify and streamline the connections, then deploy technology to automate the end-to-end process.

ERP: BUILDING BLOCK OR ROAD BLOCK

Many companies spent fortunes on ERP software and implementation only to find that the expected return on investment (ROI) is still a mirage or at least somewhat intangible. Some annual reports have gone as far as blaming ERP for lower than expected earnings. Software providers have become the likely targets of these unrealized ROIs and earnings. Are the SAPs, the Oracles, the PeopleSofts, the J.D. Edwards, and many others the real culprits of bad implementation performance? Of poor execution? On the grand scale of magnitude, there are only a few instances of technical ERP software or other IT feature/functionality performance. Although this is an unpopular statement, the largest share of the blame for ERP or any other improvement program's failed implementations rests within the organization. Why? Strategic improvement is a core competency that executives need to cultivate and develop because it is new to their organizations.

In retrospect, there were often misunderstandings of what ERP encompassed and how to implement it effectively that limited the achieved benefits. Executives were too busy and often delegated this strategically important task to their IT organization. In all fairness, the intent of many organizations was good (speed), but the purpose (Y2K versus IT-enabled business improvement) missed the mark. This is a particular area where speed kills the strategic improvement initiative, especially when you take shortcuts and skip the most critical execution steps. Recently an executive asked, "When can I expect to use the full functionality of our ERP system and achieve the benefits we were supposed to achieve?" That's the same as asking "How long is a piece of wire?" or "When will we find Huston's hidden treasure of the Sierra Madres?"

In their ERP implementations, many organizations failed to redesign business processes across the supply chain. The IT group was typically given the marching orders to make the technology transition quickly — fast and cheap. The software vendors positioned their products as an enabler for business process redesign, but many customers were entrenched in their legacy business process changes and decided not to make changes concurrent with the software implementation. Further, many implementers were keen to push extended implementation cycles because it increased revenues. Many organizations shortcut the requirements definition and business process redesign in the total order-to-delivery process. After all, clean-sheet business process redesign and the subsequent system configuration are complex, costly, and time consuming. Many organizations accepted the trade-offs of preconfigured templates in the hopes of faster system deployment and faster benefits. We did the slam-dunk implementations and accepted off-the-shelf, unvalidated templates. The purpose of these templates was to speed up implementation by incorporating industry-specific ERP practices and procedures. In effect, we took the easy way out with generic, albeit industry-specific, one-size-fits-all functionality. We glazed over the education. We skipped the infrastructure changes to become lean and started playing with menus, features, and functions. We had schedules and budgets to meet, and process improvement was viewed as something we could come back to and do later. We thumped our chests and celebrated the accelerated ERP implementations that did not work. We met our time and budget goals. But we never came back to finish what we said we would do — the tough process and infrastructure changes to become a lean organization.

One fact we discovered while conducting research for this book was the larger than expected number of organizations still limping along with their kluge of legacy and home-grown systems. The politics of change got in the way of progress for many of these organizations, which are more comfortable in the 1980s mode of MRP II systems and support. For others, they have a lot of catching up to do to even put the basic foundation in place for the Lean Extended Enterprise. We feel sorry for some organizations hung up on the debate that you can't do lean and ERP because they are in conflict! A few individuals even commented that the new ERP, supply chain management, and other applications are just too integrated! Like the familiar quote on "The Sopranos," "forget about it" if you think you can become a Lean Extended Enterprise with these antiquated black-hole legacy business systems.

ERP ENABLES LEAN AND CONTINUOUS IMPROVEMENT

Many organizations are interested in lean. However, they are still struggling with the vicious cycle of supply and demand. Figure 7.1 summarizes this age-old phenomenon. It really doesn't matter where we jump into the cycle, but let's begin with poor delivery performance.

One key to achieving lean success lies in breaking this vicious cycle of supply and demand. As we mentioned in Chapter 1, sheer value stream velocity and real-time collaboration have tipped the scales from the *supply side* to the

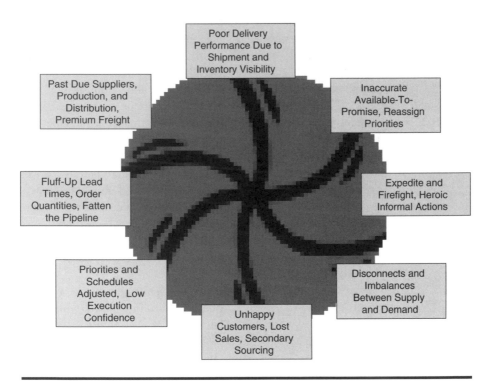

FIGURE 7.1 Vicious cycle of supply and demand

demand side. The future is a demand-driven economy. The Lean Extended Enterprise is accomplished by a combination of process redesign and integration of the correct enabling technology applications, features, and functions. There are people running around claiming that lean and ERP are at cross purposes and you cannot achieve one with the other. Some people attempt to become lean by looking for the lean module in their ERP system. Others begin with software functions and features that support lean and force-fit their process into them. Then they blame the software when the process does not work. These are all very misguided people. The fact of the matter is that ERP enables lean and vice versa. We wish we could provide you with a simple ten-step punch list, but it isn't that easy. The first step is to go back to the business process redesign stage and map out how you want to use lean principles for pull scheduling, kanban and flow control, setup reduction, maintenance management, cell and work center management, supplier integration, and visual management. Lean functionality is not a self-contained, stand-alone module: The functions and features are embedded throughout all of the major ERP software providers' products. There is a 99.9+% chance that you can enable lean with your ERP system if you follow this process and select the right functions and features and implement this functionality with improved business processes. In other words, if you start with a good process, the specific functionally to support the process is there. If you merely automate a process that is bad in the first place, ERP is not magic code that will fix this dilemma. These capabilities required to support a lean environment have always been embedded in the ERP system; the shortcuts messed up our lean journey.

There is a huge opportunity for many organizations to go back and pick up the low-hanging fruit of their ERP implementations. Many organizations have improved ERP effectiveness and achieved quick results by using the kaizen blitz approach. The goal is to identify root causes of ERP ineffectiveness and then go after these opportunities one by one. A few of the fertile areas include:

- **Master data integrity and accuracy:** This includes cleanup in the areas of part numbers, inventory balances, part locations, bill of materials, routings, and other data elements.
- **Part add practices:** This might include how to streamline this process for organizations that add and delete many parts from their offerings.
- **Planning parameter cleanup:** This includes removing the "fluff" from lead times, unit of measure, lot sizing rules, and other planning parameters.
- **Scheduling:** Implementing pull scheduling and kanban scheduling processes first, then determining how the system will enable those particular requirements.

- **ERP education:** Planners are busy executing transactions without an appreciation of the larger picture. This often results in early or late material receipts, releasing unneeded work, overloading work centers, expediting, and many other non-value-added activities. ERP competence can be improved if you commit resources to understand the ERP landscape and what it can do for you. ERP applications can only be optimized if you know how they work and what they offer.
- **Kluge cleanup:** When ERP is not working, people create their own workarounds and informal practices. Often, it's a small change to eliminate these workarounds and bring people into the formal system.

ERP improvement projects provide an excellent opportunity to reshape and streamline business along the principles of a Lean Extended Enterprise. Some of these more localized efforts are a cakewalk, but the larger scale lean strategies require more extensive mapping and planning. The problems associated with skipping this step and trying to improve through more technology add-ons are pretty obvious. ERP is a core enterprise system that other enabling technologies bolt onto to achieve the Lean Extended Enterprise.

BEYOND ERP TO THE EXTENDED ENTERPRISE ARCHITECTURE

The preceding bullet points are quick-strike activities to improve ERP effectiveness. However, we want to strike a balance between accuracy and velocity, precision and progress. Accuracy of critical information is important, but we may be reaching diminishing returns if we try to make all information 100% accurate. For example, master data accuracy is less important in a dynamic environment, assuming that appropriate corrective actions are executed. Further, accuracy of forecasts and schedules is less important in a real-time environment. Figure 7.2 illustrates this point. It is much simpler to manage demand and velocity minute by minute than to try to predict and execute a monthly schedule. Regardless of the level of perfection we could reach in ERP, it isn't enough to enable the Lean Extended Enterprise. ERP is focused on monitoring and transaction tasks, and it has limited use in terms of large-scale collaboration, value stream modeling, velocity improvement, and demand stream optimization. The Lean Extended Enterprise needs a new brain to decide the actions of the body (value stream). We relied on ERP as the brain when we were internally focused on manufacturing with six- to eight-week lead times, two-week frozen schedules, and inventory all over the place. ERP by itself does not cut it in terms of enabling the Lean Extended Enterprise, and it really falls apart in terms of supporting collaborative design, planning, and execution across multiple plat-

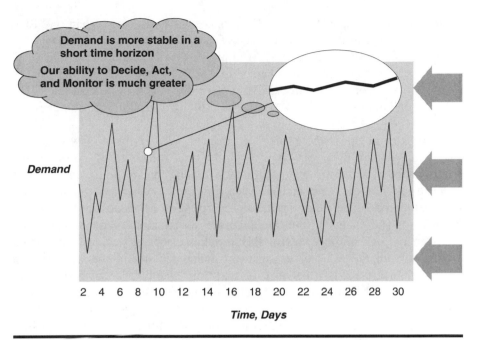

FIGURE 7.2 The velocity factor and variation

forms. Later in this chapter we will cover the *super booster* applications such as supply chain management (SCM), advanced planning and scheduling (APS), customer relationship management (CRM), product life cycle management (PLM), supplier relationship management (SRM), and networks and portal technology to facilitate total value stream collaboration and optimization. These are the new brain cells of the Lean Extended Enterprise.

Beyond ERP, we need to deep dive and understand total value stream variation. Variability and demands change daily, and velocity in actions is the key to success. Organizations need to begin developing the characteristics of the Lean Extended Enterprise and learn how to better manage value stream velocity and variation. It requires a mind-set to achieve more granularity of understanding by interjecting constraints and improving value stream capability. It involves an architecture that permits us to model and squeeze processes until they pop, so that we can better understand the root causes, bandwidth limits, and improvements needed to outperform all competitors. It requires institutionalizing the ability to Plan-Deploy-Execute across the total value stream in more real time.

Integration is a huge challenge for the Lean Extended Enterprise. Based on benchmarking data from the 2002 I2 Planet Conference:

- 65% of companies have ERP in place; 49% have more than one ERP vendor, and there is an average of 2.0 ERP vendors per company
- 44% of companies have SCM in place; 39% have more than one SCM vendor, and there is an average of 1.7 SCM vendors per company
- 44% of companies have CRM in place; 36% have more than one CRM vendor, and there is an average of 1.6 CRM vendors per company

It's pretty obvious where this is all headed. We are into a new economy where information flows rapidly through the total value stream, crossing corporate boundaries and striving for ultimate efficiency and responsiveness. Some of these activities are pretty archaic when compared to where we might be after the next decade. The Lean Extended Enterprise is a business model where information is exchanged, value stream processes are monitored, and responses are triggered in real time. Ideally, this all takes place via seamless automated processes with the rules of engagement embedded within them. The Lean Extended Enterprise is a network of real-time enterprises that form virtual value streams. They instantaneously adjust to business situations with a lot less human interaction than our current practices. For many organizations, the Lean Extended Enterprise is emerging in its embryonic form, and for others it is already the accepted norm of conducting business. This trend will continue to evolve because technology is enabling the changes to occur at a much faster rate.

Several organizations have already taken the next logical step beyond four-walls ERP and have linked into the supply base because the increasing deployment of e-procurement and the Internet opens new opportunities. For example, Mercerville, New Jersey–based Congoleum Corporation, which manufactures sheet and tile flooring, has had great success with its electronic procurement efforts. Another example is The Timken Company's Faircrest Steel Plant in Canton, Ohio. Throughout the day, the plant, which makes steel billet, sends electronic purchase orders across the street to an adjacent "Supplier City," where many of its key suppliers have set up shop. It takes milliseconds to communicate requirements and now costs less than 50 cents per purchase order. There are hundreds or maybe even thousands of other examples that support this trend.

The Lean Extended Enterprise is driving a whole set of adaptive supply chain management software applications that facilitate dynamic response and dynamic execution. We are moving beyond the traditional stagnant, "over-the-wall" links between various ERP platforms. Many organizations are well on their way to closing the gap between supply and demand via SCM, APS, CRM, event management, e-business, and other *super booster* Internet applications. From an IT perspective, the Lean Extended Enterprise includes:

- Automated processes that cross traditional enterprise boundaries and can be plugged seamlessly into other enterprise systems through a global network
- Event-driven applications such as APS, CRM, SCM, PLM, and other applications that build "condition-response" channels in real time
- Value stream collaboration and real-time information exchange between customers, employees, suppliers, and other trading partners, made possible by the expanding use of enterprise portals and other Internet-enabled technologies
- Process and security controls to maintain accurate, secure, and timely information (and the appropriate responses) across the value stream

The strategy of building a Lean Extended Enterprise is attractive to organizations because it creates a tremendous competitive weapon. However, it requires a tremendous commitment and an array of challenges to build the physical, technology, and cultural infrastructure. Organizations must learn how to execute quick responses to demand and supply changes while improving customer service and carrying less inventory. They must learn how to bring new products to market more quickly while collaborating downstream and upstream with customers and suppliers, respectively. They must learn how to use Internet-based commerce and integrate information across a variety of technology platforms in the total value stream. They must learn that the toughest job is executing these strategic improvements successfully and avoiding the costly mistakes they made in their ERP implementations.

We were working in a division of a multi-billion-dollar corporation when we received word of headquarters' new Internet-based sales and marketing program. The corporate sales and IT organizations developed the plans, but they left the divisions out of the picture. They launched this program with their customers and told them that, in keeping pace with technology, customers could now order over the Internet and receive next-day delivery. It was a great strategy, and it was even included in the annual report. But they forgot one critical detail — building the lean support infrastructure (i.e., building the right processes first). The divisions made thousands of products that require many processing steps and 12- to 18-hour setup times. The sales organization could not understand why this facility could not go from two-week deliveries to next-day delivery with the flick of a switch. Delivery performance went into the tank and everything was in a past-due status for months. It took about a year to implement the right lean infrastructure improvements to support this Internet-based selling strategy. As we have said in other parts of this book, organizations cannot achieve strategic improvement with software, soapbox speeches, and the flick of a switch.

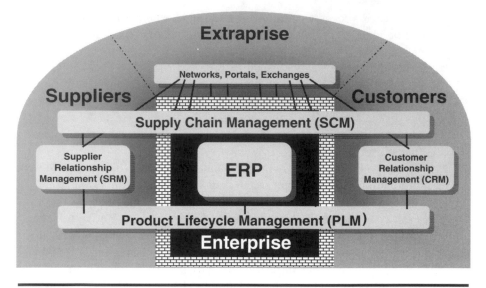

FIGURE 7.3 Enabling technology and the Lean Extended Enterprise

Value stream excellence requires a connected economy where customers, the enterprise, and the supply network are linked in real time. Leading organizations are now leveraging the external components of the value stream for competitive advantage because they understand the incredible strategic benefits. Earlier in the book we noted that as much as 80% of an organization's value stream activities, costs, and lead times are outside of its four walls. The enabling *super booster* technology exists to make this happen, and the benefits are derived by slow deliberate steps into these new technology arenas. One of the points we want to get across in this book is that technology by itself will not get you there. Figure 7.3 provides an overview of the totally connected value stream. The remainder of this chapter will focus on the enabling technologies that organizations are deploying in their pursuit of the Lean Extended Enterprise.

SUPPLY CHAIN MANAGEMENT

Today, organizations are placing much more emphasis on their supply chains because the leverage potential as a competitive weapon is enormous. Many companies have been at this game for years, using more sequential kluge approaches with a few key suppliers. Technology has progressed to the point where organizations can now build virtual networks or exchanges between themselves and their supply base and, in effect, create their value stream community as if it existed under one roof. SCM is critical to improving competitiveness because of the following factors:

■ The *demand-slide* economy is pressuring organizations to improve service levels while carrying less inventory, spending less capital, and reducing transportation costs. Warehouse space, excess and obsolete inventory, and premium freight are very expensive liabilities.

■ More and more organizations are pursuing Internet-based selling, and they need technology to monitor and ensure that business from these channels is integrated into their other supply chain activities in real time to prevent disruptions in total supply and demand.

■ Market and customer requirements change — it's a fact of life. Rather than putting the efforts into an accurate forecast, organizations must instantly adjust to these changes across the entire value stream.

■ Time to market is a critical enabler to success, and 70 to 90% of the product development activities, lead times, and costs are typically outside the four walls of the enterprise. Technology is now available to link these activities virtually together as if they were within the four walls.

■ Speed, perfection, and total value stream integration are more important than ever before in terms of standing out from the competition. Organizations must learn how to deal with preventing value stream disruptions in real time, and not let these issues affect customer satisfaction. These are the factors that increase revenues, reduce operating costs, and retain customers.

SCM allows an organization to collaborate at every detail level in the total value stream. Customer demands and forecasts can be shared instantaneously across multiple tiers in the value stream. Activities such as order status and tracking, supply chain performance, supply/demand coverage, distribution and transportation issues, and value stream modeling can be done in real time. Customers and suppliers can share accurate inventory, procurement, and invoicing information and reduce the cost of these soft processes significantly. SCM enables people to locate the status of finished goods and purchased components in real time and take action if there are any mismatches between supply and demand in an organization's various sales channels. This technology also allows users to monitor all value stream events (from the sales call to delivery) and performance in real time. This is the kind of information that organizations need to shift into a value stream problem-prevention mode because they can act on issues in real time. SCM software providers also offer networking capabilities that allow the entire value stream community to collaborate on all supply chain issues such as design, procurement, demand and supply planning, logistics, etc.

ADVANCED PLANNING AND SCHEDULING

APS systems provide highly configurable optimization capabilities to enable the Lean Extended Enterprise. APS applications include a variety of mathematical tools and techniques used to manage process constraints and optimize the total value chain. The methodologies and tools are not new, and many companies were involved back in the fifties, sixties, and seventies in APS-like manual and computerized activities to conduct critical path analysis, determine least-cost recipes for a process batch, analyze queues, and profit/margin/volume plant loading studies. Evolution of the Theory of Constraints combined with enabling technology has made it possible to simplify and automate APS tasks that used to take weeks or even quarters to perform mechanically.

Specifically, APS enables organizations to simulate value stream planning alternatives based on business objectives, evaluate and solve constraint situations, and then execute an optimal solution. APS systems compute plans and schedules for multiple simultaneous variables and constraint situations such as material availability, capacity, configuration, price, resource availability, and other factors. APS also generates optional plans to optimize the value stream for multiple critical characteristics (e.g., profitability, market share, uptime, cash-to-cash, etc.). APS uses ERP status information and other business rules, but ERP has no embedded functionality to perform these value stream modeling and optimization tasks.

The advantages of APS include:

- Simultaneous planning, action, and monitoring of value stream critical characteristics and constraints
- Multi-enterprise, multi-tier collaboration and visibility designed to help companies and their trading partners optimize limited resources and profitability
- Improved customer service, flexibility, and responsiveness through shorter cycle times and quicker collaborative resolution of problem areas
- More frequent updates of critical value stream information
- Simulation and modeling capabilities to facilitate preventive problem solving and total value stream optimization

Today's sophisticated APS technology allows users to evaluate value stream issues across several planning horizons (e.g., strategic, tactical, operational, executional). The goal of APS is to develop a plan that balances supply and demand at maximum profit and then execute and monitor the plan closely to ensure that the plan becomes reality.

CUSTOMER RELATIONSHIP MANAGEMENT

CRM is the technology that enables the organization to collaborate with customers at every level of the relationships. Organizations can interact with customers on the entire range of activities from initial marketing campaigns to post-sales service and support. Many organizations are using CRM for activities such as planning and monitoring specific sales campaigns, real-time customer segmentation, sales tracking and quick response, contract administration, and e-business.

CRM includes the following features:

- **Transactional automation:** CRM automates the more tedious transactional processes (e.g., quotations, RFPs, order administration, inventory movement, etc.) between the enterprise and its customer base.
- **Customer/enterprise integration:** CRM provides a single-pipeline view of the front end of the supply chain with multiple facilities, departments, processes, and software applications for the organization and its customers.
- **Customer demand visibility:** CRM provides visibility and real-time information and customer requirements via portals and application integration.
- **Collaboration:** CRM allows the organization and its customers to share real-time information and collaborate on various topics from new product development to order fulfillment to customer service.
- **Analytics:** CRM includes real-time analytical capabilities to measure and optimize process performance between customers and the enterprise.

CRM is critical to improving competitiveness because of the following factors. First, customer-related information is typically scattered throughout the organization. There is an enormous opportunity for organizations to consolidate this information and use it to drive sales. Second, this information is often conflicting between the engineering, marketing, and sales groups. Consolidation also enables the organization to align itself with the real requirements of its customers. Further, it allows organizations to align their business processes so they can execute effectively.

PRODUCT LIFE CYCLE MANAGEMENT

No one would argue that in most industries innovation and new product development are the key to future revenue growth. Customers are demanding more products, and they want higher performance, lower cost, and instant availability. This is a huge challenge for most organizations because traditionally they have attempted to accomplish this with disconnected and fragmented *over-the-wall* processes. Organizations have made significant improvements to their internal product development processes; however, the technology to link the entire new product development community together (e.g., customers, sales and marketing, engineering, manufacturing, quality, suppliers, etc.) has been very limited. Critical product development information is often trapped in process repositories such as an engineer's or a buyer's file cabinet, an equipment manufacturer's shop, or a test laboratory. This often leads to conflicting or incorrect information, redundant activities, increased cycle times and costs, and development process defects. Time to market may increase revenues, but it also increases the risks of increased costs, cannibalization, warranty/return issues, field performance, customer dissatisfaction, and reduced profitability without the right product development infrastructure.

PLM is the technology that enables organizations to manage new product development through the entire life cycle. It creates collaborative communities of sales executives, design engineers, quality managers, manufacturing engineers, suppliers, and customers that can share information and proactively design, build, distribute, service, and maintain products in real time. The following is a partial list of typical features of PLM:

- Fully integrated new product development process that enables value stream collaboration, concurrent engineering and development, and web-based information exchange
- Project management capabilities such as performance to schedule, cost management, resource utilization, event tracking and monitoring, and problem resolution in real time
- Knowledge management capabilities such as historical project information, CAD drawings and product structures, field reliability data, manuals, service information, previous design problems and solutions, etc.
- Quality planning and analysis from product planning and design, development information for build and service quality strategies, information relevant for Design for Six Sigma, test and validation data, etc.
- Maintenance management and engineering change capabilities to facilitate product upgrades, modifications, and refurbishments

- Compliance and regulatory capabilities to support safety, environmental, hazardous materials, and other government or regulatory requirements
- Integration with other analytical development tools for conducting profitability and product/volume/margin analysis, reliability and maintainability analysis, supplier process capability, etc.

Providing a consistent global view of products is critical to improving competitiveness. It reduces the soft administrative costs substantially and provides instant availability to the correct specification, bill of material, equipment, configuration, and process information. The non-value-added content associated with this information being incorrect is in the millions of dollars for most organizations.

SUPPLIER RELATIONSHIP MANAGEMENT

SRM is a more technically robust version of e-procurement, a technology that has been around for years. SRM is primarily concerned with extended procurement processes such as sourcing execution, payment and settlement, sourcing analysis, and sourcing performance measurement and feedback. SRM is typically integrated with PLM, SCM, and ERP because organizations need these touch points throughout the business cycle, from new product development to customer order fulfillment and post-sales service and support.

SRM has many features which can be summarized into the following categories:

- **Transactional automation:** SRM automates the tedious transactional processes between the enterprise and its suppliers. This includes activities such as sourcing, contract management, direct purchase order and invoice routing, payment and reconciliation, and real-time transactional monitoring.
- **Single-enterprise integration:** SRM provides a single-pipeline view of the supply chain with multiple facilities, departments, processes, and software applications for the organization and its supply base.
- **Supply/demand visibility:** SRM provides visibility of information and requirements between the organization and its suppliers via portals and application integration.
- **Collaboration:** SRM allows the organization and its suppliers to share real-time information and collaborate on various supply line issues.
- **Analytics:** SRM includes real-time analytical capabilities to measure and optimize process performance.

The strategic advantages of SRM are obvious in terms of leveraging the supply base for competitive advantage. SRM enables the enterprise and its supply network to make radical improvements in new product development, sourcing and buying processes, procurement velocity, information exchange, collaboration, and strategic relationships.

NETWORKS, EXCHANGES, AND PORTALS

In the traditional ERP mode, information can only be used within the context of this application. ERP stores vast amounts of structured data within the applications, and it is typically very difficult for the normal non-technical user to get access to this information. Sharing and information exchange become very difficult and have often been accomplished with unstructured processes such as special queries, report writers, e-mails, cut-and-paste exercises, and downloads into Excel. This is what we refer to as one-shot information because it is very difficult to organize, share, find, and use again. Network, exchange, and portal technology enables information to be shared across platform and application boundaries. This allows resources across the total value stream to collaborate, access relevant information, and take action in real time.

Think about all the steps required to resolve a customer complaint, find information that you downloaded from that Six Sigma website last week, locate the last customer shipment of a particular product from one of your subcontractors, figure out when your last premier customer's visit was, or access the last performance review of John Doe. This information may be scattered and "black-holed" across several sources, which makes it nearly impossible to access in any reasonable amount of time. People and organizations waste precious time looking for information, researching answers to problems, recreating redundant or conflicting information, and many other non-value-added activities. Networks, exchanges, and portals simplify this process by providing user-friendly technical interfaces and access points. True collaborative commerce is rapidly emerging as organizations continue to search for more ways to increase revenue growth, speed, flexibility, and profitability.

The idea of collaboration and information sharing across the total value stream makes some executives nervous. The technology also incorporates security and authentication mechanisms, digital security features, encryption techniques, and other common security protocol practices. In addition, things such as firewalls and routers provide network security and limited access when communicating to the external world. Without getting into the details, the technology to maintain network security is also incorporated into all network, exchange, and portal product offerings.

THIRD-PARTY SERVICES

We want you to be aware that beyond application-based technologies, there are a host of other management services offered by third-party organizations. These include areas such as logistics, transportation and freight, document and package handling, service parts and repairs, inventory management, and many other services that are compatible with the Lean Extended Enterprise. Organizations such as UPS, FedEx, and many others offer services that improve value stream performance via the seamless integration of shipments, information, and funds transfer.

A NEW IT BUSINESS MODEL IS NEEDED

Software and solution providers are beginning to respond to a changing dynamic in the marketplace. First, organizations are not interested in taking on another IT initiative of the scope of their previous ERP experience. One executive we talked to referred to it as the "5&10 IT model" ($5 million for the software and $10 million for consulting). ERP is more steady-state when compared to emerging technology because it integrates business activities within the four walls, automates transactions, and maintains historical information. Sure ERP was an expensive proposition, but we can probably expect a useful life of at least ten years, so the payback horizon is longer. By the way, we're not saying this is correct; it's just the way it is in most cases, given that the investment has already been made and the anticipated ROIs are not here yet.

In contrast, the total value stream is much more dynamic, and organizations need to achieve the IT payback quicker. The markets, products, pricing and promotions, customer and supplier relationships, collaboration channels, etc. will be different a year or two from now than they are today. From a ROI perspective, this requires a much more flexible and modularized solution for SCM, APS, CRM, PLM, SRM, or networked exchange communities. Organizations are looking for a more deliberate step-by-step deployment of the right technology enablers to the highest impact opportunities that achieve value stream excellence. Stated another way, a new IT business model is beginning to emerge where organizations purchase and implement enabling technology at a pace where they can actually digest the technology and achieve results.

One successful example of this trend is ChannelWave, which is taking CRM to the next step, called partner relationship management (PRM). This technology enables enterprises to tighten the communication and collaboration loop with their selling partners, streamline partner planning, improve lead distribution and follow-up, sharpen revenue forecasts, decrease channel conflict, and significantly reduce channel management costs. Besides being the best-in-breed PRM technology, ChannelWave's implementation strategy is aligned to this new emerging IT model. Its implementation approach includes this step-by-step deployment, focused on the high-impact opportunities. ChannelWave also introduces its customers to PRM at a pace at which they can digest the technology and achieve the ROI on their technology investment quickly.

The Lean Extended Enterprise is unfolding rapidly before our very eyes. The methodologies and enabling technology are available and work well when deployed correctly to the right opportunities. Demand-driven supply requires quick response — beyond the current capabilities of present ERP applications. It requires instant collaboration and response across the total value stream. This in turn requires a high degree of integration and comprehensive, more accurate, faster, and more actionable information. Many organizations like Dell, Steelcase, Shell, and Nokia are already at this level of performance, and many more are on their way. Table 7.1 provides a partial list of these organizations discovered during the research on this book. Sure, it requires further IT investment beyond ERP, and that might be a sore subject after the Y2K fiascoes of the recent past. But the costs, wastes, and drains on profitability are much larger because we are not taking advantage of the total value stream opportunities.

TABLE 7.1 Partial list of organizations involved in Lean Extended Enterprise improvement

3M	Del Monte Foods	Nestlé
Abbott Laboratories	Department of Defense	Nokia
Anheuser-Busch	Donnelley	Osram Sylvania
AstraZeneca	DuPont	Pacific Gas and Electric
BAE Systems	Eastman Chemical	Panasonic
BASF	Eastman Kodak	Phillips
Bayer	Ericsson	Smiths Industries
Best Buy	Federal Express	Sony
BMW	Ford	Southwest Airlines
Boeing	General Dynamics	Steelcase
Bose	Gillette	Storage Technology
Bristol-Myers Squibb	Herman Miller	Sun
Caterpillar	Hewlett Packard	Taylor Made
Colgate-Palmolive	Honeywell	Unilever
Corning	Inland Steel	UPS
Cummins Engine	Johnson & Johnson	Volvo
Daimler Chrysler	Lockheed Martin	Wal-Mart
Dell		

CHAPTER 7 TAKE-AWAYS

- IT solutions do not solve strategic and organizational problems, and they are not plug-and-play solutions to achieve the company's mission. Changing people and processes is much more difficult and time consuming. But it's the only way to get the full value out of your enormous IT investment.

- The interconnected world of the Lean Extended Enterprise requires business partners to analyze and understand each other's core business processes, then apply the right methodologies to simplify and streamline the connections, then deploy technology to automate the end-to-end process.

- Strategic improvement is a core competency that executives need to cultivate and develop because it is new to their organizations.

- ERP enables lean and vice versa. If you start with a good process, the specific functionally to support the process is there. If you merely automate a process that is bad in the first place, ERP is not magic code that will fix this dilemma. These capabilities required to support a lean environment have always been embedded in the ERP system; the shortcuts messed up our lean journey.

- ERP is focused on monitoring and transaction tasks, and it has limited use in terms of large-scale collaboration, value stream modeling, velocity improvement, and demand stream optimization. The Lean Extended Enterprise needs a new brain to decide the actions of the body (value stream).

- Organizations need to begin developing the characteristics of the Lean Extended Enterprise and learn how to better manage value stream velocity and variation. It requires a mind-set to achieve more granularity of understanding by squeezing processes until they pop, so that we can better understand the root causes, bandwidth limits, and improvements needed to outperform all competitors.

- Value stream excellence requires a connected economy where customers, the enterprise, and the supply network are linked in real time. The enabling *super booster* technology exists to make this happen, and the benefits are derived by deliberate steps into these new technology arenas.

- The Lean Extended Enterprise is unfolding rapidly before our very eyes. The super booster enabling technology beyond ERP, such as SCM, APS, CRM, SRM, PLM, networks, portals, and exchanges, is available and is enabling the Lean Extended Enterprise for hundreds of companies and their trading partners.

SUGGESTED FURTHER READING

Greenburg, Paul, *CRM: Capturing and Keeping Customers in Internet Real Time,* McGraw-Hill/Osborne, 2002.

I2 Planet Conference Proceedings CD, 2002.

Langenwalter, Gary, *Enterprise Resource Planning and Beyond,* St. Lucie Press, 1999.

Norris, Grant, John Dunleavy, James R. Hurley, John D. Balls, and Kenneth M. Hartley, *E-Business and ERP: Transforming the Enterprise,* John Wiley & Sons, 1999.

www.amrresearch.com.

www.channelwave.com.

www.demantra.com.

www.gartner.com.

www.icgcommerce.com.

www.I2.com.

www.oracle.com.

www.SAP.com.

EVERYTHING BEGINS AND ENDS WITH PERFORMANCE MEASUREMENT

We could not possibly write a book on the Lean Extended Enterprise and leave out the topic of performance measurement. Executives fully understand how to gauge the enterprise's financial performance. They have a strategic plan and know what needs to be done. The financials provide periodic information about profitability, cash flow, return on investment, dividends and equity, asset utilization ratios, market value, revenue growth, margins, market penetration, and a host of other critical business metrics. Performance measurement is the needle and thread that tie together strategy and execution and turn the Lean Extended Enterprise Reference Model into reality (Chapter 2). It enables companies to achieve alignment and integration (Chapter 8) throughout the organization. More importantly, it allows people to measure the right things so everyone can tell if things are getting better. The all-too-familiar disconnects occur in the details of the organization because there is poor alignment at the operational level. We have observed celebrations for hitting a particular performance target that was totally meaningless, like variances or indirect labor/direct labor (IL/ DL) ratios. Sure, the target was hit, but there is no clear rhyme or reason between the target and people's actions. Was it deliberate or was it an accounting adjustment? We have seen luncheons to celebrate the length of time teams have been together. (You guessed it. The obvious question — *What have they done lately?* — is always skirted.) As someone once said, "Our measurement system is about as meaningful as rewarding an anorexic person for not eating candy bars." That's a terrible analogy but, on a more serious note, people do not set these disconnects up on purpose; they just happen because of a lack of understanding about the importance of measurement and alignment. Why? We hope you appreciate the answer by now. Strategic improvement is a core competency. Performance measurement is not only concerned with measuring the right metrics. Performance measurement includes many levels, and it must be designed to link and align the organization. It must create that hard-wired spiral between the organization's strategy and its daily improvement activities. Otherwise, initiatives tend to wander away from the original objectives. In this chapter we will discuss some of the common performance measurement issues relating to strategic improvement. It is not our intent to write a measurement textbook because there are other references that cover this subject very well. Later in the chapter we provide our detailed Lean Extended Enterprise Assessment Process.

PERFORMANCE MEASUREMENT AND THE LEAN EXTENDED ENTERPRISE

In the Lean Extended Enterprise, there are multiple levels of performance that we must address (Figure 8.1). First there is the *extended enterprise* level, where we need to be concerned with the success of every player in the total value stream community. The second level is the *enterprise* level, where we must maximize the value propositions of stakeholders, shareholders, and customers and focus on strategic services that build brand image and customer loyalty. Shareholder value, market share, growth, revenue from new products, and brand image are a few of the key measures of this level. The third level is the *business process* level, where we must focus on external customer synchronization, flexibility, and quick response to existing product demand/supply issues. On-time delivery performance, target cost, warranty/returns, profitability, and customer satisfaction are a few key measures of this level. The fourth level is the *operational* level, where the focus is primarily on internal process steps with attention to *next customer* requirements. Cycle times, productivity, quality, cost, and other traditional cost accounting measures are part of this level. In the Lean Extended Enterprise, we must strive for performance measurement and alignment between each of these levels.

With regard to strategic improvement, performance measurement is one of those topics that everyone knows everything about, except in practice. Recall our previous words about the difference between knowing how to do something and doing it right every day. Here's a few examples from our recent past:

LEVEL	CUSTOMER	MISSION
Extended Enterprise	The Total Value Stream Community	Maximize Total Value Stream Performance
Enterprise	Stakeholders, Shareholders	Minimize Enterprise Performance
Core Business Process	External Customers	Maximize Individual Customer Requirements
Operational/Event	Internal Customers	Maximize and Align Process Performance

FIGURE 8.1   Level of performance measurement integration

- Consider the scandals involving Enron, WorldCom, Arthur Anderson, Tyco, Adelphia, and a few others. One might blame them on executive greed and be done with it, but a closer look has a lot to do with performance measurement. A good part of these executives' behaviors was driven by performance measures that they thought would maximize the corporation's and their own personal performance. They were too focused on the wrong measures and the wrong actions to imagine the ultimate harm they could cause millions of total value stream employees and shareholders.
- A client from a few years back had a sister division that was supposedly into lean with impressive results achieved. The general manager suggested that we visit the facility to learn more about its efforts. We attempted to set up several Friday visits with no success. One day, an innocent team leader answered the telephone and informed us that we must visit Monday through Thursday because Friday was the line re-work, repair, and build-ahead day. Moral of the story: Don't believe every "world-class" and performance measure story that is published; go look at the details.
- A division controller under pressure from headquarters would close the books five to six times during the beginning of each month, until they got it "right." Everyone was running around with different data and

versions of reports. First there was a focus on purchase price variance (PPV), then in the next breath it was material variances, then it was inventory levels, then delivery performance. Then they would schedule Saturday overtime to quickly improve absorption before they closed the books again. The numbers would change as if someone actually did something to influence these issues, but it was a big accounting game. How do you make the right decisions in a meeting when every attendee has different information and different marching orders? Moral of the story: Accounting games will ultimately kill the organization. If you can't get it right the first time, why bother? Seriously, think about all the gyrations this practice put people through and the cost of non-value-added activity and the inherent inconsistency of the messages.

■ A vice-president of operations was sitting through a review of a Six Sigma candidate's Black Belt project. The recommendations were causing this individual to squirm in his seat and make a lot of faces. In the middle of the review, he responded, "Listen, there's something wrong with your data. I know because I've been in this job for ten years." We probed politely, asking to see his data, until he finally answered, "I don't have any data, I've never seen any data. I just know what I know." This individual did not want to be confused by the facts. The Six Sigma candidate's data and analysis were correct. Moral of the story: You don't know what you don't know. In the absence of data and facts, you know only opinions and perceptions. If you're high enough in the organization, these opinions can become facts. Consequently, you lead the organization to make many wrong decisions without data and facts.

■ A centralized supply management group in the Northeast was buying raw materials (many of which were dated materials) for multiple manufacturing locations around the United States. While corporate was rewarding this group for cost reductions and favorable PPVs, the plants were in complete chaos. One facility rented 20 trailers to store corrugated packaging materials and other powdered materials (some of these trailers leaked when it rained). Besides creating a shipping/receiving nightmare in the parking lot, it was a field trip to find anything. The facility rented a highboy forklift each month to move all the obsolete material around to make room for more. Finally, they implemented a color-coded dot system to identify slow-moving stock, and many of the cartons resembled a Wonder Bread wrapper! Coincidentally, several of the raw material "A items" came from a supplier less than three miles away from the largest plant, but the facility had ten months of material on hand. Because much of this material was dated, the plants were always getting beat up for excess/obsolete inventory and spoilage, over which they had no control. Now that's a performance disconnect. Moral of the story: Performance measurement is a motivator of behaviors and actions, but not necessarily the right actions.

There are specific practices that best-in-class organizations follow to ensure alignment between the business strategy and the daily activities of improvement throughout the organization. It requires time, effort, and the right information, and it requires constant attention because the world changes quickly, organizations drift, and individuals oscillate around perceived expectations.

First, we need to make sure that there is alignment between strategic improvement projects and the strategic plan so we avoid the common trap of motion in the absence of progress. Project selection is critical, and process characterization and measurement are right behind. Otherwise, we cannot determine with data and facts that our actions are improving the process. This factor is related to the *Field of Dreams* improvement we discussed back in Chapter 3. Results just don't happen; they just don't fall out of the sky after a lot of motion and activity. Results are the product of a deliberate, well-executed improvement process that focuses on eliminating root causes of poor performance.

Second, we need to structure performance measurement in a manner which enables true enterprise performance and fosters the right behaviors at every level of the organization. A familiar saying about this topic is "Be careful what you measure, you might just get it."

A final consideration is the right measurements. Sure, there are conflicts between traditional cost accounting practices and strategic improvement, but the key to success is moving beyond the debates and building connections. For example, metrics such as overhead absorption, variances, purchase price variances, and efficiency or utilization measures tend to drive organizations in a direction contradictory to lean. One approach is to point fingers, but a more proactive approach is to put the right lean measures in place with solid data and facts. In many cases, there is a direct correlation between financial performance and operational performance. You just need to find it and educate others. In one great Six Sigma project, a Black Belt candidate quantified the cause-and-effect relationships of inventory performance and their impact on days of supply. Most intelligent people are willing to reconsider and compromise their position when you show them the real data and facts behind a situation. Many of the traditional cost accounting measures are a pay now or pay later proposition. Balance is critical, and you will not get anywhere in business by calling your financial organization Public Enemy #1 or recommending that the organization throw out its cost accounting system or keep multiple sets of books. Rather than treating the financial resources in the organization as adversaries, get them deeply involved in kaizen, lean, and Six Sigma efforts, particularly in the project selection and baseline performance efforts. Validate operational improvements and any other financial or operational data you can with these people. They can provide useful inputs about strategic alignment and pegging operational performance to financial performance.

THE LEAN EXTENDED ENTERPRISE ASSESSMENT PROCESS

The remainder of this chapter provides the detailed *Lean Extended Enterprise Assessment Process*. This performance measurement tool is based on the Lean Extended Enterprise Reference Model (LEERM) presented in Chapter 2 and in particular the Best Practices and Principles Panel (Figure 8.2).

As we mentioned earlier, this panel includes the underpinning best-in-class practices and principles of lean applied across the total value stream. Within each of the 7 categories are 6 specific criteria (42 criteria total) which serve as the underpinning practices and principles of value stream excellence. It is an expansion of the traditional notion of lean into distinct criteria covering the entire breadth and scope of the total value stream.

The performance measurement criteria for the Lean Extended Enterprise are based on the balanced scorecard methodology. As we developed the LEERM, we saw a need to develop a framework for measuring this new reference model. The performance measurement framework for the LEERM incorporates the balanced scorecard concepts of customer, finance, internal business process, and learning/growth. However, we discovered the need to clarify the methodology as it impacts the total value stream. Appropriately, we decided to name this methodology the Lean Extended Enterprise Assessment Process, or LEEAP. The acronyms are simple: LEERM is the entire reference model, and LEEAP is the performance measurement assessment process.

Refer to the LEERM Best Practices and Principles Panel again. There are 7 best practices and principles categories (or perspectives if you are familiar with the Kaplan/Norton model). Within each of these 7 categories are 6 more specific criteria (42 criteria total). The detailed LEEAP performance measurement methodology is included at the end of this chapter. The following provides an overview of the Best Practices and Principles Panel:

1. **Leadership:** This is an area that is often taken for granted. We covered this topic in great detail in Chapter 3. In a strategic improvement initiative such as the Lean Extended Enterprise, we need a more formal methodology to ensure that the right levels of leadership and commitment exist. The LEEAP measures criteria such as the organization's

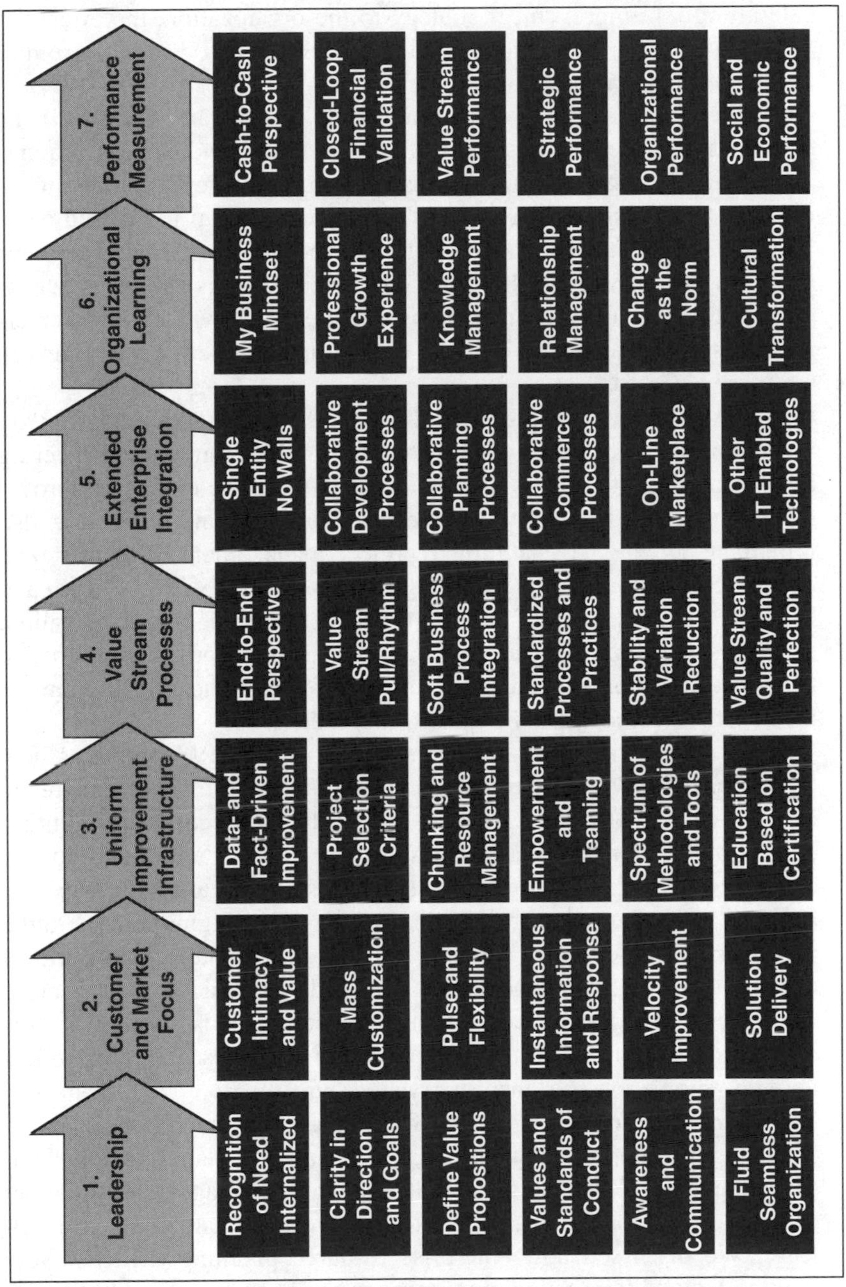

1. Leadership	2. Customer and Market Focus	3. Uniform Improvement Infrastructure	4. Value Stream Processes	5. Extended Enterprise Integration	6. Organizational Learning	7. Performance Measurement
Recognition of Need Internalized	Customer Intimacy and Value	Data- and Fact-Driven Improvement	End-to-End Perspective	Single Entity No Walls	My Business Mindset	Cash-to-Cash Perspective
Clarity in Direction and Goals	Mass Customization	Project Selection Criteria	Value Stream Pull/Rhythm	Collaborative Development Processes	Professional Growth Experience	Closed-Loop Financial Validation
Define Value Propositions	Pulse and Flexibility	Chunking and Resource Management	Soft Business Process Integration	Collaborative Planning Processes	Knowledge Management	Value Stream Performance
Values and Standards of Conduct	Instantaneous Information and Response	Empowerment and Teaming	Standardized Processes and Practices	Collaborative Commerce Processes	Relationship Management	Strategic Performance
Awareness and Communication	Velocity Improvement	Spectrum of Methodologies and Tools	Stability and Variation Reduction	On-Line Marketplace	Change as the Norm	Organizational Performance
Fluid Seamless Organization	Solution Delivery	Education Based on Certification	Value Stream Quality and Perfection	Other IT Enabled Technologies	Cultural Transformation	Social and Economic Performance

FIGURE 8.2   LEERM Best Practices and Principles Panel

recognition of the need to change, the ability to develop and communicate a uniform improvement strategy to the organization, the effectiveness of awareness and communication, and the effectiveness of promoting values and standards of conduct.

2. **Customer and market focus:** This category evaluates how well the organization understands and translates customer and market requirements into the right actions. In this category, we are interested in the organization's responsiveness, flexibility, value stream pulse, and overall alignment of customers, the enterprise, and suppliers. In this area, we are trying to answer the big questions: How well is the organization directly plugged into customer and market needs? How well is the enterprise positioned philosophically to deal with these new demand-driven realities?

3. **Uniform improvement infrastructure:** This category promotes moving away from "flavor-of-the-month" programs and focusing on unwavering improvement strategy. It is important to have a single uniform improvement program that integrates all the methodologies and tools. It is also important here to have a formal project management, selection, and execution process. Finally, this category is concerned with the depth and breadth of *hard* (technical) and *soft* (teaming) skill injections, education, and training so that people can be successful. Enterprises must fold in their various improvement programs and redirect them at a common theme. It's the ends, not the means, that matter.

4. **Value stream processes:** In this category, the LEERM promotes how the organization views, manages, and optimizes the total value stream. Moving beyond the shop floor to soft business processes and further outside of the four walls is critical to success. This category is primarily concerned with how we are eliminating waste and variation from core business processes using the kaizen, lean, and Six Sigma tools. From a pure process improvement perspective (prior to automation), it is critical to deploy the right methodologies and tools to achieve synchronized flow, variation reduction, perfection, and instantaneous adjustment. It is also critical to define and think through best practices first, then follow up with automation (not the other way around).

5. **Extended enterprise integration:** This category introduces the enabling technology to support collaborative forecasting and planning, collaborative product development, collaborative supplier management, and other enabling technologies as a means to achieve total value stream excellence. We discussed how enterprise resource planning (ERP) is very limiting beyond transaction monitoring in the Lean Extended Enterprise environment. The deployment of applications such as supply chain man-

agement (SCM), customer relationship management (CRM), supplier relationship management (SRM), product life cycle management (PLM), value stream optimizers, and network/exchange technologies is a necessary practice in the Lean Extended Enterprise.

6. **Organizational learning:** This category focuses on professional development and growth, knowledge and relationship management, behavioral adjustment and alignment, change and improvement as daily subconscious activities, and cultural transformation. It is our premise that learning and growth based on facts and knowledge are important factors in permanent cultural transformation. Learning is much more than education programs. It involves applying these skills to real-world problems, feeling success, and growing to new levels of competence.

7. **Performance measurement:** The last category of the Best Practices and Principles Panel is concerned with achieving balance across the total value stream. We must put the right measurement/monitoring structure and processes in place to achieve optimization of the value stream community. No longer is it acceptable to be successful in a particular machine in the plant or for a company to succeed at the expense of its suppliers. We cannot be successful with unactionable weekly or monthly performance reports. We need real-time, closed-loop validation and feedback that the right actions are being managed and executed across the total value stream.

The LEEAP instrument and scoring criteria are provided at the end of this chapter.

CHAPTER 8 TAKE-AWAYS

■ Performance measurement is the needle and thread that tie together strategy and execution and turn the LEERM into reality. It enables companies to achieve alignment and integration throughout the organization. More importantly, it allows people to measure the right things so everyone can tell if things are getting better.

■ Often there are disconnects between strategic performance and daily improvement activities. People do not set these disconnects up on purpose; they just happen because strategic improvement is a core competency that organizations must develop over time.

■ Performance measurement is not only concerned with measuring the right metrics. Performance measurement includes many levels, and it must be designed to link and align the organization. It must create that hard-wired spiral between the organization's strategy and its daily improvement activities. Otherwise, initiatives tend to wander away from the original objectives.

- Performance measurement is one of those topics that everyone knows everything about, except in practice. Remember the other theme throughout this book: There is a difference between *knowing how* to do something and *doing it right* every minute of every day.
- In the LEERM, the scope of performance covers the extended enterprise, the enterprise, core business processes, and daily operations performance.
- The LEEAP is the framework for measuring our LEERM model. The LEEAP framework incorporates the balanced scorecard concepts of customer, finance, internal business process, and learning/growth via 7 best practices and principles categories and 42 criteria (subcategories).

SUGGESTED FURTHER READING

Bossidy, Larry, Ram Charan, and Charles Burck, *Execution: The Discipline of Getting Things Done,* Crown Publications, 2002.

Kaplan, Robert and David Norton, *The Balanced Scorecard: Measures That Drive Performance,* Harvard Business School Press, 2000.

Nightengale, Deborah and the LAI, The Lean Enterprise Self Assessment Tool (LESAT) — Research Sponsored MIT Lean Aerospace Initiative, http://lean.mit.edu/Events/workshops/files_pu.

Niven, Paul, *Balanced Scorecard Step-by-Step,* John Wiley & Sons, 2002.

THE LEAN EXTENDED ENTERPRISE
ASSESSMENT PROCESS
Methodology and Definitions

The LEEAP is the formal performance measurement tool for the LEERM. The objective of this tool is to evaluate status and progress in migrating toward a Lean Extended Enterprise. A second objective is to provide a quantitative assessment of the organization's ability to execute, sustain, and realign itself for strategic improvement. The LEEAP consists of the following framework elements:

- **Categories:** There are seven major evaluation areas in the Best Practices and Principles Panel of the LEERM:
  1. Leadership
  2. Customer and market focus
  3 Uniform improvement infrastructure
  4. Value stream processes
  5. Extended enterprise integration
  6. Organizational learning
  7. Performance measurement
- **Criteria:** An expansion of the traditional *five basic principles of lean* into 42 distinct practices and principles of value stream excellence. There are 6 distinct practices and principles for each of the 7 categories, or 42 in total (refer to the Best Practices and Principles Panel in Figure 8.2).
- **Practice elements:** The specific evaluation points within each practices and principles criterion.
- **Frequency score (F):** A relative measure of the organization's sustainability and commitment on each of the practice elements (i.e., leadership, commitment, strategy).
- **Excellence score (E):** A relative measure of how well the organization is capable of achieving results on each of the particular practice elements (i.e., execution, technical competence).
- **Strategic focus score (S):** A measure of the organization's ability to detect a loss of focus and realign itself to achieve the desired strategic and operational results (i.e., measurement, alignment, sustainability).
- **LEEAP score (F $\times$ E $\times$ S):** A composite measure represented by the product of the frequency score, the excellence score, and the strategic focus score.
- **Comments and actions required:** Documentation of corrective actions required to improve the individual and composite scores for a particular practice element.

Matrix and Scoring Criteria

We have adopted a Likert scale scoring methodology similar to the approach used in failure mode and effects analysis or FMEA. In the LEEAP scoring criteria (Figures 8.3 and 8.4), a high score is "bad" and a low score is "good" for each of the criteria. This increases the mathematical ease of Pareto analysis and identifying areas for further focus.

Frequency Score (F)

0 — We are experts and this is a daily practice throughout the organization

2

4 — We have knowledge about this practice and are implementing

6

8

10 — We have never been involved in and have no knowledge about this practice

Excellence Score (E)

0 — We have achieved Best-in-Class performance with this practice

2

4 — We are beginning to achieve some measurable results

6

8

10 — We have achieved no measurable results

Strategic Focus Score (S)

0 — We have a formal alignment process throughout the value stream

2

4 — We are prioritizing efforts and need improvement in making adjustments to markets and customers

6

8

10 — We do not have the ability to detect misalignment and activities "off track"

FIGURE 8.3   LEEAP rating scale

	Frequency	Excellence	Strategic Focus
0	This is a subconscious daily practice throughout the enterprise.	We have achieved Best-in-Class performance with this practice across the total value stream.	We have formal systems and processes in place to monitor and adjust the total value stream.
1	This is almost a daily practice throughout the enterprise with occasional customer annoyances.	We have achieved competitive advantage and significant benefits from this practice.	We collaborate with customers and suppliers in real time about all business issues.
2	Customers experience annoyance when the practice is not followed.	We have achieved enterprise benefits and are migrating the practice beyond the four walls.	We collaborate with customers and suppliers on selected topics, not always in real time.
3	Customers experience dissatisfaction when the practice is not faithfully followed.	We have achieved benefits at the enterprise level in several key areas of our business.	We are working with selected customers and suppliers, with work-around versions of this practice.
4	Customers experience degradation in productivity and downstream customer service.	We have achieved good pilot results and are beginning to migrate the practice to other areas.	We have achieved benefits with a few suppliers on a few targeted projects with this practice.
5	Inconsistency in practice leads to warranty, repair, supply chain disruptions, and major complaints.	We are beginning to achieve islands of localized benefits as a result of this practice.	Need improvement in aligning activities to customers and markets and understand practice.
6	High degree of customer dissatisfaction and lost revenue opportunities.	We have been piloting the practice but have not achieved any measurable improvements yet.	We have been piloting the practice but have no way of telling if it's working or not.
7	Extremely high customer dissatisfaction without any impact on safety or governmental regulations.	We are beginning to pilot this practice.	We are beginning to pilot this practice.
8	Customers, the enterprise, and suppliers financially impacted by bad practice.	We understand the importance of this practice and have identified pilot implementation areas.	We recognize the need to realign ourselves with customer and market needs.
9	Customers endangered by product use and severe adverse customer service problems.	We are just beginning to understand the importance of this practice.	We limp along with a dysfunctional ERP system and many other homegrown or kluge systems.
10	Customer injured or severe consequences for bad performance (lost sales, legal, contractual penalties, etc.).	We have no understanding and experience in applying this practice.	We have no way of detecting problems and misalignment of activities until after the fact.

FIGURE 8.4 LEEAP scoring guide

THE LEAN EXTENDED ENTERPRISE ASSESSMENT PROCESS

Categories and Criteria	Frequency Score (F)	Excellence Score (E)	Strategic Focus Score (S)	LEEAP Score (F) (E) (S)	Comments and Actions Required
1. LEADERSHIP **Recognition of Need Internalized**					
The organization understands core competencies and limitations					
The improvement strategy is grounded to the organization's core competencies					
The organization is satisfied with the current state					
Best-in-class performance is known and we measure ourself against it					
The organization is very familiar with customer critical-to-customer (CTQs) and market requirements					
The gaps between current and best-in-class performance are known and documented					
The strategic plan addresses mandatory improvement expectations					
The organization is on track with meeting or exceeding the strategic plan					

THE LEAN EXTENDED ENTERPRISE ASSESSMENT PROCESS (continued)

Categories and Criteria	Frequency Score (F)	Excellence Score (E)	Strategic Focus Score (S)	LEEAP Score (F) (E) (S)	Comments and Actions Required
The organization has a clear vision for improvement					
The organization has defined additional resources and skills needed to support strategic improvement					
The improvement vision has been communicated and embraced by the entire organization					
The executive team is passionate about the improvement vision					
The executive team can articulate the organization's challenges and improvement vision uniformly					
Clarity in Direction and Goals					
A formal lean improvement strategy is in place					
The organization is able to monitor improvement needs and revise priorities					
The organization has a formal structure and process to ensure that it is engaged in the right value stream opportunities					
There is a documented Strategy of Improvement					

THE LEAN EXTENDED ENTERPRISE ASSESSMENT PROCESS (continued)					
Categories and Criteria	**Frequency Score (F)**	**Excellence Score (E)**	**Strategic Focus Score (S)**	**LEEAP Score (F) (E) (S)**	**Comments and Actions Required**
There is a formal process to continuously collect and synthe-size information and integrate the findings into the Strategy of Improvement					
The Strategy of Improvement balances needs across the total value chain					
The enterprise's response to known customer problems is more proactive and preventive, rather than reactive					
Goals and objectives are aligned to customer requirements, business plan, financial plan, and core competencies					
Improvement goals and objectives are quantified and documented					
Improvement goals are discussed openly and frequently					
Everyone in the organization understands the improvement goals					
The improvement goals are concise, quantitative, baselined, and physically measurable					
The barriers to improvement are identified and addressed promptly					

THE LEAN EXTENDED ENTERPRISE ASSESSMENT PROCESS (continued)

Categories and Criteria	Frequency Score (F)	Excellence Score (E)	Strategic Focus Score (S)	LEEAP Score (F) (E) (S)	Comments and Actions Required
The Strategy of Improvement is integrated into the business plan and financial plan					
Define Value Propositions					
Roles and responsibilities of improvement are defined (infra-structure)					
Business improvement is everyone's responsibility					
Leadership sets the expectation of business improvement					
Business improvement goals are part of the formal performance review process					
The Strategy of Improvement is aligned and cascades throughout all levels of the organization					
The potential concerns about change are evaluated and responses are prepared for employees					
There is a formal strategy to handle barriers, naysayers, union objections, etc.					

THE LEAN EXTENDED ENTERPRISE ASSESSMENT PROCESS (continued)

Categories and Criteria	Frequency Score (F)	Excellence Score (E)	Strategic Focus Score (S)	LEEAP Score (F) (E) (S)	Comments and Actions Required
Leadership has the courage to discuss potential outcomes — good and bad					
Values and Standards of Conduct					
Leadership has an unwavering commitment to improvement					
Executives walk the talk and champion improvement efforts					
Leadership deals head on with and removes the barriers to change					
Management understands and embraces empowerment					
Cross-functional barriers are being addressed					
People embrace teaming and employee involvement					
Leadership has defined expectations for behavior and professional standards of conduct					
The organization practices dignity, honesty, respect for others, and openness					

THE LEAN EXTENDED ENTERPRISE ASSESSMENT PROCESS (continued)

Categories and Criteria	Frequency Score (F)	Excellence Score (E)	Strategic Focus Score (S)	LEEAP Score (F) (E) (S)	Comments and Actions Required
People modify their own behaviors in the interest of the total value stream					
The organization is focused on process, not on politics and localized silos					
Awareness and Communication					
The organization is fully aware of the need to change					
The organization understands what needs to change					
Executives and key resources are fully accessible					
People understand how the organization will change					
The organization has achieved full acceptance and active involvement of the Lean Extended Enterprise vision					
People understand and accept their role in the change process					
The consequences of doing nothing are well understood by the organization					

THE LEAN EXTENDED ENTERPRISE ASSESSMENT PROCESS (continued)					
Categories and Criteria	Frequency Score (F)	Excellence Score (E)	Strategic Focus Score (S)	LEEAP Score (F) (E) (S)	Comments and Actions Required
There is a uniform, top-down improvement message delivered to the organization					
There is a two-way communication strategy in place					
There is a formal reinforcement process with regularly scheduled updates					
The organization conducts "improvement broadcasts" so everyone has a shared notion of goals, status, and planned activities					
Fluid Seamless Organization					
The organizational culture embraces change and is intolerable of protective functional silos					
Departmentalized functional silos have been eliminated					
The organization generates a high level of political push-back for change and improvement					
The organization views itself as a value stream component, not a stand-alone entity					

THE LEAN EXTENDED ENTERPRISE ASSESSMENT PROCESS (continued)					
Categories and Criteria	Frequency Score (F)	Excellence Score (E)	Strategic Focus Score (S)	LEEAP Score (F) (E) (S)	Comments and Actions Required
There is a comfort level with individuals working out of their norms and in cross-process activities					
There is a comfort level on the part of process owners when other people in the organization evaluate and critique their key business processes					
The organization and culture make it simple for teams to recruit resources based on skill needs					
Culture supports and encourages challenging of the norms					
The organization endorses skill-driven versus title-, political-, or longevity-based activities					
2. CUSTOMER AND MARKET FOCUS **Customer Intimacy and Value**					
The organization understands customer products, CTQs, markets, plans, and values					
There is a full understanding of the value stream and its issues					
The organization has initiated collaborative improvements					

THE LEAN EXTENDED ENTERPRISE ASSESSMENT PROCESS (continued)					
Categories and Criteria	Frequency Score (F)	Excellence Score (E)	Strategic Focus Score (S)	LEEAP Score (F) (E) (S)	Comments and Actions Required
Four-wall actions are aligned to increase customer success					
The enterprise has identified the highest impact opportunities					
There is also an understanding of emerging opportunities					
The enterprise is integrated into customer business plans					
Mass Customization					
The organization has identified custom solutions for its market needs					
The organization is positioned to design, produce, and deliver a wide variety of custom products and services					
The organization is proactive in steering customers to the right product and service offerings					
The organization is flexible and responsive to a variety of customer demand streams					
The organization manages demand across the total value stream in order to achieve flexibility and quick response					

THE LEAN EXTENDED ENTERPRISE ASSESSMENT PROCESS (continued)					
Categories and Criteria	Frequency Score (F)	Excellence Score (E)	Strategic Focus Score (S)	LEEAP Score (F) (E) (S)	Comments and Actions Required
The mass customization strategy is clearly linked to the organization's core competencies					
There is a proactive effort to balance standardization and product proliferation					
Pulse and Flexibility					
The organization has the capability to monitor and manage demand across the total value stream					
Upstream and downstream demand changes are managed in real time					
The value stream incorporates surge capacity and buffers to accommodate changes in demand					
The organization collaborates with customers and suppliers on value stream demand issues					
The enterprise has formal supply chain agreements with customers and suppliers					

THE LEAN EXTENDED ENTERPRISE ASSESSMENT PROCESS (continued)					
Categories and Criteria	Frequency Score (F)	Excellence Score (E)	Strategic Focus Score (S)	LEEAP Score (F) (E) (S)	Comments and Actions Required
Instantaneous Information and Response					
Channels are established for internal and external customers and suppliers					
Formal communication and response protocols are established					
The enterprise maintains a real-time data warehouse information system for customers and suppliers					
Priorities and urgency/escalation process guidelines are in place					
The roles and responsibilities for communication and response are clearly defined between the enterprise and its customers and suppliers					
Velocity Improvement					
The enterprise understands the importance of the value stream and its components and inefficiencies					
The organization has analyzed value stream variation and constraints and has many improvement initiatives in place					

THE LEAN EXTENDED ENTERPRISE ASSESSMENT PROCESS (continued)					
Categories and Criteria	Frequency Score (F)	Excellence Score (E)	Strategic Focus Score (S)	LEEAP Score (F) (E) (S)	Comments and Actions Required
The organization is collaborating with customers and suppliers to achieve value stream improvement goals					
There are several improvement initiatives under way to reduce cycle time, increase responsiveness, and eliminate value stream variation					
Solution Delivery					
The organization offers the best delivery, quality, and value for products and services in its markets					
The organization understand its customers' market directions and service delivery channels					
Enterprise resources are integrated into customers' marketing and new product development initiatives					
The organization provides new product solutions for customers' total value stream					
The organization provides collaborative technical, operations, and planning support for suppliers and customers					

THE LEAN EXTENDED ENTERPRISE ASSESSMENT PROCESS (continued)

Categories and Criteria	Frequency Score (F)	Excellence Score (E)	Strategic Focus Score (S)	LEEAP Score (F) (E) (S)	Comments and Actions Required
There is a formal strategy for delivering the enterprise's total capabilities and competencies					
3. UNIFORM IMPROVEMENT INFRASTRUCTURE **Data- and Fact-Driven Improvement**					
The organization has conducted a thorough self-assessment diagnostic and understands its strengths and weaknesses					
The self-assessment diagnostic has identified specific improvement needs and goals					
The organization understands the improvement goals, metrics, and baseline performance					
The plans for improving the value stream are based on data, facts, and customer leverage potential					
A formal project infrastructure and project management practices are in place					
The organization has the capability to conduct real-time project management and tracking of results					

THE LEAN EXTENDED ENTERPRISE ASSESSMENT PROCESS (continued)

Categories and Criteria	Frequency Score (F)	Excellence Score (E)	Strategic Focus Score (S)	LEEAP Score (F) (E) (S)	Comments and Actions Required
There is a uniform approach to value stream improvement that is fully integrated throughout the enterprise					
Project Selection Criteria					
There is a detailed implementation plan that defines activities, responsibilities, timelines, deliverables, and expected results					
There is a formal process to align business strategy and daily improvement activities					
The organization has a formal project selection process so that it can evaluate, align, and prioritize the highest impact opportunities					
The project selection process evaluates benefits, risks, completion time, resource commitment, and likelihood of success					
Project selection is a dynamic process that acts as a litmus test for improvement activities					
Value stream improvement projects are collaborative and include customers, suppliers, and other stakeholders					

THE LEAN EXTENDED ENTERPRISE ASSESSMENT PROCESS (continued)

Categories and Criteria	Frequency Score (F)	Excellence Score (E)	Strategic Focus Score (S)	LEEAP Score (F) (E) (S)	Comments and Actions Required
Customer and financial impacts are well understood before improvement projects are assigned to teams					
Value stream improvement projects are continually assessed against new opportunities					
Project selection ensures that limited resources are working on the most important value stream opportunities					
Chunking and Resource Management					
Leadership is committed to providing the right resources and the commitment to ensure project success					
The organization is committed to assigning individuals full time to strategically important improvement projects					
Projects and opportunities are broken into manageable implementation segments					
Projects are well defined at point of assignment					

THE LEAN EXTENDED ENTERPRISE ASSESSMENT PROCESS (continued)

Categories and Criteria	Frequency Score (F)	Excellence Score (E)	Strategic Focus Score (S)	LEEAP Score (F) (E) (S)	Comments and Actions Required
Leadership takes an active role in making time and resources available by prioritizing, postponing, and eliminating less important responsibilities					
Objectives, scope, improvement goals, timeline, resources, and deliverables are clearly defined					
Team members understand their responsibilities, commitments, and assignments					
The organization has a formal process to prevent resource overload and total team/individual ineffectiveness					
Contingency plans support the ease of reassigning and backfilling improvement projects as needs change					
There is a formal process to align projects, teams, and resources to the Strategy of Improvement					
The value stream implementation infrastructure regulates project flow, validation of results, and closure					

THE LEAN EXTENDED ENTERPRISE ASSESSMENT PROCESS (continued)					
Categories and Criteria	Frequency Score (F)	Excellence Score (E)	Strategic Focus Score (S)	LEEAP Score (F) (E) (S)	Comments and Actions Required
Empowerment and Teaming					
Employees embrace empowerment and teaming as the norm					
The organization has provided formal education on basic teaming, facilitation, group dynamics, basic problem-solving tools, conflict resolution, etc.					
People are comfortable taking risks, challenging norms, and making mistakes as part of the learning process					
Team activities are effective and produce tangible results (i.e., personalities, status, etc. checked at the door)					
Decision making is delegated to the point of process impact and control					
Individuals have the power to shut down a process that is generating recurring and out-of-control problems					
Teams are virtual, and turnover and redeployment are frequent occurrences					
Teams complete a single project and are not in place for long periods of time to conduct many projects					

THE LEAN EXTENDED ENTERPRISE ASSESSMENT PROCESS (continued)

Categories and Criteria	Frequency Score (F)	Excellence Score (E)	Strategic Focus Score (S)	LEEAP Score (F) (E) (S)	Comments and Actions Required
The word "team" is not a convenient name given to a production line or a department					
People take the initiative to volunteer for team-based improvement events					
Teaming is considered to be a normal responsibility of an individual's job					
Spectrum of Methodologies and Tools					
People understand the complete spectrum of improvement tools (kaizen, lean, Six Sigma, ERP, etc.) and how they fit different value stream situations					
People are focused on solving problems, not on implementing tools					
People view improvement tools as the means, not the ends					
Teams know how to deploy a broad spectrum of improvement tools					

THE LEAN EXTENDED ENTERPRISE ASSESSMENT PROCESS (continued)					
Categories and Criteria	Frequency Score (F)	Excellence Score (E)	Strategic Focus Score (S)	LEEAP Score (F) (E) (S)	Comments and Actions Required
Teams deploy the right tools correctly and to the right opportunities to achieve tangible improvements					
The organization has sponsored formal education on kaizen, lean, Six Sigma, ERP, and the integration of these methodologies					
Teams implement improvements without really thinking about whether they are involved in a kaizen, lean, or Six Sigma activity					
The organization discourages silos and camps of improvement methodologies					
The organization recognizes the importance of enabling information technology (IT) in value stream process improvement					
Achievement-Based Education					
Kaizen, lean, Six Sigma, and ERP education is customized to the specific requirements and business needs of the enterprise					
Value stream education and training are relevant and aligned to the Strategy of Improvement					

THE LEAN EXTENDED ENTERPRISE ASSESSMENT PROCESS (continued)					
Categories and Criteria	Frequency Score (F)	Excellence Score (E)	Strategic Focus Score (S)	LEEAP Score (F) (E) (S)	Comments and Actions Required
Education programs incorporate concepts and theory, plus relevant improvement issues					
Education programs include how to apply the concepts to the enterprise's specific operating environment					
Education requires that participants complete both classroom and real-life problem-solving assignments					
Participants in various education programs have completed mandatory projects for kaizen, lean, Six Sigma, and other improvement methodologies					
The enterprise has many certified lean and Six Sigma employees who champion improvement efforts and provide a spectrum of technical support					
The organization evaluates the effectiveness of its various education programs and makes the necessary changes					
The education program develops people on the correct application of various improvement methodologies and mentoring and leading teams					

THE LEAN EXTENDED ENTERPRISE ASSESSMENT PROCESS (continued)

Categories and Criteria	Frequency Score (F)	Excellence Score (E)	Strategic Focus Score (S)	LEEAP Score (F) (E) (S)	Comments and Actions Required
Education stresses the need to execute with data and facts and achieve results					
The organization develops individuals who become instructors and mentors of subsequent education and teaming activities					
4. VALUE STREAM PROCESSES **End-to-End Perspective**					
The organization views itself, customers, and suppliers as a single entity					
Collaboration occurs regularly between the enterprise and its customers and suppliers					
The organization initiates improvement activity outside of its own four walls					
Key business process owners have a value stream perspective					
There are direct dialogues between internal process owners and their external counterparts and stakeholders					

THE LEAN EXTENDED ENTERPRISE ASSESSMENT PROCESS (continued)

Categories and Criteria	Frequency Score (F)	Excellence Score (E)	Strategic Focus Score (S)	LEEAP Score (F) (E) (S)	Comments and Actions Required
The organization promotes co-location of internal and external resources to facilitate a value stream perspective					
Value Stream Pull/Rhythm					
The organization has the methodologies and tools in place to monitor demand and variation across the total value stream					
Logistics/material flow and information flow are seamless and real time across the value stream					
Lean Extended Enterprise practices and methodologies are in place and producing measurable results for customers, suppliers, and the enterprise					
The organization has implemented event-driven applications such as APS, CRM, SCM, and PLM					
The enterprise has specific techniques to manage process constraints and optimize the total value stream					
The enterprise has the ability to simulate what-if conditions and prevent critical value stream issues before they occur					

THE LEAN EXTENDED ENTERPRISE ASSESSMENT PROCESS (continued)					
Categories and Criteria	Frequency Score (F)	Excellence Score (E)	Strategic Focus Score (S)	LEEAP Score (F) (E) (S)	Comments and Actions Required
Soft Business Process Integration					
The organization understands the cash-to-cash implications of order administration, warranty/return, purchasing, invoicing, new product development, and other soft process activities					
The organization has documented performance gaps in key business processes and is aggressively pursuing value stream improvements in its soft process areas					
The organization has a defined, prioritized, ready-to-go pool of improvement projects in its soft process areas					
The majority of the organization's improvement efforts are focused on the soft process areas					
The organization has achieved dramatic results in cycle time, quality, and cost in its soft process areas					
Standardized Processes and Practices					
The Strategy of Improvement is the driver for structuring and standardizing business processes					

THE LEAN EXTENDED ENTERPRISE ASSESSMENT PROCESS (continued)

Categories and Criteria	Frequency Score (F)	Excellence Score (E)	Strategic Focus Score (S)	LEEAP Score (F) (E) (S)	Comments and Actions Required
Hard and soft processes are uniform and structured to optimize the total value stream					
The enterprise has avoided "one size fits all" and is structured along a variety of specific customers, products, and processes					
The value stream strategy embraces an "all customers are not equal" approach and enterprise resources are focused on serving various customer segments in different ways					
The enterprise collaborates with customers and suppliers to maximize revenues and profitability of the total value stream					
There is a formal, real-time "red-yellow-green light" management practice in place to monitor process performance					
Improvement programs follow a uniform approach and methodology across the entire organization					
Stability and Variation Reduction					
Process variation is quantified and the associated root causes are documented					

THE LEAN EXTENDED ENTERPRISE ASSESSMENT PROCESS (continued)

Categories and Criteria	Frequency Score (F)	Excellence Score (E)	Strategic Focus Score (S)	LEEAP Score (F) (E) (S)	Comments and Actions Required
Six Sigma is a very active improvement program to reduce variation in the soft process areas					
Individuals routinely apply the concepts of process mapping, process capability, root cause analysis, and corrective action					
FMEAs, fishbone diagrams, and basic statistical analysis are frequently applied in the soft process areas such as accounting, marketing, engineering, supply chain, etc.					
Six Sigma methodologies are routinely used to rationalize new product designs and evaluate supplier capabilities to deliver to these requirements					
The enterprise conducts replication activities to ensure that root causes of variation have been eliminated					
Value Stream Quality and Perfection					
The enterprise embraces process quality and perfection in every aspect of the total value stream					

THE LEAN EXTENDED ENTERPRISE ASSESSMENT PROCESS (continued)

Categories and Criteria	Frequency Score (F)	Excellence Score (E)	Strategic Focus Score (S)	LEEAP Score (F) (E) (S)	Comments and Actions Required
Individuals throughout the enterprise think in terms of process, inputs, outputs, defects, root causes, and corrective actions					
The organization has implemented IT solutions beyond ERP to enable perfection and quality beyond its four walls					
Process improvements are due to real preventive actions, not changes in volume, mix, or other irrelevant factors					
The organization focuses on process improvement first, followed by process automation					
5. EXTENDED ENTERPRISE INTEGRATION **Single Entity, No Walls**					
Upstream, downstream, and enterprise values are quantified, balanced, and aligned for the benefit of the total value stream					
Doing business with customers and suppliers feels like a four-walls process where everyone is seamlessly integrated					
The enterprise and its customer and supplier organizations are virtual					

THE LEAN EXTENDED ENTERPRISE ASSESSMENT PROCESS (continued)				
Categories and Criteria	**Frequency Score (F)**	**Excellence Score (E)**	**Strategic Focus Score (S)**	**LEEAP Score (F) (E) (S)**	**Comments and Actions Required**
Trust, security, honesty, and mutual respect are practiced be-tween the enterprise, its customers, and its suppliers					
The organization has implemented IT to enable collaboration and communication across a wide variety of customer and supplier application platforms					
Collaborative Development Processes					
Customers and suppliers collaborate globally on new product ideas and market opportunities					
Customers and suppliers are jointly involved in new product development					
Product and process development is fully integrated across total value stream					
There is value stream collaboration on concurrent engineering, project management, cost, resource utilization, and real-time problem resolution					

THE LEAN EXTENDED ENTERPRISE ASSESSMENT PROCESS (continued)

Categories and Criteria	Frequency Score (F)	Excellence Score (E)	Strategic Focus Score (S)	LEEAP Score (F) (E) (S)	Comments and Actions Required
Collaborative development is integrated with SCM, CRM, SRM, and other activities					
Collaborative development includes Design for Six Sigma					
Collaborative development addresses regulatory, safety, environmental, and hazardous issues across the total value stream					
Collaborative Planning Processes					
Value stream processes are designed to accommodate dynamic change					
Collaborative planning facilitates instantaneous communication and response on all business relationships					
Collaborative planning provides a single-pipeline view of the total value stream					
Visibility of information and requirements between facilities is instantaneous and real time					

THE LEAN EXTENDED ENTERPRISE ASSESSMENT PROCESS (continued)

Categories and Criteria	Frequency Score (F)	Excellence Score (E)	Strategic Focus Score (S)	LEEAP Score (F) (E) (S)	Comments and Actions Required
Tedious transactional processes between the enterprise and its suppliers have been improved via enabling IT solutions beyond ERP					
The enterprise and its customers and suppliers share real-time planning information and collaborate on various supply line issues					
Collaborative planning analytics to simulate and optimize value stream performance					
Collaborative Commerce Processes					
The enterprise defines, anticipates, and accommodates customer and supplier activities across the total value stream					
Supplier capabilities are quantified, followed by specific collaborative improvements					
Kaizen, lean, and Six Sigma improvement methodologies are standardized across the total value stream					
Supplier relationships are seamlessly synchronized to the total value stream					

THE LEAN EXTENDED ENTERPRISE ASSESSMENT PROCESS (continued)

Categories and Criteria	Frequency Score (F)	Excellence Score (E)	Strategic Focus Score (S)	LEEAP Score (F) (E) (S)	Comments and Actions Required
The tedious processes of order administration, inventory movement, and other transactions between customers and suppliers have been simplified					
The enterprise has defined and eliminated redundancies between itself and its trading partners					
The organization is pursuing non-traditional web-based sales and marketing channels as a growth strategy					
Online Marketplace					
Customer/supplier exchanges and networks are defined to ensure optimum value stream performance					
The organization has web-based applications to support product sourcing, application and technical data, and configuration options					
The enterprise makes it easy for customers to conduct e-business transactions for placing and checking the status of orders					
The enterprise supports web-based customer service and warranty activities					

THE LEAN EXTENDED ENTERPRISE ASSESSMENT PROCESS (continued)

Categories and Criteria	Frequency Score (F)	Excellence Score (E)	Strategic Focus Score (S)	LEEAP Score (F) (E) (S)	Comments and Actions Required
The enterprise has simple processes in place to manage sourcing, contract management, payment settlement, performance measurement, and problem resolution					
Other IT Enabled Technologies					
Business systems enable real-time seamless information availability across the total value stream					
Information is fully available and accessible across the Lean Extended Enterprise					
The enterprise has moved beyond ERP and has implemented SCM, CRM, SRM, PLM, networks and portals, and other Internet-based enabling value stream technology					
Total value stream interface processes are documented and standardized					
Individuals and value stream stakeholders share information in real time					
IT enabled "chat-room-like" processes are in place across the total value stream					

THE LEAN EXTENDED ENTERPRISE ASSESSMENT PROCESS (continued)					
Categories and Criteria	Frequency Score (F)	Excellence Score (E)	Strategic Focus Score (S)	LEEAP Score (F) (E) (S)	Comments and Actions Required
6. ORGANIZATIONAL LEARNING **My Business Mind-set**					
Individuals have a business process orientation and place a higher emphasis on process versus area performance					
Employees think and act like business owners					
The organization is serious about value stream improvement, and individuals are intolerant of others who are "winging it"					
People look beyond their own areas for opportunities to enhance organizational performance					
Professional Growth Experiences					
The enterprise fosters a learning and professional development environment					
The enterprise recognizes and rewards individuals for collective experiences and contributions outside of their normal duties					
The organization encourages a constant flow of new ideas and its people to challenge the accepted business practices					

THE LEAN EXTENDED ENTERPRISE ASSESSMENT PROCESS (continued)					
Categories and Criteria	Frequency Score (F)	Excellence Score (E)	Strategic Focus Score (S)	LEEAP Score (F) (E) (S)	Comments and Actions Required
Education and professional development are designed to concurrently expand the organization's core competencies and develop the individual's skills					
The culture encourages out-of-the-box thinking, risk taking, and making mistakes as part of the individual learning experience					
Knowledge Management					
A formal knowledge management repository is in place					
Individuals are able to learn from the collective experiences of other individuals in the organization					
The organization leverages its combined internal knowledge through collaboration and information sharing					
The organization leverages its ability to service customers and markets via total value stream knowledge					
The enterprise has formal practices to ensure that knowledge is disseminated and integrated into the organization's decision-making processes					

THE LEAN EXTENDED ENTERPRISE ASSESSMENT PROCESS (continued)					
Categories and Criteria	Frequency Score (F)	Excellence Score (E)	Strategic Focus Score (S)	LEEAP Score (F) (E) (S)	Comments and Actions Required
Relationship Management					
Organizational boundaries are seamless and encourage direct communication between value stream stakeholders					
The organization and culture encourage relationship building and knowledge sharing across key business processes and beyond the four walls					
Individuals are provided with opportunities for personal and career growth through interim assignments in other areas of the organization					
The organization fosters an environment characterized by direct peer-to-peer collaboration regarding value stream issues					
Politics is replaced by trust, mutual respect, collaborative problem solving, and performance					
Change as the Norm					
Change is occurring across the extended enterprise, not in pockets or isolated areas					

THE LEAN EXTENDED ENTERPRISE ASSESSMENT PROCESS (continued)

Categories and Criteria	Frequency Score (F)	Excellence Score (E)	Strategic Focus Score (S)	LEEAP Score (F) (E) (S)	Comments and Actions Required
People except and embrace change as the norm of conducting business					
The organization provides professional development opportunities for its people, so they are equipped with the right tools and skills for change					
The status quo and lack of change create a sense of nervousness in the organization					
People have learned to benefit from change, rather than become victims of change					
Cultural Transformation					
The organization stresses learning and personal discovery as an enabler of cultural change					
The organization invests the time and effort to transform culture, rather than through edicts or hopes					
Executives lead cultural transformation by example					

THE LEAN EXTENDED ENTERPRISE ASSESSMENT PROCESS (continued)					
Categories and Criteria	Frequency Score (F)	Excellence Score (E)	Strategic Focus Score (S)	LEEAP Score (F) (E) (S)	Comments and Actions Required
The Strategy of Improvement provides a structured process for individuals to learn and apply new skills, benefit from their experiences, and modify their perspective about change					
Executives create inertia and critical mass so that individuals accumulate a wealth of new positive experiences with change					
7. PERFORMANCE MEASUREMENT **Cash-to-Cash Perspective**					
The organization leverages key business processes to reduce cash-to-cash cycle time					
The organization has aggressive but fair cash management practices rather than relying on accounting games to achieve financial goals					
The organization is pursuing multiple improvements across the total value stream, which are geared to improve cash and asset management					
Relevant performance measures are defined and in place to measure cash-to-cash effectiveness					

THE LEAN EXTENDED ENTERPRISE ASSESSMENT PROCESS (continued)

Categories and Criteria	Frequency Score (F)	Excellence Score (E)	Strategic Focus Score (S)	LEEAP Score (F) (E) (S)	Comments and Actions Required
There is alignment between the Strategy of Improvement and daily improvement activities					
The organization deploys IT to enable cash-to-cash improvements					
Closed-Loop Financial Validation					
There is a formal feedback process to link the Strategy of Improvement to actual improvement outcomes					
The organization has formal feedback systems to evaluate the effectiveness of key business processes					
The organization uses a balanced scorecard approach for measuring performance					
Potential benefits of proposed improvement projects are validated by the financial organization					
Executive leadership promotes the practice of linking operational improvements to financial performance					
The financial organization is heavily involved in value stream improvement programs					

THE LEAN EXTENDED ENTERPRISE ASSESSMENT PROCESS (continued)

Categories and Criteria	Frequency Score (F)	Excellence Score (E)	Strategic Focus Score (S)	LEEAP Score (F) (E) (S)	Comments and Actions Required
Savings from improvement projects are validated by the financial organization					
Value Stream Performance					
The organization has implemented specific practices to monitor demand, quality, cost, and velocity across the total value stream					
Performance measurement practices identify value stream constraints in real time and allow people to collaborate and resolve problems					
The enterprise proactively assists customers and suppliers on critical value stream issues					
Strategic Performance					
The enterprise has a "bead" on mission-critical customer requirements and uses this information to drive strategic performance					
The enterprise forecasts and commits to future levels of improvement during the budgeting process					

THE LEAN EXTENDED ENTERPRISE ASSESSMENT PROCESS (continued)

Categories and Criteria	Frequency Score (F)	Excellence Score (E)	Strategic Focus Score (S)	LEEAP Score (F) (E) (S)	Comments and Actions Required
Formal benefit-sharing practices are in place with customers and suppliers					
The performance measurement system closes the loop between the strategic business plan, the Strategy of Improvement, and actual improvement outcomes					
The organization has the right metrics in place to gauge strategic activities such as market penetration, new product launch effectiveness, strategic alliances, etc.					
Organizational Performance					
Improvement is part of the individual's performance plan					
Formal recognition and rewards practices are in place and linked directly to team and individual performance					
The organization has an established gainsharing program in place with employees					
Formal skill- and knowledge-based compensation practices					

THE LEAN EXTENDED ENTERPRISE ASSESSMENT PROCESS (continued)					
Categories and Criteria	Frequency Score (F)	Excellence Score (E)	Strategic Focus Score (S)	LEEAP Score (F) (E) (S)	Comments and Actions Required
The organization uses 360-degree performance review practices					
The organization has metrics in place to measure the climate for change and cultural acceptance					
The organization has metrics in place to measure learning, individual development and growth, and educational effectiveness					
Social and Economic Performance					
The business strategy includes initiatives that positively impact the enterprise, the total value stream, the community, and other legal and ethical considerations					
The enterprise collaborates and provides resources to help other stakeholders in the value stream					
The enterprise promotes excellence and provides employee resources to conduct community service					
The enterprise provides external education assistance and services such as tuition reimbursement, counseling, ESL, financial planning, etc.					

THE LEAN EXTENDED ENTERPRISE ASSESSMENT PROCESS (continued)					
Categories and Criteria	Frequency Score (F)	Excellence Score (E)	Strategic Focus Score (S)	LEEAP Score (F) (E) (S)	Comments and Actions Required
The enterprise supports and encourages local community service by its employees					
The enterprise is viewed as a vital part of its community					

9

VALUE STREAM INTEGRATION: A KEY ELEMENT OF SUCCESS

We have covered a lot of ground about the Lean Extended Enterprise and strategic business improvement. This chapter provides additional information and insights about value stream integration and other related topics.

CONSISTENCY OF INTEGRATION

As we have mentioned several times, many organizations have consumed a lot of time flitting from buzzword program to buzzword program. Blindly following a guru's latest buzzword fad reduces the organization's creativity to a rigid set of commoditized improvement actions. Ultimately it creates a tremendous amount of confusion as the organization moves from fad to fad, and it also destroys leadership credibility when these "flavor-of-the-month" programs fail. When you walk into an organization that is anti-change, leadership usually has a lot to do with it. We have seen many organizations that did total quality management (TQM) in 1994, reengineering in 1995–1997, enterprise resource planning (ERP) in 1999, lean in 2000, and Six Sigma in 2002 and have failed miserably at all of these efforts. What is the appetite for another improvement program for these organizations? The larger challenge is getting organizations like this to change once they have been through the disappointing spin cycle of improvement programs. These organizations must step out of their "paintball and smorgasbord" approaches and learn quickly how to benefit from improvement before they become victims of their competitors' improvements. We came across the following quote in our research which proves that the challenge of consistent improvement is not a new concept:

> We trained hard — but it seemed that every time we were beginning to form up into teams we would be reorganized. I was to learn later in life that we tend to meet any new situation by reorganizing; And a wonderful method it can be for creating the illusion of progress while producing confusion, inefficiency and demoralization.
>
> *—Petronius, 70 A.D.*

Consistency of the message and focus are important; that's why the "flavor-of-the-month" programs fail. Consistency avoids feeding people 50 different versions of the same thing and confusing them. Consistency and focus lay down the right set of priorities, expectations, and thought processes to drive the right actions. Consistency of the message must be followed by consistency in actions and behaviors. Otherwise people will become very cynical if they hear one message and observe a different action. Organizations must adopt the philosophy that they only have one chance to get these things right, then pour in the leadership, commitment, improvement infrastructure, and measurements to ensure success. With the right unwavering leadership, strategy, and successful execution, we can make changes at clockwork speed because the methodologies and enabling information technology (IT) are available to us. Those organizations that do this right will make giant-step improvements before their competitors know what hit them.

THE DIMENSIONS OF VALUE STREAM INTEGRATION

Integration is a key to the Lean Extended Enterprise. Figure 9.1 displays this graphically. First, organizations must expand their focus *vertically* and get off the shop floor. We have beat the shop floor to death with previous improvement programs and that is not where the large opportunities exist. In many cases, manufacturing groups are ahead of the improvement power curve, and we can learn several good lessons from their experiences. The largest opportunities in most organizations lie in their soft process areas. Many of these soft processes are untouched territory and ripe for improvement, and organizations can make dramatic improvements rapidly. Opportunities in the warranty/returns, invoicing, quotations, customer service, purchasing, sales and marketing, new product development, and human resource areas are in the millions of dollars. Organi-

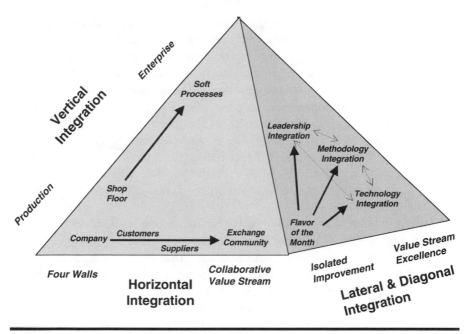

FIGURE 9.1   Total business integration

zations can get at these opportunities by applying many of the improvement methodologies familiar to their manufacturing groups, such as structured kaizen events, lean assessments (e.g., value stream mapping and waste elimination, cycle time reduction, flow synchronization, basic quality improvement, etc.), and Six Sigma to situations that have more complex process variation.

Migrating into the soft process areas requires strong leadership with a consistent message about improvement. In too many organizations, it's easy to point fingers at the manufacturing group and take the status quo or automation route in the soft process areas. It's easy to blame the ERP monster when business processes fail, but the reality is that improvement is 95% process and 5% system. One of the most rewarding experiences is watching people conduct Six Sigma projects in their backyard. The education changes their perspective, but they are required to deep dive into causals and follow the methodology. They discover that the *problem is me,* and then they make the necessary changes and *live* the improvements. Humbling experiences turn soft process employees around, and it is much more effective than lectures and improvement edicts. Encourage, don't penalize, because this is the best way to develop change agents. You get a lot more out of people through encouragement rather than threats and punishment.

We need to get everyone in the organization thinking about process improvement, root cause, and solving problems. People's employee status may be exempt, but no one is exempt from improvement. Everyone in the organization is part of one or many processes that can be dissected and improved. As we mentioned earlier, think *root causes* for the issues in manufacturing because the majority of them are defects in the soft processes. Take a hard look at these soft process areas and their potential impact on the enterprise's *cash-to-cash* position, design or delivery performance, costs, and customer satisfaction. Process improvement, simplification, and defect reduction in the soft areas has a positive residual impact on the IT world. Enough said. We must move beyond the production floor to the high-impact "soft process" areas. We need to go *vertical* with our lean efforts.

Another aspect of integration involves transforming our lean thinking *horizontally* beyond the four walls to the total value stream. The opportunities beyond the four walls are enormous because 70 to 95% of the customer-impacted activities, cycle times, and costs are generated in these segments of the supply chain. The benefits of instantaneous demand and supply adjustment, business collaboration, and information exchange are pretty obvious, and we have covered these benefits earlier in the book. Part of this horizontal integration includes building the value stream community. This may also include relooking at core competencies and deciding to outsource or insource activities. It may include rationalization of product offerings, customers, suppliers, logistics, manufacturing locations, distribution, third-party service providers, and the like. These activities are focused on simplifying link paths in the total value stream to facilitate speed and collaboration. Some people are referring to these efforts as spiral or fractal collaboration structures. The most challenging effort in this stage is connecting the links electronically to facilitate collaboration and instantaneous upstream/downstream activities. This is where the focus on ERP, supply chain management (SCM), advanced planning and scheduling (APS), customer relationship management (CRM), product life cycle management (PLM), networks, exchanges, and portals, and other enabling technology comes into play.

We caution organizations not to take on another multi-million-dollar IT effort like ERP. These horizontal links can be built "a chunk at a time" with a deliberate and well-thought-out horizontal integration strategy and plan. You don't need another big-bang IT approach, and technology is not the sole enabler of the Lean Extended Enterprise. Take a more manageable, calculated building-block approach with smaller incremental successes. Learn a lesson from the ERP days: Don't write a blank check and rely on the promises of technology and software to solve all of the Lean Extended Enterprise issues. The bottom line here is that we need to step outside of the four walls, focus our lean integration efforts *horizontally,* and harvest these new opportunities across the total value stream.

The other focus of lean thinking is *lateral* and *diagonal* integration. This includes success through empowered people and teams, through creative leadership and cultural transformation, and through the integration of various improvement methodologies, ERP, and other enabling IT. The total value stream encompasses the full spectrum of process opportunities. Lateral and diagonal integration broadens our toolbox and our knowledge about applying the right tools to these situations. It helps us to move away from our preoccupation with the methodologies and tools themselves and focus on solving critical business problems. Lateral and diagonal integration also replaces functional silos and rigid chains of command with person-to-person knowledge networks.

Earlier in the book we covered the need for a Strategy of Improvement and our Plan-Deploy-Execute model. We also discussed how people have always had a fascination with the methodologies and tools of improvement. Lateral and diagonal integration includes the topics in Chapter 3. We need to take the time to develop a solid Strategy of Improvement. We need to let go of our old binary choice practices about improvement. We need to expand our toolbox because the total value stream includes the full array of problems and opportunities. Like your toolbox at home, you are very limited with just a hammer and a few screwdrivers. Pretty soon every problem starts to look like a nail or a screw. We need to stop the debates about kaizen, lean, Six Sigma, ERP, SCM, APS, CRM, PLM, and other improvement enablers and recognize that they all have their place in the Lean Extended Enterprise. The methodologies and tools are not magic mantras; they are simply tools of the trade that work well when deployed correctly and to the right opportunities. We need to provide new injections of skills so that people understand how all of the improvement methodologies fit together. We need to focus on integrating processes, people, and information across the total value stream. We need a more carefully planned and executed IT strategy focused on the most critical elements of value stream integration and to not let our IT investments skyrocket out of control like the last ERP cycle. Finally, we need to close the loop with real-time performance measurement. Everything begins and ends with performance measurement. This is what *lateral* and *diagonal* integration is all about.

INTEGRATION OF IMPROVEMENT METHODOLOGIES

In the Lean Extended Enterprise and in the realities of business improvement in general, there is a continuum of problems. If we blindfold ourselves and randomly select touch points in the total value stream (i.e., the production floor, purchasing, customer service, sales and marketing, engineering, IT, suppliers, customers, third-party distributors, etc.), this continuum of issues is a reality. Refer to Figure 9.2, which displays this graphically. On one end of this continuum there are the no-brainer improvement situations that require little to no analysis to resolve. Some of these require just action. There's a piece of crumpled paper on the floor that someone might trip over; pick it up. Another good example of this is housekeeping and the general physical organization and appearance of a work area. Kaizen-like events and in particular the 5S principles (sort, set in order, shine, standardize, sustain) are the best tools of choice. As we progress further along this continuum, we encounter more complicated situations that require further analysis. While we may still be in the realm of quick-strike improvement, the basic blocking and tackling tools (e.g., Pareto analysis, checksheeting and charting, fishbone diagrams, spreadsheet analysis, etc.) are best suited for these situations. As we continue across this continuum, we discover hard/soft process waste and material/information flow situations that are best eliminated by the lean principles such as value stream mapping, work cells, kanban and pull systems, quick changeover, and the like. Continuing further, we discover situations that are totally unexplainable — processes that contain very complex variation. Why does the molding machine produce scrap? What are the factors that contribute to excess/obsolete inventory or warranty and returns? Why is there so much unplanned maintenance? Why is there so much variation in productivity and quality across 50 operators running the same equipment? How can we improve the reliability of new products? What practices have the greatest impact on cash position? These are more complex problems that lend themselves to the Six Sigma methodology and tools. So far, we have discussed the methodologies and tools that are best suited to process improvement.

ERP, APS, SCM, CRM, SRM, PLM, and all of the other enabling technologies in Chapter 7 also play a critical role in this continuum and in the total architecture of the Lean Extended Enterprise. We need good information to solve any kind of problem in the continuum. More importantly, we need good *real-time* information to prevent problems from occurring in the first place. Some may argue that ERP and other enabling technologies are also tools to improve processes. In some earlier implementations, these technologies forced a discipline on organizations that was previously missing. In other cases, they added complexity and confusion, particularly when the organization began with bad processes and practices, and there was a lack of both business process education and application user education. One of the problems with many ERP implementations was the compression of education. In the interests of budgets and schedules, we rounded people up and gave them the abbreviated user manuals and the ERP crash course, and then we told them to go out and do great

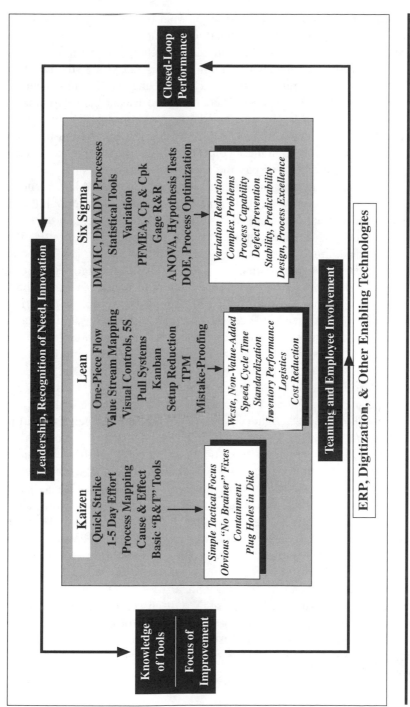

FIGURE 9.2 Integrating methodologies, tools, and enabling technologies

things. Many people understandably forgot what they learned almost immediately and began pushing buttons without understanding the implications up and down the total value stream. Others are still searching for the functionality or module that enables lean and many other things they're trying to do. For the past few years, people have muddled their way out of their Y2K implementations, but at great pain, waste, and cost. There's a good lesson here: Organizations need concurrent process improvement and automation, coupled with education. Time and budgets are certainly reasonable constraints, and we must learn how to improve and operate within these constraints. If the constraints are unreasonable, we must change them or pay the consequences.

The kaizen and lean methodologies discussed in Chapters 4 and 5 tend to be more *compensating* improvements in practice. Many people overlook the complex deep-rooted variation within each step of their key business processes and compensate via quick localized fixes, synchronized pull kanban, buffer inventories, cell scheduling/loading practices, visual management, and other techniques. This achieves improvement to a certain level. Six Sigma is more of a *perfection-driven* improvement, where we attempt to understand and eliminate variation and improve process capability. Six Sigma drives process performance to a new level. In Chapter 7, we covered the role of enabling IT for real-time collaboration and *instantaneous* improvement. The most important point is that *all* of these improvement methodologies have a role in achieving best-in-class performance. Correct deployment of the right methodologies to the right opportunities and priorities for improvement is always driven by the customer.

In summary, integration of the various improvement methodologies and tools is critical to success. Organizations will never see the Lean Extend Enterprise with a single "flavor-of-the-month" improvement program. You can't blitz yourself there in the next two to three months. You can't get there with the five basic principles of lean. You can't kanban yourself there. You can't get there solely with complex statistical tools. And you certainly can't get there by relying on technology. But you can get there with all of the above, deployed deliberately and correctly to the right value stream opportunities. *All* means a solid Strategy of Improvement, unwavering and relentless leadership, and integration of all the improvement methodologies and enabling technologies we have discussed in this section.

The remaining elements of Figure 9.2 are also critical infrastructure requirements for the Lean Extended Enterprise. We discussed the need for leadership and infrastructure development in Chapter 3 and performance measurement in Chapter 8. The next factor we will discuss is education, knowledge, and skills development, another critical infrastructure requirement for the Lean Extended Enterprise.

EDUCATION, KNOWLEDGE, AND SKILLS DEVELOPMENT

The need for education and knowledge development is obvious. Without education, knowledge, and new skills, people and organizations cannot develop the core competency of strategic improvement. When the purse strings get tight, it's difficult to justify investing in education, which is often the first casualty of budget-cutting exercises. Organizations hope things will still change when they tell their people to "make do" or "do the best you can," but for the most part, things remain the same. People in the organization need various levels of education to support a strategic improvement effort. They need to understand the need to change, the strategy of change, and their roles in the process. They need to understand and feel the organization's challenges and the consequences of doing nothing. They need a uniform implementation plan and approach. We have already discussed how confusing it can be when people are flying different banners of improvement. They need injections of new process improvement skills such as the kaizen, lean, Six Sigma, and other problem-solving tools we discussed earlier in the book. People need to be aware of customer and supplier expectations and then bolt on the right enabling technologies to their improvement initiatives.

Achievement-Based Education

As we all consider the billions of dollars invested in education for TQM, just-in-time, reengineering, lean, Six Sigma, ERP, etc., it is often difficult to justify the expenditures based on a straightforward return-on-investment calculation. About ten years ago, we began experimenting with different approaches to continuous improvement education, and to be honest, we have kept a low profile with our methodologies for obvious reasons.

There are two basic options for educating organizations on the methodologies of improvement:

1. **Provide off-the-shelf, generic education on the philosophies, concepts, and tools:** In this scenario, we hope for a critical mass that is smart enough to make the connection between concepts and reality and run with the ball. This approach usually leaves participants with some level of doubt and confusion about how to proceed. Often, the emphasis is on the mechanics of the tools themselves, with limited focus on the larger scope of improving competitiveness and profitability. Nothing much changes. When people return to their regular jobs, the knowledge begins to degrade until it's almost as if they never attended the training

at all. How many seminars and workshops have our employers sent us off to in our careers that had this kind of feeling? Education is only a piece of the total puzzle, and we hope that you're beginning to see that strategic improvement is a core competency by now.

2. **Customized, focused education integrated with the improvement strategy and focused on mission-critical opportunities:** In this scenario, the organization first identifies the strategic improvement infrastructure where education follows the improvement strategy, implementation plan, teaming assignments, and identification of opportunities. Next the education is customized around the organization's specific knowledge and skill set needs. The education includes the strategy and mission-critical opportunities that we need to improve. The education also includes real-life examples of how to apply the methodologies and tools to specific improvement areas. People walk away with a connection between concepts and reality and get right to work on their assigned projects. There's not the usual debates about applicability and whether we should change or not.

Most organizations have followed the first alternative because, on the surface, it makes so much sense. Many responses fall into the category of "Before we kicked off lean we needed to learn something about it first." There is so much groundwork that should be laid down before an organization thinks about education. Education without a strategy is like a mathematical vector with magnitude but no direction. Education without strategy also drives people on the trivial pursuit of implementing tools versus solving problems. For the past decade, we have adopted a real-world approach to education that we refer to as Achievement-Based Education (option 2 above). It has taken years of experimenting with various alternatives to improve education effectiveness, and the Achievement-Based Education model works well. During the classroom component, participants understand the strategy and implementation plans for change. They learn both the concepts and the nuts-and-bolts methodology of how to apply these concepts to their projects. One of the techniques we have used for years is called Half Fast, Inc.™,* a *Legos-based* participant simulation exercise where the company purchases, builds, and distributes products. This simulation exercise is designed and modeled around the participants' own value chains. In the first iteration, they experience the same frustrations as they do on a daily basis. Then they have the opportunity to apply the improvement concepts and experience the benefits during several subsequent iterations. Not only does it

---

* Half Fast™ is patented by The Center for Excellence in Operations, Inc. Legos® is a registered trademark of the Lego Company.

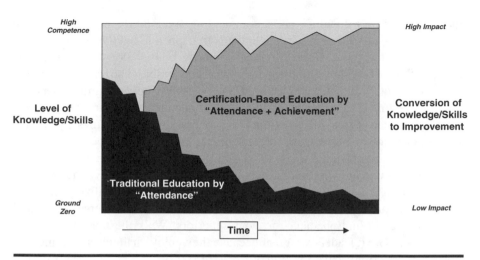

FIGURE 9.3 Achievement-Based Education

make the connection to their specific challenges, it drives home the point that you can always get better. This approach to education also has a more sustaining effect, as shown in Figure 9.3.

One of the major factors why Six Sigma has been so successful is because it has taken this Achievement-Based Education a step further to certification. Candidates complete the classroom time, but they also must complete a mandatory project and solve a real-world business problem, demonstrate their understanding of how to apply the Six Sigma methodology and tools correctly, and achieve a defined level of benefits.

We have covered the importance of project selection many times in this book. It is appropriate to remind you about how education and project selection go hand in hand. When education is coupled with the right projects, people experience the victory of improvement. These victories are the molecules of cultural transformation.

FIND THE LEADERSHIP AND HERO WITHIN YOURSELF

Think about why 80%+ of the people who most of us work with are unhappy at work. Some people are simply unhappy, no matter what they do. But the majority of these people are unhappy because they have allowed themselves to settle into comfortable routines. They might look outwardly and wish they could be promoted into a more responsible and challenging position, but their actions have allowed their thinking to become proceduralized and stagnant. They spend their days in "ain't it awful" mode, commenting about all the problems and the causes outside of their area. If we allow this to happen to ourselves, we become prisoners of the process. Then, when someone comes along to change the process that people have embraced forever, they resist change. Whether you know it or not, you're sitting on top of a very professional rewarding opportunity, but you need to break out of the mold, challenge what is around you, and take action. If you're involved in the soft processes of your business, you have the opportunity to solve many organizational problems and become a hero. Don't be afraid to take a few risks and find that new improvement opportunity. Tap the skills and knowledge of others, and work together to solve the problem. Don't be afraid of ambiguity. Deal with data and facts and revitalize your mind. Leadership comes from all directions. You will stifle your leadership potential by politics and blind obedience to your superiors. Walk the line, but be your own person. Great leaders are great because they enjoy challenges, and most of these leaders do not have the title VP or CEO.

In retrospect, I (TB) feel blessed that I learned *the fine art of stirring the pot* early in my career. Was I ever humbled or pushed back? Sure, many times. But it really bugged me when people sat in their cubicles resigned to inefficiency and bad performance when there was an obviously better, simpler, faster, cheaper way of doing things. The important point here is that when you're aggressive and armed with data and facts, you will get more people to notice and listen to you than those who flatly reject your ideas and push back. Great leaders recognize that they do not have all the answers, and they inspire their organizations to generate a constant flow of ideas. They appreciate initiative, good ideas, and well-thought-out game plans based on facts. They reward initiative, superior performance, and risk taking.

Another reality of the improvement business is resiliency: *the fine art of learning to run through walls.* Sometimes there's enough resistance to change — even if you're armed with the facts — and you bounce off! Did I ever provoke emotions? Sure, many times. It's a prerequisite for change. Did I have bosses who counseled me about politics and how "I can't" do something or "it's not the XYZ Co. way"? Sure, many times. Did I ever experience "You're right, but we're not changing it" situations? Yes, and so will you. Over the years, I learned that it's easier to ask for forgiveness than permission, especially when your analysis and facts are correct. Success is always forgiven. I was also fortunate to have a prior manager who taught me that "It's not the big news, it's how you package the facts and deliver the big news." Granted, many of these situations have wreaked of ambiguity, high emotion, and stress. A good change agent armed with data and facts helps people discover for themselves that these perceived barriers are 90% imaginary and 10% real. That's very rewarding. A bad change agent without data and facts helps to reinforce that these things are

90% real and 10% imaginary and nothing changes. I've had a hundred times more successes than disappointments, and the latter often taught me valuable lessons. I was not born with these skills, and I do not hold a Ph.D. in "stirring the pot." It only takes initiative — a quality that everyone has within them. Initiative is the first step in developing the core competency of strategic improvement. Starting today, don't let that quality within you lie dormant. Go out there and *stir your own pot*. Take the initiative to seek out opportunities for improvement and make yourself happy. Don't wait for permission; go out and push the envelope a little. When the walls knock you down, get up, look for the lessons learned, refocus your efforts, and be persistent if you are right.

Some leaders create these perceived barriers to upward communication. When you think about it, it's pretty ludicrous that people would look up to these people for direction, and so they use these barriers as an excuse to sit around and do nothing. In many cases, these executives are so busy with other issues like acquisitions, shareholder concerns, broader financial issues, and customers that they might not even be aware of their influence on the organization. We are not making excuses for these individuals, because great leaders make themselves accessible and available. But the reality is that the demands placed on executives these days are mammoth. When executives realize that these unintentional barriers exist, they do everything in their power to remove them. The point is that these individuals always welcome the help, especially on the topic of business improvement. For the most part, these barriers are an illusion, a mirage in your own mind. If you really believe that these barriers exist, you will probably act accordingly and make sure that there are barriers. Go out and bust the barriers because they are not real. You have a responsibility to your own conscience to take the initiative for business improvement because everyone in the organization has the power to lead and make a difference. Executives are extremely interested in improvement these days because everyone is under pressure to do more with less. If you sit around and do nothing long enough, you may end up on the *less* side of the *do more with less* equation.

Another organizational dilemma is the perception that asking for help or admitting that a process is not working is a sign of weakness and mismanagement. Sometimes people cover their tails or point fingers, and the organization suffers accordingly. Others postpone change or are not willing to admit that they need to change and are missing the internal skills to make it happen effectively. If your processes are broken, chances are they will not fix themselves for you. These are the true signs of weakness and mismanagement — knowing that there's a problem and not doing anything about it. Two different medical products manufacturers that were interested in lean and Six Sigma had very familiar stories: growth rates of 30 to 80% annually, record profitability, strong market positions, building new facilities, launching many new products, couldn't hire people fast enough, a real upbeat environment. Both CEOs commented that they were extremely pleased with their organization's performance, but they know they could do even better. They also wanted to protect their competitive position because when organizations are this successful, you can bet that someone else is looking to get into the action with a competitive or substitute product. The moral: What a paradigm shift — making improvements while you're healthy and successful. These two CEOs are true leaders.

IMPROVEMENT IS ALWAYS NECESSARY

The fact is, no matter where your current performance lies, it simply is not good enough beyond today. The world is moving at clock speed, technology and product life cycle are very short, and everyone is involved in business improvement. The diagonal vector and bandwidths in our Kano diagram (Figure 9.4) are rising at a much faster speed than many organizations can keep up with. However, this also provides the opportunity to leapfrog and surprise the competition with the right strategy. The Kano diagram represents this phenomenon graphically. For example, let's say you want to buy a $299 notebook PC. You call up HP Computer and learn that the price is $2,199. You are in the lower right

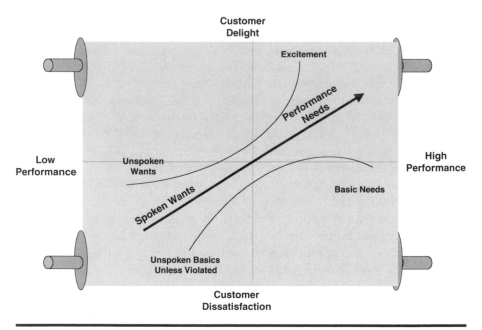

FIGURE 9.4   Demand-slide Kano diagram

quadrant — you're looking for performance but you are disappointed at the quoted price. Next you call Hell Computer and learn that it just introduced a notebook with everything you're looking for and the price is $99.95. Now you are elated and in the upper right quadrant of the Kano diagram. You are excited and place the order. When you receive your new notebook, the display is 1″ × 1″, the hard drive is 40 KB, not MB (a typo on the web site), and it doesn't come with a power cord. Now you're in the lower left quadrant of the Kano diagram because your assumed expectations were violated. Finally, you open the rest of the contents of the box and find three extra batteries, a bunch of CDs for AOL, QuickTime, CD Creator, game subscriptions, another catalog, a Hell umbrella, and a few other things that are not relevant to your needs. Now you are in the upper left quadrant of the Kano diagram. You return the box with all of its contents to Hell. In the process, you learn that Dell Computer has just introduced a notebook for $799. You compromise your price expectations, order the notebook, and are very happy with your decision. Now you are back in the top right quadrant and everyone else has slipped down and to the left. We are spending time on the Kano diagram because the combined dynamics of your customers, the organization, and your competitors are continually moving relative positions around on this model. In addition, customer and market needs and the combined responses to these dynamic requirements are causing the model to scroll up to higher expectation levels. Customer expectations (the diagonal bar) keep rising. Great organizations execute strategies that delight customers and in the process keep themselves in the top right quadrant of the Kano diagram. Organizations that do nothing will see their relative position slip quickly in the new demand-slide economy.

The best time to change is now. Great leaders recognize opportunities for improvement and the challenges faced by the people around them. They also find the time to initiate and lead improvement initiatives even thought it may look like the last thing they need to worry about. They have an overwhelming and unwavering resolve to prevail, no matter what may jump out at them. They have the faith and confidence that the organization can change without compromising current customer obligations. Finally, they create an open culture and problem-solving environment where improvement and celebrations replace blame and substandard performance.

STOP THE HAM SANDWICH IMPROVEMENTS

A familiar saying in the legal profession is that "attorneys can indict anything, including a ham sandwich." Unfortunately, many of our previous improvement efforts have resembled this statement. Sure, we can rearrange equipment and print kanban cards. We can hang up signage and shadowboards, purchase color-coded totes, and label everything in the place. We have seen organizations literally tie their business in knots with the various buzzword tools. Then they become so infatuated with trying to make their tools work that they forget about the original objective. One particular organization was a bit obsessive with its 5S program. It labeled every file cabinet and piece of equipment in the office — as if people needed help identifying the copy machine, the water fountain, the paper cutter, and the paper shredder. Amazingly, everything in the men's room was also labeled: the sink, urinal, toilet, paper towels, trash. What is the point? What is the purpose of our actions? How will the customer benefit from our actions? If we itemized the customer's invoice, would he or she be willing to pay for those labels in the men's room and the pretty cell signs as value-added activities? What particular problem are we trying to solve? How will our actions change the dynamics of our Kano diagram?

Each improvement tool by itself can provide some gains, but there is a danger of going overboard. It's like our analogy of a hammer looking for a nail earlier in the book. The most significant benefits are achieved by combining and integrating tools and deploying the right tools correctly to the highest impact opportunities. We need to ask ourselves these questions constantly because sheer motion is not improvement. Remember the ham sandwich analogy the next time you're thinking about improvement.

Mistakes are part of learning, unless you fail to learn from your mistakes. Learning is a lot like improvement: For some, it's a passion; for others, it's a knee-jerk reaction to a particular need. People are most successful when they develop a passion for both of these things, because one feeds the other. Learning is not always vital to the task at hand, but it rounds out and enhances careers and life in general. Improvements are not always successful on the first try either. Remember, the passion for learning and improvement is never wasted.

CHAPTER 9 TAKE-AWAYS

- Blindly following a guru's latest buzzword fad reduces the organization's creativity to a rigid set of commoditized improvement actions. Ultimately, it creates a tremendous amount of confusion as the organization moves from fad to fad, and it also destroys leadership credibility when these "flavor-of-the-month" programs fail.
- Consistency of integration avoids feeding people 50 different versions of the same thing and confusing them. Consistency and focus lay down the right set of priorities, expectations, and thought processes to drive the right actions.

- Organizations must expand their focus *vertically* and get off the shop floor. The greatest opportunities in most organizations lie in their soft process areas. Many of these soft processes are untouched territory and ripe for improvement, and organizations can make dramatic improvements rapidly.

- Organizations must transform their lean thinking *horizontally* beyond the four walls to the total value stream. The most challenging effort in this stage is connecting the links electronically to facilitate collaboration and instantaneous upstream/downstream activities. This is where the focus on ERP, SCM, APS, CRM, PLM, networks, exchanges, and portals, as well as other enabling technology comes into play.

- Lateral and diagonal integration ties the appropriate improvement methodologies, ERP, and other enabling technologies together. Lateral and diagonal integration broadens our toolbox and our knowledge about applying the right tools to these situations.

- Organizations need concurrent process improvement and automation, coupled with education. Integration of the various improvement methodologies and tools is critical to success. Organizations will never see the Lean Extend Enterprise with a single "flavor-of-the-month" improvement program.

- Achievement-Based Education follows the improvement strategy, implementation plan, teaming assignments, and identification of opportunities. The education is customized around the organization's specific knowledge and skill set needs, includes the strategy and mission-critical opportunities that need to improve, and incorporates real-life examples of how to apply the methodologies and tools to specific improvement areas.

- Great organizations execute strategies that delight customers and in the process keep themselves in the top right quadrant of the Kano diagram. Organizations that do nothing will see their relative position slip quickly in the new demand-slide economy.

SUGGESTED FURTHER READING

Devenport, Thomas, *Mission Critical: Realizing the Promise of Enterprise Systems,* Harvard Business School Press, 2002.

Godwin, Malcolm, *Who Are You: 101 Ways of Seeing Yourself,* Penguin Publications, 2000.

Waterman, Thomas, *Adhocracy,* Whittle Books, 1990.

THE LEAN EXTENDED ENTERPRISE: BRING IT ON

We have covered the critical elements of the Lean Extended Enterprise. We have also mentioned that strategic improvement is a core competency that companies must develop within their organizations. The world of real-time collaboration and virtual exchanges is here. The methodologies, tools, and enabling technologies are available to streamline and optimize critical value delivery processes across the total value stream. The Lean Extended Enterprise Reference Model (LEERM) provides a structured reference model to follow and integrates strategy and execution via the Plan-Deploy-Execute process. Hopefully, you have a better picture of how all of these things fit together to create the Lean Extended Enterprise. The next step is to become more familiar with the concepts, principles, and practices of the Lean Extended Enterprise. It all begins with leadership.

The Lean Extended Enterprise is an enormous improvement opportunity for every organization. The upside potential is almost unbelievable. Some organizations are reporting savings in the hundreds of millions to billions of dollars. The downside risk is manageable with great leadership. Chapter 3 outlined the ten pitfalls of strategic improvement, and we learned that the methodologies, tools, and enabling technologies are the least of our problems with success. We also learned that many of the methodologies and tools go back to before you were born. The following short article is reprinted from *Breakthrough!*, a quarterly newsletter published by The Center for Excellence in Operations, Inc.

Kaiser: A 1940s Version of Dell

It's amazing that many of the leading-edge management topics aren't really new at all. In 1941, Henry J. Kaiser was commissioned by the U.S. government to build a few very large cargo-carrying vessels. The first one took an astounding 90 days to build. (By the way, that was considered very impressive.) Henry quickly realized that this level of production was insufficient to sustain war efforts so he standardized on a common product platform. Aiming to become the Model T of shipbuilding, he created the Liberty Ship platform, which adopted identical subsystem features such as the engine, the control room, the gun turrets, and the total design. Then he began multiplying and standardizing on production facilities around the West Coast. He created a healthy, competitive team spirit among the shipyards. He roamed around constantly and acted on his workers' suggestions, and cycle times began falling dramatically.

Henry was a visionary of the leveraged supply chain. Rather than building the boat from the hull outward, Kaiser outsourced several modules such as the living quarters and control deck, which were fully assembled at other sites and then installed as a module at the shipyard. Henry also began one of the first successful concurrent engineering, design for manufacturability, group technology, and part reduction efforts, replacing, for example, millions of rivets with welding technology. This also contributed to the expansion of women employees in the shipbuilding industry.

Henry Kaiser was short on buzzwords, but he really understood the Lean Extended Enterprise. Kaiser's innovations enabled American war workers to produce great ships at an unheard of pace. Henry quickly standardized on common parts, materials, and subsystem interfaces. He also broke the rules about assembling ships by applying the concepts of design for modularity, lean manufacturing, and z-axis assembly. Henry recognized that Kaiser couldn't do everything well or fast enough, so he leveraged the competencies of other outside suppliers. Most important of all, Henry understood the customer's latent requirements. Riveted boats might last 100 years or more and take a greater beating on the high seas. But many of Henry's boats were sunk on their maiden voyage. The key was production faster than destruction. Welding was good enough: It was much faster, cheaper, and met the form/fit/function criteria of war.

The other shipbuilders were leery of maverick Henry and his new technology and methods. But Henry gained market dominance, leapfrogging over competitors who had been in the shipbuilding business 50 to 100 years. By 1945, Henry Kaiser had built over 2,700 battleships and had reduced the cycle time from 90 days to 4 days. During the war years Henry Kaiser increased his company's and his own personal wealth by billions.

Moral to the story: It doesn't matter what you call the latest management techniques. What really matters is leadership, commitment, vision and strategy, and a solid Plan-Deploy-Execute process across the total value stream. These factors worked for "Hurry-Up Harry" from 1941 to 1945, and they will work just as well for you today.

LEAN BEGINS WITH LEADERSHIP

Leadership is the turbo-charged engine that drives a successful Lean Extended Enterprise. It comes from all directions and also from beyond the four walls. After reading this book, you may feel overwhelmed as to where to begin your journey. We suggest that you begin with the following steps:

1. Build the courage and openness to see reality as it is. Every organization is involved in improvement, and it needs to become a daily business practice, like processing orders, checking e-mail, and sending out invoices. *No news is bad news* in the Lean Extended Enterprise. You are either gaining on or falling behind your competition, and *close enough is no longer good enough.*

2. Take the initiative to improve your business model now. Regardless of what has been done in the past, it simply isn't good enough beyond today. Strategic improvement is not dependent on industries, programs, life cycles, or silos. It resides within you as a leader. Take the bold step. It will be one of the most rewarding experiences of your career.

3. Conduct the right due diligence and understand gaps between current and best-in-class performance. Create a bold vision of where you would like the organization to be in the next 12 to 36 months. Don't be afraid to go for levels beyond which any other competitor has achieved. It's called breakthrough improvement, and the only limits are the limits you place upon yourself and the organization.

4. Revisit the organization's value system and cultural norms. Identify what needs to change, and then begin by setting the example for others. Begin developing and mentoring the leadership talent in others and assembling the champion change agents.

5. Develop the Strategy of Improvement and send a uniform message to the rest of the organization about the challenges, need to change, expectations,

and what's in it for all stakeholders. Deal with the barriers up front. Then execute, execute, and execute through everyone in the organization.

Leadership is not clustered at the top of the organization, and it can spawn from many directions. Leadership is within an individual, not within an office or a title. CEOs and executives must take the initiative personally to point their organizations in the right direction because leadership, vision, and the Strategy of Improvement are the most critical elements of change. Managers and individual contributors must also lead by pointing out the inequities in business processes rather than tolerating them. We are not insinuating that people should complain about every little detail. We are saying that everyone should put the principles in this book to work and Plan-Deploy-Execute. Think about the organization's *as is* state in terms of the Lean Extended Enterprise concepts, principles, and practices. Then let your mind go and imagine Lean Extended Enterprise utopia. Brainstorm and share your thinking with others; make the ground move. Lead and help the executive team think through where and how the organization needs to change. Stop tolerating waste and mediocrity in your business processes. As one individual said, "That's easy for you to say because you do not work here. It's better not to make waves and let the chips fall where they may in this economy because it's difficult to find another job." In our opinion, this is a very career-limiting perspective. These people wake up one day and wonder what happened to their careers, their personal values, and their lives. It's a fundamental career decision: Do you want to be a *champion* of change or a *victim* of change? It's that simple, and the risks of speaking out are imaginary if you use data and facts, professionalism, and logical analysis of current conditions.

CULTURE IS THE FOUNDATION

Another topic we discussed in the book is culture, the foundation of the Lean Extended Enterprise where ordinary people grow to do extraordinary things. Everyone may be at a different starting point. If your organization has the demonstrated core competency of strategic improvement in place, then hit the starting line. It's an anomaly that the best organizations use outside assistance because there is tremendous power, focus, and velocity with the injection of new thinking coupled with internal knowledge and experience. If you're new to strategic improvement and the concepts of the Lean Extended Enterprise presented in this book, the first thing you should consider is getting outside assistance. Keep in mind that many organizations have been working on these principles for a decade, and outside assistance will help you to accelerate the improvement process. On the surface, these things look easy to implement, but the devil is in the details of Plan-Deploy-Execute. If you're an organization with a track record of "flavor-of-the-month" programs, this is probably the toughest starting point to overcome. How do you convince an organization with a string of failed improvement programs that "this time we're really serious." It's about as difficult as trying to convince a herd of goats that they need quantum physics. You can't do it with a speech; it's a slow process based on demonstrated leadership, commitment, and results. It requires many hits of consistent communication, awareness, and dialogue — and sometimes an admission that we screwed up! It also requires extreme levels of patience and perseverance, and it may feel like you're turning the Queen Mary around in Boston Harbor. If you try to move quickly into another set of improvement frameworks and tools, it will only add to the confusion of mixed messages, and the barriers will be raised. Maybe you built this culture, maybe you didn't — but this type of culture will eat your strategy for breakfast if you do not recognize it and deal with it. Communication, awareness, rebuilding confidence, and change management are all critical to avoid another failed fad program. The Lean Extended Enterprise will manifest itself in direct proportion to the organization's collective leadership and passion to succeed.

Cultural transformation is not geography or industry or market or product or program or local culture dependent. We have heard so many excuses why organizations cannot change. They run the gamut from "we're located in Europe" to "we're out in the middle of Nowheresville, USA" to "we have a union" to thinking that "our employees are not smart enough to implement lean or Six Sigma." Is there a difference in improvement from enterprise to enterprise? Sure there is. But overall, business improvement is portable, and any organization can be successful with the right Plan-Deploy-Execute process. Recall an earlier chapter in which we talked about only two things in business and in life: performance and excuses. The right leadership doesn't let the excuses get in its way. Leaders develop and grow ordinary people to do extraordinary things in their organizations regardless of the particular characteristics of geography, markets, or products.

IT TAKES FOCUS, NOT HOCUS POCUS

The Lean Extended Enterprise may seem like an enormously overwhelming initiative to take on. It is a major strategic undertaking, and it will take years to get there. Many of the organizations listed in Chapter 7 have been at it for years. But to be successful, it requires focus.

The Strategy of Improvement is critical to the success of the Lean Extended

Enterprise or any other strategic improvement initiative. Organizations that short-circuit this important step end up with a significant disconnect between means and ends. They fail to establish a dynamic process for defining new opportunities, establishing priorities, aligning and managing critical resources, and judging success. They embark on another "flavor-of-the-month" program destined for failure because:

- The primary focus ends up on activities and tools, not results.
- A focus on activities and tools leads to improvements in unimportant areas, cosmetic/transparent improvements, and political/fictional improvements.
- There is no alignment between the strategic needs of the organization and the daily improvement activities that people are involved in, and it also fosters a false sense of improvement.
- Limited improvement resources are misallocated and consumed by trivial or symptomatic efforts, and people are intelligent enough to question the value of their assigned improvement projects.
- Many improvements are claimed; however, overall business performance fails to improve.

Regardless of the specific approach used to develop a Strategy of Improvement, the goal is not to solve problems at this point. The goal is to understand core value-creating processes, identify gaps and opportunities, calibrate pain points and opportunities, think through the implementation approach, and begin communication and awareness efforts. Tangible and significant business improvement comes from understanding and improving the core business processes in the total value stream. Failure to develop a solid Strategy of Improvement is analogous to a balloon full of hot air. We can blow it up and let it go and it will fly around the room, but quickly it falls to the floor — just like "flavor-of-the-month" programs do.

During the Strategy of Improvement stage, it is often helpful to conduct executive brainstorming sessions and create a high-level enterprise business map. This identifies the core business processes in the value stream, their interdependencies and interrelationships, and key performance issues that need to be addressed. The enterprise business map should also be populated with descriptive data such as value-added, cost, waste, cycle time, and pain points. We can take this down a level of detail and conduct preliminary data analysis to validate our collective insights. The enterprise business map usually provides excellent insights about where to focus initial efforts.

One of the characteristics of a solid Strategy of Improvement is focus. We want to avoid sending limited resources off to *boil the ocean* or *solve world hunger*. The best and easiest way to accomplish this is by using multi-level

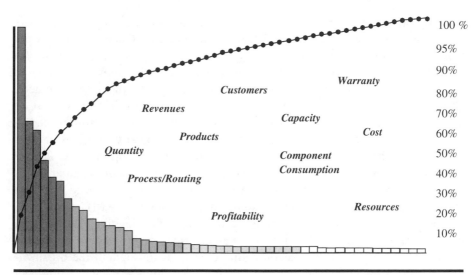

FIGURE 10.1   Multi-level Pareto analysis

Pareto analysis (Figure 10.1). When you consider all of the content in this book, the Lean Extended Enterprise is overwhelming. Multi-level Pareto analysis enables us to analyze various factors of our business in relation to each other. In essence, the objective of focus is to answer questions such as:

- What 20% of our customers generate 80% of revenues?
- What 20% of our products generate 80% of revenues?
- What 20% of our products generate 80% of profits?
- What 20% of our inventory items represent 80% of our inventory investment?
- What products flow through what process steps or routings?
- What 20% of our products consume 80% of capacity?
- What products consume what raw materials?
- What is the distribution of risk priority numbers (RPNs) in the failure mode and effects analysis for an inefficient cash-to-cash cycle?
- What are the stratified expenditures by supplier?
- What is the distribution of root causes for unplanned downtime?
- What are the warranty costs by product and by customer?
- What is the distribution of ECNs versus obsolete inventory?

What insight does this type of analysis provide to us? It helps us to focus on the critical 20% of the problems that will generate 80% of the results. If we try to focus on everything, we will spread our resources too thin and end up working on the other trivial 80% of the problems. As you deep dive into the relationships between these critical factors, the Lean Extended Enterprise becomes a lot less overwhelming. Multi-level Pareto analysis is also very useful for the chunking and project selection activities covered earlier.

Another characteristic of a solid Strategy of Improvement is alignment. Everyone talks about this concept, but few organizations do it well, at least on a continuous basis. Alignment is not a natural phenomenon. It requires leadership and a formal alignment process that links strategy to daily activities in more real time. It's not an alignment module per se in a software application. It's the culmination of people, processes, and enabling technology in collaboration across the total value stream. Supply chain management (SCM), advanced planning and scheduling (APS), customer relationship management (CRM), supplier relationship management (SRM), product life cycle management (PLM), and portals enable real-time collaboration and alignment. Without alignment, there's a natural tendency to drift into conflicting objectives throughout the organization, rather than staying focused on mission-critical improvements. Alignment provides a crystal-clear link between the Strategy of Improvement and the day-to-day improvement activities throughout the organization.

SUCCESS CAN BE FAILURE IN DISGUISE

Another observation that has always frustrated us personally is an organization's failure to recognize the need to improve. Many executives are indecisive and spend too much time in denial mode. Reality is about to run them over, but they hang on to their hopes and wishes that things will turn around. Hopes and wishes are not strategies or methodologies of improvement. Others foster an attitude of "We're doing okay, let's hold off for now." This really frustrates indignant people who want to do the best they can at their jobs. Improvement is not bad, — it's a good thing! About 90% of the time it requires a catastrophic event to turn the organization's lights on, because people think of improvement as a response to problems, not something you do when you're experiencing success. The best examples of this situation are the high-revenue growth organizations in emerging markets. When many organizations are repeatedly successful, they begin to believe that they have found the magic success formula and are not subject to the human fallibility or the same economic constraints of other organizations. The 30 to 50% revenue growth situations are temporary. When an organization is growing at this rate, it cannot install the infrastructure fast enough to support these levels. Revenue growth is only camouflage for waste. Every organization has waste: it is less visible in high-growth organizations. There are many successful organizations out there that could probably *double* their margins if they were serious about strategic improvement. The interest levels increase as it becomes painfully obvious that the growth and margins can no longer hide the inefficiencies of bad processes.

ON A ROLL VERSUS OWNING THE ROLL

Successful organizations go through a familiar evolution in high-growth situations. The first stage is referred to as the *on-a-roll* stage. During this stage, the organization is multiplying its more-of-the-same strategy at an accelerated rate. It is too busy to focus on improving current practices, so it supports growth by cloning current practices. Specifically, this is the hiring of people and increased capital spending for additional equipment and facilities. This is the right first response to high growth, because organizations must do something immediately. Many organizations stay in this mode too long, and eventually a stronger competitor catches up to them. In fact, many organizations get stuck in this *more-of-the-same ten times over* mode to their ultimate detriment. They get *rolled over* by their competitors.

Another common practice, particularly in high-growth technology hardware and software organizations, is *process push-back.* This is the situation where there is no standard process for developing new products/processes, except in the ISO manuals. Product development is viewed as a craft; individuality of designs, component parts, and suppliers are promoted. Worse yet, margins are high and the organization has a track record of success with this operating model: first to market, followed by high warranty/repair costs, software downloads, and other patches. Executives in these organizations have been heard to make comments like "We have to run our business this way...We would not have been as successful if we had a formal stage/gate process or used Design for Six Sigma techniques to improve designs and processes...Is this software or black magic? Customers do not expect perfection...We have schedules to meet." There is a perception in these organizations that standardized, more capable processes would only get in their way. The sad truth is that it would make them even more successful by enabling more leverageable and robust designs and higher quality products, in half the time and with a reduced life cycle cost of 50 to 85% or more. This is a tremendous competitive and financial opportunity for a forward-thinking organization, even if it owns its market.

Smart organizations ultimately recognize that *more of the same* is not good enough to lead their markets in the long term. They constantly reinvent and rewrite the rules of competitiveness in their markets and in effect *own the roll.* For example, look at organizations such as Dell, Nokia, and Sony, to name a few. These and many other market leaders constantly reinvent the rules of their industries and dominate them in the process. The way each of these organizations conducts business is significantly different today than it was three, five, or ten years ago.

If you're successful, you can bet that someone is clocking you. Organizations are involved in technology scanning, opportunity assessments, and new business/new market development activities as part of their strategic planning process. If you're a small player who landed luckily in a market opportunity of a large multi-national, remember that they can out-spend, out-resource, out-invest, and out-deal you. It's only a matter of time before the growth stops or new entrants jump in or substitute technology is available. That's business. Organizations such as Dell and Nokia were fortunate to have evolved to a point where strategic improvement is no longer viewed as a program. It's a subconscious minute-by-minute response to the marketplace. If you're missing the foresight, leadership, decisiveness, culture, velocity, nimbleness, technology, or Internet marketing savvy of a Dell or Nokia, the organization may become a victim of clock cleaning if it is too arrogant to improve in good times.

Regardless of industry or financial status, organizations must also recognize that business improvement is asymmetrical in nature. The velocity and magnitude of improvement oscillate up and down over time, and immediate urgency is often the driver. The dynamics of the total value stream inject constant variability in velocity, demand, mix, and choices. Organizations implement improvements to strengthen their competitive position. Their competitors are doing the same thing to improve their relative market position and, in the process, offset gains of their competitors. Some organizations have more sustaining improvements than others. Some organizations rise and fizzle because they were great at the wrong things. The only way to win at this game is to embed improvement deep enough in the organization's culture so that people live and breathe improvement without even thinking about it. Ideally, the best time to improve is when you're healthy, but in all cases the best time to improve is now.

The Lean Extended Enterprise presents an opportunity for the organization to differentiate itself from other competitors. It also enables companies to transition away from a "me-too" organization to a "me-only" organization. In the Lean Extended Enterprise, being a "me-too" organization could be a vulnerable position (e.g., victim of Internet auctions and margin squeezing because the only differentiator is price). We've all read the book *Who Moved My Cheese?* In the Lean Extended Enterprise, there's a lot more at stake than cheese. Organizations that fail to pay attention to these rapidly emerging trends will be wondering *Who Moved My Customers?* and *Who Moved My Profits?* very soon. Market leadership and profitability will be highly influenced by the practices and principles of the LEERM.

PERSONAL DISCOVERY MOMENTS TRANSFORM CULTURE

The ability to sustain improvement is directly associated with culture. In our Six Sigma practice, we coined the term *Personal Discovery Moments* to describe the personal experience of feeling project success. In the past, too many improvement programs have attempted to change behaviors and culture directly. The fact is, nothing really changes in an organization until people change. We can't do it by edict, we can't do it by threats, and we can't hope it. Personal Discovery Moments occur in the context of individual experience with change, particularly when individuals feel inner success and personal growth. Improvement programs that stress this context of personal discovery are much more successful at promoting learning and behavioral change.

Personal Discovery Moments can be very rewarding, and they can be very disappointing. The outcome shapes a particular individual's behavior and response to more change. As we said earlier, project selection is critical to a positive outcome. By now, we hope you understand the components and interdependencies of the LEERM. We mentioned the example of a Six Sigma Black Belt candidate who was assigned a kaizen-like mandatory project for certification. He solved the problem in a few days, but he went through the full four-month certification process literally creating make-work demonstrations of the methodology and tools. His efforts were non-value-added, except to satisfy an academic need. Education for the sake of education, with no learning opportunities on his assigned project. Every step of the DMAIC (Define Measure Analyze Improve Control) process after the first few days was a big waste of his time. He received his Black Belt certification, but is he a believer? Absolutely not. Will he speak positively about his experience to others? Absolutely not. Can an organization be successful with Six Sigma when it produces hundreds of people with this experience? Absolutely not. These individuals will probably benefit most from their experiences on their resumes.

Positive personal discovery experiences create a positive spiraling effect on the organization. They set the stage for creating believers in improvement and change. They transcend the Strategy of Improvement to a level of meaningful reality by achieving results. They raise individual confidence and commitment to new levels where these people begin mentoring others. This in turn leads to more positive personal discovery experiences and more behavioral change. After we cultivate hundreds of believers and accumulate thousands of positive personal discovery experiences, the organization begins to transform culture.

The inverse is also true. People with negative personal discovery experiences are not believers. They will complain and discourage others about improvement. The rumor mill will carry this message just like the one unhappy customer who tells his friends, who tell their friends, and suddenly 300 people know about the bad experience. Bad news always travels faster than good news. The e-mail cartoons start flying around. People become standoffish and reluctant to join in, and pretty soon the improvement initiative loses momentum. Behavior and culture never change. Soon the initiative fades away as if it never existed.

Personal discovery experiences shape our thinking, our beliefs, and our careers. If you live and breathe business improvement long enough, you will be involved in hundreds and thousands of these experiences. In the process, you will also discover that helping the organization reach its next level of improvement has the residual effect of helping you reach your next level of growth. It's a two-way street of professional development when done correctly, and it's also extremely rewarding to help organizations and people reach new planes of improvement and accomplishment. In consulting, there are the emotions of leaving clients and people whom you may never see again with a feeling of wishing that they could do something to repay you for everything you've done for them. Then you realize that they already have. You thank your stars for these new nuggets of wisdom and knowledge, and then it's time to go on to the next personal discovery opportunities. We hope these stepping-stones of wisdom mentioned at the beginning of Chapter 1 are now clearer to you.

THE CYCLE OF IMPROVEMENT

There is a cycle of improvement in organizations that is consistent with sustained success or failure. We represent this concept with the *Improvement Cog Model* (Figure 10.2). It works at both the organizational and individual level, but it must begin at the individual level. Think about your organization in the context of concepts, principles, and practices of the LEERM presented in this book. Think about your organization's capability to Plan-Deploy-Execute and sustain a strategic improvement initiative. Then release the brake on the *Cog Model*. Which direction does your improvement cog move, up or down? In our model, it depends on the following factors:

- The process begins with a need for continuous learning, and this is accomplished through education.
- With the right Plan-Deploy-Execute process in place, we can define customer requirements, identify high-opportunity areas of improvement, and apply this new education to specific opportunities and experience success.
- We have now sharpened our skills because we understand how to retrofit these methodologies and tools to the specifics of our environment. We have a few successes, but this is not good enough. We need to create

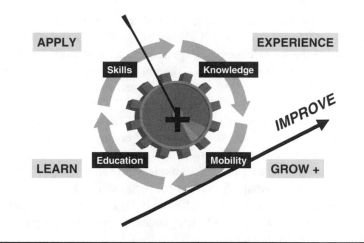

FIGURE 10.2a Improvement Cog Model +

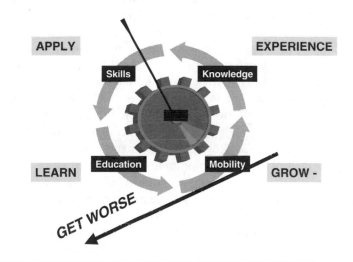

FIGURE 10.2b Improvement Cog Model –

inertia and critical mass, so we need hundreds of people in the organization on the improvement cog.

■ When individuals do this over and over, they accumulate a wealth of new experiences that can be shared by the rest of the organization. This is knowledge.

■ Finally, when individuals and organizations are involved in enough of these positive improvement activities, they grow and the organization grows. This is the point where cultural transformation occurs. Another aspect of this phase is that it allows organizations and people to grow based on the knowledge and experiences accumulated during the positive improvement cog. In effect, the improvement cog moves uphill, the organization improves, and individuals grow.

The opposite is also true. If you released the brake and thought about the lack of leadership and direction, the limited pockets of individual expertise that exist in the organization, and the training budget frozen due to budget constraints, this is a very bad first state. Without learning and education, we become stuck in the Chapter 1 formula: Same People + Same Thinking + Same Process = Same Results. Organizations and individuals do not have the opportunity to develop new skills, knowledge, and experiences. So growth is negative and the improvement cog rolls downhill.

There are a few interesting dynamics to the Improvement Cog Model that are relevant to change in organizations. First, think of the forces required just to keep the improvement cog in the same position on the plane. Second, think of the inertia and momentum required to move the improvement cog uphill versus downhill. Uphill requires a ratcheting of improvement, and sometimes you move farther forward than during other times. When the improvement cog moves uphill, there are always dynamics in the total value stream introducing variation, complexity, and change toward the downhill direction. When the improvement cog first begins to roll downhill, there is a better chance of changing its direction than if one waits until the momentum is established. This is analogous to the parade of fad programs. The direction can be changed, but it will take a great deal of leadership, commitment, and hard work. Now add in the enabling technology. Imagine if you could predict what's ahead so you could plan the activities and number of people pushing and pulling uphill on the improvement cog to keep the direction positive.

The LEERM is a serious matter, and the benefits are enormous. Strategic improvement is not a part-time assignment you give to someone who isn't busy enough. It is an inter-enterprise and extra-enterprise effort that requires constant focus and momentum to sustain improvements.

TEN MOST VALUABLE LEERM LESSONS LEARNED

As we approach the end of our book, it is important to summarize the most salient points of the Lean Extended Enterprise or any other strategic improvement initiative. We have made the point over and over in this book that the methodologies and tools by themselves play a minor role in success. The remainder of this section provides, in our opinion, the ten most important lessons learned of this book.

1. Strategic Improvement Is a Core Competency

Most organizations do not have this core competency internally by osmosis, and they underestimate the difficulty of strategic improvement. Organizations must learn how to define, lead, and execute strategic improvement. You don't get there by developing a grand strategy and then delegating it to a powerless organization. You don't go to a seminar or a plant tour and become an instant change master. You don't wake up one day, flip a switch, and have these competencies in place throughout your organization. And it certainly is not attached as an addendum to an organization's latest crisis situation. It takes a big commitment to define and organize a strategic improvement initiative and then integrate strategy, leadership, execution, the right methodologies, and permanent culture change. Those organizations that have achieved impressive results from their improvement programs do so because they understand this fact.

Organizations must learn how to define and organize a strategic improvement initiative and then integrate strategy, leadership, execution, the right methodologies, and permanent culture change. This skill is not automatically derived by osmosis or stature in the organization. Strategic improvement is 80 to 90% leadership, strategy, and execution and 10 to 20% the tools themselves.

2. The "Demand-Slide" Economy Is Here and Will Continue to Evolve

A few years back, the Kano bar rose and made quality and on-time delivery givens. The next stage is dynamic mass-customized demand streams that provide instant availability of products, in whatever quantity and flavor that appeals to the particular customer. Think about the challenges: As much as 70 to 95% of product cost is generated outside of your company. As much as 75 to 95% of lead time is consumed outside of your company. As much as 95%+ of the key activities of design, supply chain planning, and manufacturing (and the associated employees) are outside of your company. The Lean Extended Enterprise represents a gold mine of collective value stream opportunity. That's why this Lean Extended Enterprise is so critical to future success and collaborative competitiveness. *Demand-slide* is not a Freudian slip. It's short for *demand landslide* because that is exactly how it is hitting organizations that are ill prepared to respond to these new order-of-magnitude market demands.

3. Leadership Is the Turbo-Charged Engine That Drives a Successful Lean Extended Enterprise

It comes from all directions and also from beyond the four walls. Leadership is not clustered at the top of the organization, and it can spawn from many directions. Leadership is within an individual, not within an office or a title. CEOs and executives must take the initiative personally to point their organizations in the right direction because leadership, vision, and the Strategy of Improvement are the most critical elements of change. Managers and individual contributors must also lead by pointing out the inequities in business processes rather than tolerating them. We are not insinuating that people should complain about every little detail. We are saying that everyone should put the principles in this book to work and Plan-Deploy-Execute.

4. The Strategy of Improvement Is Critical to the Success of the Lean Extended Enterprise or Any Other Strategic Improvement Initiative

Organizations that short-circuit this important step end up with a big disconnect between means and ends. They fail to establish a dynamic process for defining new opportunities, establishing priorities, aligning and managing critical resources, and judging success. The Strategy of Improvement enables collaboration, focus, and alignment across the total value stream. Another important element of strategy is consistency of integration. This practice avoids feeding people 50 different versions of the same thing and confusing them. Consistency and focus lay down the right set of priorities, expectations, and thought processes to drive the right actions.

5. The Integration of Kaizen, Lean, Six Sigma, ERP, and Other IT Enabling Technologies Is Required in the Lean Extended Enterprise

Across the total value stream there is a spectrum of improvement opportunities ranging from simple solutions to complex process variation to great slow stand-alone practices that need to be automated and connected further. The Lean Extended Enterprise is not an "either/or" decision. It can only be achieved by applying all of these methodologies correctly, to great opportunities, and to achieve great results. Improvement methodologies by themselves are neither sufficient nor exhaustive. The tools themselves are also ineffective and short-lived without the right improvement strategy and infrastructure bundled around them. Improvement methodologies, tools, and enabling technologies are the means, not the ends. There is no need to discuss the compatibility of lean and enterprise resource planning (ERP) or kaizen versus lean versus Six Sigma any further. We have the enabling technology such as SCM, APS, PLM, CRM, SRM, networks and portals, and other Internet-based applications. We also have a variety of third-party options ranging from UPS logistics and fulfillment services to simplified document management and distribution. There is no need to wait for the next silver bullet. We have everything we need to achieve total value stream excellence. If your organization has achieved less than desirable results with previous improvement programs, the Lean Extended Enterprise is a huge opportunity to cultivate these dormant improvements and save millions or billions of dollars.

6. "Flavor-of-the-Month" Programs and Tools-Based Approach to Improvement Are Short-Lived and Produce Few Results

Buzzwords and the tools-based approach are shortsighted as they limit the lean initiatives to a few selected lean tools that are applied without properly conducting a lean assessment of their current extended enterprise. Blindly following a guru's latest buzzword fad reduces the organization's creativity to a rigid set of commoditized improvement actions. Ultimately, it creates a tremendous amount of confusion as the organization moves from fad to fad, and it also destroys leadership credibility when these "flavor-of-the-month" programs fail. Moving from one generation of lean to the next generation requires a broader toolbox and integration of improvement methodologies, a higher focus on the soft business processes, and the right applications of enabling technology.

Focus most of the organization's efforts on strategy, project selection, problem solving, and execution. These elements of the LEERM will guide organizations and individuals to the right tools for the right situations. The Lean Extended Enterprise requires successful deployment of all methodologies, tools, and enabling technologies correctly, and to the right improvement opportunities.

7. Understand and Manage Total Value Stream Velocity and Variation

It is important to get the entire organization focused on understanding the value streams so that waste can be identified and eliminated beyond the shop floor. The soft process areas are the most fertile ground for strategic improvement. Success requires a mind-set to achieve more granularity of understanding by squeezing processes until they pop, so that we can better understand the root causes, bandwidth limits, and improvements needed to outperform all competitors.

Value stream excellence requires a connected economy where customers, the enterprise, and the supply network are linked in real time. The enabling super booster technology exists to make this happen, and the benefits are derived by deliberate steps into these new technology arenas.

8. Everything Begins and Ends with Performance Measurement

Performance measurement is one of those topics that everyone intuitively knows everything about, except in practice. Remember the other theme throughout this book: There is a difference between knowing how to do something and doing it right every minute of every day. There is a huge difference between knowing how to implement improvement and implementing improvement and getting results. These words should raise a big red flag if you hear people saying they know how to do something but are not doing it.

Performance measurement is not only concerned with measuring the right metrics. Performance measurement includes many levels, and it must be designed to link and align the organization. It must create that hard-wired spiral between the organization's strategy and its daily improvement activities. Otherwise, initiatives tend to wander away from the original objectives.

9. Positive Personal Discovery Experiences Transform Culture

They transcend the Strategy of Improvement to a level of meaningful reality by achieving results. Personal Discovery Moments occur in the context of individual experience with change, particularly when individuals feel inner success and personal growth. Improvement programs that stress this context of personal discovery are much more successful at promoting learning and behavioral change. After we cultivate hundreds of believers and accumulate thousands of positive personal discovery experiences, the organization begins to transform culture. Cultural transformation is not geography or industry or market or product or program or local culture dependent. The right leadership can develop and grow ordinary people to do extraordinary things in any organization.

10. The Lean Extended Enterprise Is Unfolding Rapidly Before Our Very Eyes

Demand-driven supply requires quick response — beyond the current capabilities of present ERP applications. It requires instant collaboration and response across the total value stream. This in turn requires a high degree of integration and comprehensive, more accurate, faster, and more actionable information. The methodologies and enabling technology are available and work well when deployed correctly to the right opportunities. The super booster enabling technology beyond ERP such as SCM, APS, CRM, SRM, PLM, networks, portals, and exchanges is available and is enabling the Lean Extended Enterprise for hundreds of companies and their trading partners.

PARTING THOUGHTS

Once upon a time, there was a famous magician named Harry Houdini, a master of misdirection. Houdini could make people around him see things that he wanted them to see. Houdini knew that "seeing is believing," because people trust their sight more than the other four senses. Motion by itself can be a very powerful and most convincing form of misdirection. Houdini could also make his audience hear things he wanted them to hear. Audible signals can also be a powerful form of misdirection. For Houdini, his objective was misdirection: "What the body sees and hears, the mind believes." After reading this book, you know exactly where we're going with this one by now. There have been far too many Houdini improvement programs in the past decade. There is the perception of improvement caused by enough motion and verbal claims. Organizations have spent millions of dollars on Houdini improvement programs, and their customers have not noticed any differences. Leadership, a solid Strategy of Improvement, deployment of the right methodologies correctly to the right opportunities across the total value stream, and closed-loop performance will put your previous misdirected improvements back on track.

We were having dinner recently with the executive group of one of our clients. We were discussing why some organizations are more successful than others with strategic change. The conversation drifted to something like "Some organizations are great, and some are mediocre. There are strong leaders and weak leaders. Some organizations get it and are quick to change, and others don't get it and operate in the slow lane. Some organizations are market leaders, and others are followers. Some have better and brighter people than others. Culture is different in Boston than it is in Austin, San Jose, Appleton, London, or Kuala Lumpur. It's that 80/20 thing at play. That's what creates competition and makes the world go round." One executive finally said, "If you look inwardly at our own successes, I don't buy any of this discussion. It all comes down to choices. There's nothing special about our organization except the choices we've made to become market leaders and build the right infrastructure to support this strategy. It's the choices we've made to become the best at everything we do. We're just ordinary people doing extraordinary things." When you think critically about strategic change, it really comes down to choices, doesn't it. We all have the choice of leading change or hanging around and becoming victims of someone else's change. We all have the opportunity to learn, to apply new knowledge, and grow professionally or sit around and become stagnant thinkers. We all have the choice of operating in the slow lane or displacing our competition in the upper 20% echelon. The Lean Extended Enterprise also represents a strategic change of choice, and the *choice* and the *outcome* are directly in your control.

The Lean Extended Enterprise is a profound evolution/revolution in the making. The demand-slide economy is the major driver of this next frontier of improvement. This is a gold mine of opportunity because 70 to 95% of many organizations' product cost, lead time, design, supply chain planning, and manufacturing are outside of their four walls. This book has provided a reference model for the Lean Extended Enterprise (LEERM) and a performance measurement framework called the Lean Extended Enterprise Assessment Process. We have provided a Plan-Deploy-Execute methodology that you will find helpful in developing and implementing your particular strategic improvement initiative. We have told you about the top ten pitfalls and provided suggestions to avoid them. We have discussed the need to integrate all of the improvement methodologies, tools, and enabling technologies because no single buzzword will get you there. We discussed migrating beyond ERP to other enabling technologies such as SCM, APS, CRM, PLM, SRM, PRM, network and portal technology, and other Internet-based applications. We discussed the topics of performance measurement and the need to integrate change horizontally, vertically, laterally, and diagonally across the total value stream. We suggested next steps and reiterated the most important factors as organizations begin their journey. And we provided many real-life examples which we hope made the book more interesting to read. The rest is up to you, and the risk of doing nothing is much greater than the risk of improvement. Go out and turn that initiative on, stir the pot, and have fun — and best of luck on a very challenging and rewarding journey to the Lean Extended Enterprise.

CHAPTER 10 TAKE-AWAYS

- The world of real-time collaboration and virtual exchanges is here. The methodologies, tools, and enabling technologies are available to streamline and optimize critical value delivery processes across the total value stream. No more silver bullets needed!
- The Lean Extended Enterprise is an enormous improvement opportunity for every organization. The upside potential is almost unbelievable. Some organizations are reporting savings in the hundreds of millions to billions of dollars.

- The LEERM provides a structured reference model to follow and integrates strategy and execution via the Plan-Deploy-Execute process.
- Leadership is the turbo-charged engine that drives a successful Lean Extended Enterprise. It comes from all directions and also from beyond the four walls.
- The Strategy of Improvement is critical to the success of the Lean Extended Enterprise or any other strategic improvement initiative. Organizations that short-circuit this important step end up with a big disconnect between means and ends. They fail to establish a dynamic process for defining new opportunities, establishing priorities, aligning and managing critical resources, and judging success.
- One of the characteristics of a solid Strategy of Improvement is focus. The best and easiest way to accomplish this is by using multi-level Pareto analysis, which enables us to analyze various factors of our business in relation to each other.
- There's a big difference between being *on a roll* and *owning the roll*. Most organizations spend their time on and off rolls, and a much smaller number implement the right improvement strategies to *own the roll*.
- Ideally, the best time to improve is when you're healthy, but in all cases the best time to improve is now. The Lean Extended Enterprise presents an opportunity for the organization to differentiate itself from other competitors. It also enables organizations to transition away from a "me-too" organization to a "me-only" organization.
- Positive personal discovery experiences transform culture. They transcend the Strategy of Improvement to a level of meaningful reality by achieving results. After we cultivate hundreds of believers and accumulate thousands of positive personal discovery experiences, the organization begins to transform culture.
- The Lean Extended Enterprise is a profound evolution/revolution in the making. The demand-slide economy is the major driver of this next frontier of improvement. This is a gold mine of opportunity because 70 to 95% of many organizations' product cost, lead time, design, supply chain planning, and manufacturing are outside of the four walls.

INDEX